SOVIET BLITZKRIEG

The Stackpole Military History Series

THE AMERICAN CIVIL WAR
Cavalry Raids of the Civil War
Ghost, Thunderbolt, and Wizard
Pickett's Charge
Witness to Gettysburg

WORLD WAR II
Armor Battles of the Waffen-SS, 1943–45
Army of the West
Australian Commandos
The B-24 in China
Backwater War
The Battle of Sicily
Beyond the Beachhead
The Brandenburger Commandos
The Brigade
Bringing the Thunder
Coast Watching in World War II
Colossal Cracks
D-Day to Berlin
Dive Bomber!
Eagles of the Third Reich
Exit Rommel
Fist from the Sky
*Flying American Combat Aircraft of
    World War II*
Forging the Thunderbolt
Fortress France
The German Defeat in the East, 1944–45
German Order of Battle, Vol. 1
German Order of Battle, Vol. 2
German Order of Battle, Vol. 3
Germany's Panzer Arm in World War II
GI Ingenuity
Grenadiers
Infantry Aces
Iron Arm
Iron Knights
*Kampfgruppe Peiper at the Battle
    of the Bulge*
Luftwaffe Aces
Massacre at Tobruk
Messerschmitts over Sicily

Michael Wittmann, Vol. 1
Michael Wittmann, Vol. 2
Mountain Warriors
The Nazi Rocketeers
On the Canal
Packs On!
Panzer Aces
Panzer Aces II
The Panzer Legions
Panzers in Winter
The Path to Blitzkrieg
Retreat to the Reich
Rommel's Desert War
The Savage Sky
A Soldier in the Cockpit
Soviet Blitzkrieg
Stalin's Keys to Victory
Surviving Bataan and Beyond
T-34 in Action
Tigers in the Mud
The 12th SS, Vol. 1
The 12th SS, Vol. 2
The War against Rommel's Supply Lines

THE COLD WAR / VIETNAM
*Flying American Combat Aircraft:
    The Cold War*
Here There Are Tigers
Land with No Sun
Street without Joy

WARS OF THE MIDDLE EAST
Never-Ending Conflict

GENERAL MILITARY HISTORY
Carriers in Combat
Desert Battles

SOVIET BLITZKRIEG

The Battle for White Russia, 1944

Walter S. Dunn, Jr.

STACKPOLE
BOOKS

Published in paperback in 2008 by
STACKPOLE BOOKS
5067 Ritter Road
Mechanicsburg, PA 17055
www.stackpolebooks.com

Cover design by Tracy Patterson

Printed in the United States of America

10 9 8 7 6 5 4 3 2 1

ISBN 0-8117-3482-X (Stackpole paperback)
ISBN 978-0-8117-3482-0 (Stackpole paperback)

The Library of Congress has cataloged the hardcover edition as follows:

Dunn, Walter S. (Walter Scott), 1928–
    Soviet blitzkrieg : the battle for White Russia, 1944 / Walter S. Dunn, Jr.
    Includes bibliographical references and index.
    ISBN 1-55587-880-6 (hc. : alk. paper)
    1. World War, 1939-1945—Campaigns—Belarus. 2. Belarus—History—20th century. I. Title
    D764.7.B38D86 2000
    940.54'21781—dc21
                                            99-36041

To David McNamara,
a valued friend and colleague

Contents

Illustrations

Maps

Tables and Figures

Preface

This presentation of a factual account of the Battle for White Russia in July 1944 places the battle in historical perspective. I have made a determined effort to compare quantitative data from numerous sources and to present rational interpretations of events.

Compressing a description of World War II's greatest battle, fought by 2 million Russians and nearly 800,000 Germans, into a few hundred pages without losing the feeling of the engagement was quite a task. My approach was to separate the operation into six drives. Because of the unfamiliarity of most readers with the place names, the rivers, and the military units involved, I reduced the references to obscure towns and rivers and concentrated on the major objectives of the six spearheads. Relating the drives to objectives in six cohesive chapters gives the reader an opportunity to become familiar with the units and towns in each of the areas and to follow the action as a continuous narrative.

The disadvantage of this type of organization is that on occasion action in one area spills over into an adjoining sector and some repetition and duplication result. However, this is a small price to pay, considering the alternative of reviewing an entire operation on a day-by-day basis. Dividing the action into separate drives allows the reader to appreciate the amazing performance of the Soviet armored columns as they plunged forward in true blitzkrieg fashion, bypassing German resistance, cutting roads and rail lines, and effectively isolating the German units and leaving retreat as the units' only option.

Occurring simultaneously with the dogged advance of the British and U.S. forces in Normandy, prior to the breakout in early July, the Soviet gains in the first two weeks of the operation received scant mention in Western newspapers. After the U.S. forces' breakout in France, there was even less coverage of the steady but slower advance of the Russians in July and August.

In any description of a battle one of the first priorities is to determine who participated. The previous dearth of information concerning the Red Army has been alleviated by the recent Russian release of some information. The Russian order of battle data presented here came from my data base of 9,100 units compiled from published Soviet order of battle data and German intelligence records based on information from spies, prisoners of war, intercepts of radio transmissions by units, Soviet publications and broadcasts, and captured documents. When the German information was compared with the Soviet data remarkably few irregularities surfaced. The German order of battle information came from hundreds of published sources, the most notable being the series by Georg Tessin.[1]

*　*　*

Many individuals deserve recognition in completing this work. Foremost was Tom Johnson, who read the manuscript with great care and made many valuable suggestions. He provided the tables and maps without which the narrative would be difficult to comprehend. Colonel David Glantz gave permission to use maps that he had painstakingly created over many years. David McNamara years ago first suggested that I look into the White Russian operation. George, Bill, and Bob Wendeberg brought my attention to weather changes in late June in Eastern Europe based on a tradition passed on from their grandfather. Many others have provided information, support, and encouragement.

No scholarly work could succeed without resources. The librarians of the Memorial Library of the University of Wisconsin were unstinting in their support. No one has contributed as much as my wife, Jean, who has edited the manuscript and helped turn the mass of detail into a readable piece.

Notes

1. Georg Tessin, *Verbände und Truppen der Deutschen Wehrmacht und Waffen SS in Zweiten Weltkrieg 1939–1945,* 14 vols. (Osnabrück: Biblio, 1965–1980).

Introduction

The Battle for White Russia erupted south of Vitebsk on the morning of 22 June 1944, when Russian artillery began a thundering barrage of over a thousand guns, mortars, and rockets that blasted away for 2 hours and 20 minutes in an 18-kilometer-long sector. At the same time a Soviet fighter corps, two bomber divisions, and a ground attack division pummeled the bunkers of General Pfeiffer's VI Corps with bombs and strafed any foolhardy German troops in the trenches with machine gun fire. The sheer weight of explosives that rained down on the German dugouts and bunkers paralyzed the defenders, especially the new replacements who had arrived during the previous few months. Even the older, experienced men had never suffered through such an intense pounding for so many hours. When the heavy artillery and rockets finally quieted the relentless air attacks intensified; *landsers* (German foot soldiers) leaving a dugout invited instant death. Finally, the rumbling of engines and the clatter of steel tracks signaled the approach of the dreaded Soviet tanks, sounds greeted with a sigh of relief, for at least the rain of death from the skies soon would cease.

However this bloody havoc was but a prelude to what was still to come. A torrent of tanks and riflemen from four divisions of General N. I. Krylov's 5th Army stormed the German trenches along the 18-kilometers sector, about 36,000 men, or two men for every meter. With the shouting Red Army riflemen came two tank brigades and five assault gun regiments with over 120 tanks and 100 assault guns, double the strength of a panzer division. The hurricane struck nine battalions of the German 299th Division and one regiment of the 256th Division with their 4,500 men against 36,000 Soviet soldiers. The Russians quickly overran all three trench lines of the first defense zone, and two more Soviet divisions rushed forward to add weight to the onslaught. Within hours a gap of 50 kilometers

1

opened in the German defenses, and Soviet mobile columns of tanks, assault guns, and motorized infantry poured through to exploit the success.

The crushing breakthrough by the 5th Army south of Vitebsk was but one of six major breakthroughs north and south of Vitebsk, north of Orsha, east of Mogilev, and east and south of Bobruysk. The six eruptions opened one of the biggest battles of all times in terms of the number of men involved, 2 million Russians and nearly a million Germans and their allies, one-third of all the troops on the Eastern Front. The destruction of fifty divisions imposed on the defenders altered the course of the war. After the first 2 weeks of the White Russian operation, Hitler had no chance to withdraw any troops from the east to check the British and Americans in France, and instead stripped the other German army groups in the east of their reserves to close the yawning void that had been Army Group Center. The gains of the first 2 weeks were accomplished with minimal Soviet losses—unlike the future bloodbath at Berlin. In that same 2-week period the number of Germans killed and captured far exceeded the number of Soviet casualties.

This greatest of all Soviet victories in World War II, except taking Berlin, came from the application of blitzkrieg tactics and strategy. Most Soviet victories were the result of overwhelming the Germans with superior numbers of men and machines in frontal attacks, which were demanded by the need for quick results; but the Red Army was capable of waging blitzkrieg-style warfare. The first phase of the Battle for White Russia ending in the destruction of the German Army Group Center is an outstanding case study of Soviet blitzkrieg.

Eight elements made up the successful execution of the White Russian operation: local superiority, deception, surprise, leadership, timing, use of terrain, training, and technology. The success of the elite armored spearheads resulted from an ideal combination of factors.

Local Superiority

The first requirement was the concentration of force in the breakthrough sectors to secure a huge margin of superiority. This the Red Army achieved in June 1944. North of Vitebsk the elite 1st Tank Corps, commanded by General V. V. Butkov, had been completely refitted with 195 new T34/85 tanks and forty-two new assault guns in the spring of 1944 and was much stronger than a German panzer division. Butkov drove due west after the breakthrough in General Wuthmann's IX Corps sector, while the Soviet 6th Guard Army commanded by General I. M. Chistyakov supported by tank and assault guns equivalent to a tank corps turned south to cut off Vitebsk from the north.

South of Vitebsk, General I. I. Lyudnikov's 39th Army turned north after the breakthrough to cut off Vitebsk and the four divisions of General Gollwitzer's LIII Corps in Vitebsk from the south. General N. S. Oslikovskiy's Horse-Mechanized Group with the famous 3rd Guard Cavalry Corps, which had retaken Smolensk in the summer of 1943, and the 3rd Guard Mechanized Corps, equipped with sixty-five new Sherman M4A2 tanks with high-velocity 76mm guns in its tank brigade and forty-two assault guns, drove southwest to Senno.

North of Orsha, General A. S. Burdeyniy's 2nd Guard Tank Corps, at full strength with new T34/85 tanks, sped quickly to Borisov to close the escape route of General K. Tippelskirch's Fourth Army. Marshal P. A. Rotmistrov's 5th Guard Tank Army followed and played a major role in creating the pockets east of Minsk.

East of Mogilev, General I. T. Grishin's 49th Army with tank-supported infantry hammered away to hold Tippelskirch in place, while the Russian pincers closed behind from the north and south.

East of Bobruysk, General A. B. Gorbatov's 3rd, with General B. S. Bakharov's 9th Tank Corps, coming back from 6 months behind the lines with 195 new T34/85 tanks and forty-two assault guns, broke through General Freiherr von Lützow's XXXV Corps of General Jordan's Ninth Army and General Müller's XII Corps of Tippelskirch's Fourth Army. Bakharov plunged ahead to cut off Bobruysk from the north, while Gorbatov turned north to cut off Mogilev from the south.

South of Bobruysk, General A. A. Luchinskiy's 28th and General P. I. Batov's 65th Armies broke through General Weidling's XXXXI Corps. General I. A. Pliev's Horse-Mechanized Group plunged through the hole and dashed west toward Slutsk. (Two months earlier, Pliev's group had been awarded the Order of the Red Banner for its spectacular breakthrough to take Odessa in the Ukraine in April 1944.) General M. F. Panov's 1st Guard Tank Corps, another crack unit that had been refitted with 195 new T34/85 tanks and forty-two assault guns, turned northwest to cut off Bobruysk from the south. After surrounding Bobruysk, Panov joined Bakharov in the drive toward Minsk, the capital of White Russia.

Deception

A second blitzkrieg requirement was deception to minimize the availability of enemy reserves that could contain the armored spearheads once the breakthrough had been accomplished. The Russians cleverly diverted the German reserves in June 1944 by an elaborate deception plan that convinced Hitler that the main attack would come at Kovel to the south, leading him to retain his powerful panzer divisions there until his Army Group Center was annihilated. (In a previous example, in May 1940, the Germans had enticed the British and French to string out their forces through northeastern France and through Belgium all the way to the Dutch border, leaving the Germans' breakthrough sector at Sedan without adequate reserves.

Deception played a major role in the White Russian offensive. In view of the identified Soviet troop concentrations north and south of the Pripyat Marshes salient, neither Hitler nor the German OKH (Oberkommando des Heeres–Army High Command) could comprehend a frontal attack on White Russia. The Soviets had concentrated a number of highly visible offensive units, including tank armies, in the Kovel area, well to the southwest, in the spring of 1944. Even after the offensive began, days passed before the Germans were able to appreciate that the attacks were anything more than a ruse devised to draw German reserves away from the crucial points at Kovel and Ostrov far to the north. Hitler reasoned that pulling German reserves into the marshes would increase the size of the bag of captured Germans when the real attacks began and cut off the Pripyat salient with a gigantic encirclement with pincers from north and south. Given this interpretation of Soviet intentions, the pleas of the army and corps commanders in Army Group Center that a major offensive was about to erupt on the face of the salient were ignored.

The elaborate plan of deception was aimed at the higher German command levels. German front-line units were, of course, aware that something major was brewing across the barbed wire entanglements. To deceive the Germans, the Russians made an elaborate show of building defenses in depth to indicate a passive role for the Red Army units on the face of the Pripyat salient. However, the German front-line commanders detected the movement of units and the ever increasing density of Russian infantry, tanks, and artillery in front of them.

The Soviet leadership made a concerted effort to prevent the Germans from learning the true extent of the buildup. Assault units remained in the rear until the last few days, while the front continued to be occupied by the same divisions. Troop movements were made at night, and the units were concealed in forests during the day. Although the 5th Guard Tank Army moved from the Ukraine to the area south of Vitebsk, German intelligence maps still placed it in the south on 22 June 1944. The 11th Guard Army was moved by rail from the Crimea to concealed training grounds in the forests around Nevel in May. The 11th Guard Army prepared for the upcoming offensive without being detected by German reconnaissance aircraft, which were kept away by special efforts of the Red Air Force.

Although scores of units, such as the 11th Guard Army or the 5th Guard Tank Army, were added to the four Soviet fronts, most did not have a high profile. The two newly assembled horse-mechanized groups, nearly as powerful as tank armies, went undetected. (The presence of tank armies usually signaled Soviet offensives, just as German offensives earlier in the war had been marked by the concentration of panzer corps.) Since German intelligence did not detect the presence of any tank armies opposing Army Group Center, Hitler and the OKH were convinced that no major offensive would take place in the area, and German panzer reserves were held opposite the Soviet tank armies that had been located. Even when the catastrophe was well under way, Hitler was reluctant to move the panzer divisions to help and instead sent a few infantry divisions and assault gun brigades.

Much of the Soviet buildup came in the form of independent tank brigades and regiments and new assault gun regiments from the Stavka (Army Headquarters) reserve and the Moscow Military District. Although these additions individually were minor and, if detected, aroused little interest, the sum total represented over a thousand tanks and assault guns, mostly of the latest types. During the opening weeks of the offensive, Soviet rifle divisions were amply supported by tanks and assault guns whenever needed. In the accounts of an advancing rifle division, the presence of a tank brigade or an assault gun regiment was usually noted.

Surprise

The third blitzkrieg factor was surprise. In June 1944 the Germans believed that the four fortified cities of Vitebsk, Orsha, Mogilev, and Bogushevsk effectively blocked the four good roads, the paths usable by armored forces. The Red Army broke through the German lines between the fortified cities in marshy sectors and caught the Germans by surprise. The Russians were able to sustain the breakthroughs with four-wheel-drive American-made trucks, a factor the Germans had not anticipated. Once through the German defense zones, the Russians were able to surround the four strongpoints and take them from the rear.

Similarly in France in May 1940, the Germans had come through the Ardennes, which the Allies believed impassable for armored units. The German panzers were able to brush aside the weak French divisions guarding a supposedly safe sector and dash to the English Channel.

Leadership

Boldness was also a major component of a successful blitzkrieg. Russian division, corps, and army commanders risked everything as they dashed ahead, relying for protection on the speed of their advance and the disorganization in the German rear. Both the Red Army in June 1944 and the Germans in May 1940 acted boldly, although the destruction of the British army in 1940 was denied when Hitler stopped the advance short of Dunkirk.

Bolder leadership in the Red Army resulted from a vital change that had occurred by the spring of 1944 as the relationship between Stalin and his generals moved from their fear of him to working in harmony as Stalin came to trust his subordinates. In 1941 the Russian generals were more afraid of Stalin than the Germans (an army commander was shot for losing a battle) and were careful to make conservative decisions that would meet with Stalin's approval even though the decisions would cost many lives. As the war progressed, Stalin became more concerned about the loss of millions of soldiers. The Soviet generals came to strike a more equitable balance between fear of failure and that of losing men, and by 1944 the aim of the Red Army was containment of losses unless there was a worthy objective.

An example of Stalin's search for professional leadership was the career of General I. S. Lazarenko. In June 1941 Lazarenko commanded the 42nd Rifle Division in the 4th Army defending Brest. After a determined resistance the Germans finally drove the division out of Brest, but Stalin did not believe that Lazarenko had done enough and had him arrested for indecisive action, negligence, and surrendering his command to the enemy. Lazarenko was convicted and ordered to be shot, but the sentence was reduced to 10 years in prison. In 1943 he was released, and in June 1944 he was in command of the 369th Rifle Division of the 49th Army in White Russia. Unfortunately he was killed by a German land mine during the battle.

While the Russians were becoming more concerned with retaining commanders who would contain losses, Hitler was moving in the opposite direction. The Germans had used defense in depth to reduce casualties by withdrawing from one defense zone to another as soon as the effectiveness of the first zone had been reduced—in essence, ground being traded for reduced casualties. By 1944, however, Hitler had reversed this tactic and was demanding that ground be held regardless of casualties, as exemplified by his order establishing that fortress cities be held to the last man and the last bullet. Hitler's obsession with holding ground worsened the relationship between Hitler and his generals and gave the Russians an additional advantage in 1944.

Timing

Timing was essential because deception cannot last indefinitely. The Russians completed their deployment for this battle, including two armies that had been engaged in the liberation of the Crimea in May 1944, in about 6 weeks, in contrast to the 3-month buildup of Russian forces before the Battle of Kursk. German intelligence lost contact with entire Soviet armies and learned of their presence only when attacked.

Use of Terrain

The Red Army used the terrain to its advantage and overcame Army Group Center despite the German strategy of the fortified cities. In only 2 weeks the Red Army advanced over 275 kilometers, farther than the distance covered by Rommel from the Belgian border to the Channel coast in May 1940. Whereas in May 1940 the Germans had broken through third-rate territorial divisions holding poor defensive positions, the Russians broke through top-quality German divisions in well-prepared lines. Rommel's tanks, half-tracks, and trucks rolled over one of the best road networks in the world in bright sunny weather after emerging from the Ardennes Forest. In 1944 the Russians fought bitterly for the four good highways, and most of their advance was over rain-soaked, thinly surfaced gravel roads, and even dirt roads, churned up into rivers of mud by the heavy traffic. Rommel's advance had paralleled the course of major rivers and, because of poorly coordinated Allied defense, crossed bridges that should have been destroyed. The Russians moved against the grain of the terrain, encountering one rain-swollen river after another that had to be crossed first by infantry in small boats, then artillery on ferries, and finally tanks and assault guns on pontoon bridges because the Germans had blown most of the bridges.

The German army had held White Russia for 3 years, a vast expanse of wetlands intersected by numerous small rivers with primarily north-south courses. Soviet offensives early in 1944, north and south of White Russia, had created a vast salient held by German Army Group Center. The Pripyat Marshes severely hampered rapid movement and limited heavy travel to the major highways and roads and the few railroads that crossed the marshes.

This densely wooded wet ground had provided an impenetrable haven for Soviet Partisans since 1941. Many Red Army stragglers left behind in 1941 had joined the local residents in partisan units that continued to harass the Germans despite several efforts to wipe them out. In attempts to control the partisans and protect the roads and railways, the Germans had assigned numerous security units to keep the supply lines open.

Based on the success of the strongpoints on the major roads that had blocked the Red Army counteroffensive during the winter of 1941–1942, Hitler and his generals had created heavily fortified areas with large garrisons of up to four infantry divisions on the four major roads crossing the marshes at Vitebsk, Orsha, Mogilev, and Rogachev.

The theory behind the German fortified regions was that although the Soviet infantry and possibly a few tanks might penetrate the weakly held sectors between the regions, German reserves would quickly counterattack with tanks, infantry, and artillery to drive back the unsupported Russians before they could create havoc in the rear of German forces. Before the arrival of American-built Lend Lease trucks, the combination of wetlands and forests made it difficult for the Soviet forces to bring forward enough heavy weapons, antitank guns, artillery, tanks, and assault guns to hold gains against German counterattacks.

The German appraisal of these limitations worked well for over 2 years; Soviet attacks were repulsed with heavy losses by German artillery and tank-supported counterattacks. The German theory worked so well that little serious effort was made to create and man reserve positions behind the first defense zone. Both German and Soviet defensive theories called for a succession of defense zones, each consisting of multiple trench lines. Should the first zone be penetrated, the troops were expected to withdraw to the second zone, and if the second zone was penetrated, the troops would fall back to the third. Especially sensitive areas would have additional zones. At Kursk, in 1943, the Soviets had seven defense zones protecting the shoulders of the salient, and the German attack was halted in the third zone. The Germans neglected their second and third zones in White Russia because of the shortage of troops, the difficulty of the terrain, and their confidence in the four strong points.

Terrain played a major role in limiting German movement and

therefore deceived the Germans, who expected the attack at the south shoulder of the salient, rather than against well-established German defenses on the salient's face. Even though the dry weather in May and early June firmed up the marshlands, a heavy rain at any time would confine movement to the roads and limit the operations of Soviet aircraft, further reinforcing the German conviction that an attack would not come on the face of the salient.

The weather combined with the terrain, in fact, did make the Soviet attack more difficult. More time was needed for the Soviet 5th Guard Tank Army to complete its move from the south, the original date of the attack being postponed for 9 days. The delay had serious consequences: 22 June marked the point when the days began to shorten, and even a slight variation in temperature increased the likelihood of heavy rain.

White Russia stands on the border between the movement of cold air southwest of the cold air mass over the northern Urals meeting the warm air moving northeast from North Africa that picks up moisture from the Mediterranean Sea. The collision of the cool dry air and the warm moist air produces the heavy rainfall that created the Polesian Marshes and the Dnieper Lowland that form the southern and eastern sides of the White Russian salient. The heaviest rain usually falls in late June and July, and the 9 days' delay increased the expectation of heavy rain during the crucial early days of the offensive. Heavy rain did fall the first few days and greatly impeded the advance of Rotmistrov's 5th Guard Tank Army.

The Germans assumed that the Russians would be unable to penetrate the marshlands and that the strongly fortified towns of Vitebsk, Orsha, Mogilev, and Rogachev would block the main highways, especially because Soviet forces had failed to take Vitebsk in the winter of 1943–1944 after a determined effort. The terrain west of Vitebsk was heavily forested, and the Ulla River was a formidable barrier. However, once over the Ulla, there was a good corridor to the town of Molodechno, and the Obol River to the north provided a barrier to flank attacks by Army Group North.

North and south of Orsha the terrain was favorable for offensive action, and these paths were used successfully by the Russians. West of Mogilev, the Berezina and Drut Rivers were extremely difficult to cross, especially when the marshes on both banks were flooded by the heavy rain. These two rivers were serious obstacles to the advancing Russians.

Bobruysk was surrounded with marshlands, but once the Russians crossed the River Ptich and cleared the lowlands, the ground was favorable all the way to Slutsk and Baranovichi. This path was taken by Pliev's Horse-Mechanized Group.

Although the heavy rain on the first few days limited their movements, the Red Army units took advantage of the difficult terrain to surprise the Germans by moving through the wetlands and bypassing the roadblocks. After a few days, the roads had dried and the Soviet armored columns were able to move ahead swiftly, leaving the fortified cities behind.

The southern flank of the Pripyat Marshes was even more treacherous with very little dry land, more numerous rivers, denser forests, and no significant north-south roads. The impassable nature of this sector affected both sides. Earlier in the year the Soviets had been able to assume a secure northern flank when driving to Kovel, using only a thin screening force as they advanced westward. Similarly, the Germans had little fear that the Red Army would try to widen the breadth of the advance to Kovel to the north and felt confident in leaving the defense in the hands of a few scattered German and Hungarian units.

In June 1944 the Germans maintained only a light screen of forces on the line from Zhlobin in the east to Kovel in the west. Again the terrain appeared to dictate the next Soviet offensive, an advance northwest from Kovel with the ultimate goal of linking up with a drive south from the Baltic states, trapping most of Army Group Center. The salient dictated a strategy of hitting from both the north and the south. The strategic situation seemed obvious to the Germans, particularly after the Soviet offensive south of Leningrad had established an excellent startline for the northern pincer to match the position at Kovel for the southern pincer.

Training

The Red Army's use of terrain was only possible if its troops and commanders were specially trained to make the fullest use of new techniques. Liaison between the ground and air forces had to be developed and the commanders schooled in the use of air support. Additional training of Soviet units was possible because the Red Army had sufficient reserves to pull entire armies out of the line to be carefully taught about the special problems expected in crossing multiple rivers and establishing bridgeheads complete with antitank guns, assault guns, and tanks. Soviet units were trained to quickly fortify the bridgeheads before the Germans could launch tank-supported counterattacks.

General K. N. Galitskiy's 11th Guard Army spent weeks practicing with engineers to develop techniques for the construction of temporary roads through the wetlands and forest. The troops also worked with the engineers in constructing pontoon bridges over rivers and streams. The artillery units rehearsed their role in preparatory barrages and support fire for the advancing infantry.

In addition the troops were trained to use the new weapons available to the assault armies, including the Model 1943 76mm gun, the PPSh machine pistol, the SU-152 assault gun, and other weapons. Thousands of new replacements arrived from the infantry replacement regiments, and these new inductees, along with veterans returning from hospitals, had to be integrated into the rifle companies. (The combat-experienced veterans sharpened the skills of the younger men.) These well-trained replacements were superior to the raw recruits who had been drafted to fight in the Battle of Kursk the previous year.

Technology

Technological factors completely disrupted the German command's assumptions based on a defensive theory grounded in strongpoints on the major roads. The first factor was the breakdown of the rail system. The movement of the panzer divisions by rail to threatened areas was delayed by the limited rail network in White Russia and persistent Partisan attacks on the rail lines. Because of these attacks, the Germans were forced to use the roads despite the fuel shortage caused by air attacks on the synthetic fuel factories in Germany. Although the detonation of a few kilograms of explosive by the Partisans did relatively little damage, repairable in a matter of hours, hundreds of these incidents created a nightmare for the German repair crews. Should the Partisans be courageous enough to wait for a passing train and blow the charge under the locomotive, the effect was devastating, although the Partisans risked serious danger from the reaction of the German troops on the train. Removing a wrecked train was a lengthy process and, depending on the extent of the damage and the number of cars damaged, returning the track to use could take several days.

German logistical problems were the second technological factor. Once the trains arrived at a station close to the front, the trains had to be unloaded and the supplies moved to the combat divisions. The weak link was between the railhead and the front. In 1941 and 1942, both the Germans and Russians had relied heavily on horse-drawn wagons and roadbound rear-axle-drive trucks to transport weapons and supplies to the front from the railhead. Incoming troops marched from the railhead, while tracked vehicles were unloaded from flatcars at the railhead and used some of their precious limited track life to move from the railhead to the front. All units depended on the wagons and trucks to carry to the front the daily quota of rations, fuel, fodder, munitions, and other supplies.

The wagons could travel up to 30 kilometers from the front in 1 day and return loaded the following day. Advancing German and Soviet armies increased the distance from the railhead to the front and soon exceeded 30 kilometers. Any greater distance necessitated stables for the horses at a halfway point, and the round-trip was lengthened to at least 3 days, assuming the horses were able to pull the empty wagons a longer distance on the return-trip from the front. When the front was more than 60 kilometers from the depot the trip was lengthened to 4 days, increasing the need for wagons and horses. But additional wagons were seldom available, nor were stables and other facilities to care for more horses. As a result the advancing troops were inadequately supplied with fuel, food, fodder, and munitions, effectively halting the offensive more conclusively than enemy action until the railroad was repaired and the depots moved forward. To place these distances in perspective, Senno (south of Vitebsk), one of the first objectives of the Soviet 5th Army, was 50 kilometers from the original front. The West Dvina River, the first objective of the Soviet 6th Guard Army, was more than 30 kilometers from the original front. Had the Red Army also depended on horsedrawn supplies, the offensive potential of both the 6th Guard and 5th Armies would have been seriously reduced and the German counterattacks would have been far more successful, validating the German defensive theory of holding the four fortified cities.

On a good improved road with sufficient gravel for adequate drainage the rear-axle-drive trucks could supplant the horsedrawn wagons. Trucks were flexible and more easily moved to a sector needing supplies, and required less daily maintenance than horses and could travel longer distances. However, such roads were rare in the Soviet Union, and all the more so in the Pripyat Marshes. Even in the prosperous Kursk region in 1943, the roads were so poor that a moderate rain reduced them to bogs. There, the inability of the German ammunition trucks to move forward in July 1943 caused severe shortages for the artillery at a crucial point in the Battle of Kursk. The poor roads also had constrained the German ability to transfer units by truck from one sector to another. Given this fact, the German denial of the Red Army's use of the four good roads crossing the wetlands on the face of the White Russian salient was practical and had been successful for several years.

The third technological factor was the arrival of thousands of American-built four-wheel-drive trucks, weapons carriers, and jeeps that overturned the German assumptions. There are few mentions of U.S. Lend Lease trucks in Soviet writings, but German intelligence reports contain extracts from captured Soviet documents that reveal the widespread use of such vehicles. In November 1943 the 17th Tank Destroyer Brigade used Studebaker 2.5-ton trucks to tow the 76mm guns in the 389th Regiment, Soviet ZIS trucks for the 76mm guns in the 478th Regiment, and Willys Jeeps for the 45mm guns in the 712th Regiment.[1] In January 1944 the 1071st Tank Destroyer Regiment had all American-built vehicles and towed its 76mm guns with Willys Jeeps.[2] In March 1944 the Soviet 615th Howitzer Regiment was armed with M38 122mm howitzers. The official table of organization called for Soviet vehicles: one automobile, 18 GAZ-AA trucks (the Soviet version of the Ford Model A truck of the 1930s), 29 ZIS-5 trucks, 12 special trucks, and 35 tractors for towing howitzers. In fact the regiment had 7 Russian GAZ-AA trucks but the rest were from the United States: 1 Willys Jeep replacing the automobile, 21 International Harvester 2.5-ton trucks, and 14 Studebaker 2.5-ton trucks. The 35 Lend Lease trucks replaced both the tractors and the 59 trucks.[3]

Material from the United States was arriving despite the German success in stopping the summer Atlantic convoys to Murmansk and Arkhangelsk. In March 1944 a Soviet prisoner informed the Germans that six U.S. ships had arrived in Arkhangelsk (presumably from one of the four convoys that slipped past the Germans in the winter of 1943–1944 during the almost continuous darkness of the winter nights). The cargoes included 50 Hurricane and Airacobra fighter planes (from Britain and the United States, respectively), 100 medium tanks, 50 Ford 1.5-ton trucks, 40 tractors, some 155mm howitzers, spare parts for tanks, and food including sugar, bacon, rye flour, and dried white beans. The ships then were loaded with lumber in Arkhangelsk for the return journey.[4]

The American-built trucks could travel over practically impassible country as well as muddy roads. Even if mired down, many trucks were equipped with winches on the front that could pull the truck or other trucks from impossible situations with only a slight delay. Given this capability, the Soviet divisions were no longer roadbound and could advance across open country. With the help of engineers, rough trails were cut through the woods immediately behind the advancing troops to facilitate the movement of antitank guns, mortars, and artillery to fend off the German counterattacks. Jeeps carried heavy mortars and their crews. Chevrolet and Dodge weapons carriers pulled 57mm and 75mm antitank guns. Studebaker 2.5-ton trucks pulled heavier guns and carried supplies.

The trucks carried pontoons and bridging equipment that enabled the Soviet engineers to quickly bridge a river once the infantry had established a slender bridgehead. By the time the Germans were able to react with a tank-supported counterattack, the bridgehead bristled with Soviet antitank guns, mortars, and heavy weapons, while well-supplied artillery was in position immediately behind the front.

The Soviet philosophy of the field army service units delivering the supplies to the front-line divisions made full use of the flexibility of the American-built trucks. By contrast, the Germans had horse-drawn wagons from divisional service units to fetch supplies from the railhead.

A fourth technological factor was the margin of air superiority achieved by the Red Air Force. Most of the German fighter aircraft were in Germany defending the Reich and, particularly, the armaments industry from British and U.S. air raids. With few German fighters to harass them, even the relatively slow and vulnerable Sturmovik ground-support aircraft were free and unhindered to attack German tanks, artillery positions, and troop columns. The Sturmoviks were a valuable addition to the antitank resources of the Red Army and were used to break up German tank-supported counterattacks. German panzer divisions could no longer rove at will around the battlefield crushing Soviet breakthroughs. Only at night could the German troops and tanks move safely; during the day the roads were the province of the Red Air Force. When vehicles of the retreating Germans clogged the road leading to the bridge over the Berezina River, Soviet aviators were able to devastate the German forces.

Adding to German distress was the length of the days: 22 June is the longest day of the year in the northern hemisphere, and Minsk at about 55 degrees latitude is nearly two-thirds the distance from the equator to the North Pole, where the sun shines 24 hours a day in mid-June. There were over 18 hours of daylight during the Soviet offensive, giving the Germans only a few hours of darkness to avoid the Soviet air attacks. At the same time, the long days gave the Red Army ample daylight hours to press their crushing attacks.

Conclusion

The general trend in German military literature is that the catastrophic defeat of Army Group Center was Hitler's fault by his requiring that Vitebsk, Mogilev, Orsha, and Bobruysk be held to the last man. However, Hitler's faulty strategy was not the full reason for the German failure. Much of the blame can be attributed to the German headquarters intelligence officers who were hoodwinked by the Soviets and who refused to accept data from the front line that indicated an attack was imminent. The movement of four to six panzer divisions from the south to Army Group Center would have given the Germans one or two panzer divisions on each of the four major axes of the Soviet attack. This would have entailed the return of the four panzer divisions removed from Army Group Center in the weeks before the attack plus a few more, not a major reshuffle. These additional panzer divisions would have been able to respond in the same fashion as Russian tank units at Kursk, in the summer of 1943, when the Russian tanks counterattacked continuously after the Germans broke through the first zone of defense, giving the Soviet units time to occupy the second zone.

In the White Russian operation in June 1944, the Soviet forces were able to burst through the second and third zones of defense within the first few days in true blitzkrieg fashion, unhampered by serious German counterattacks, and the first zone defenders were to have no time to occupy the reserve positions.

Russian trickery and deception had encouraged the Germans to expect the attack at Kovel on the south shoulder of the salient and led them to hold their panzer divisions in that area even after the offensive was well under way. The broad-front offensive came as a surprise to the German high command.

Because of the deception, the Germans believed that the attacks were feints to draw reserves into the salient and that the strong attack would then be launched from Kovel, cutting off the salient by driving north toward Lithuania. Had the Germans at Kursk launched a feint at the face of the bulge and tricked the Red Army into committing the two tank armies to counterattack, the German attacks from the north and south shoulders would have had greater success. In contrast, during the summer of 1944, the Russians were able to conceal their troop movements to the face of the bulge and still have powerful forces at Kovel to support the German fear that the main attack would come from there.

The first 2 weeks of fighting in White Russia gave a classic demonstration of the Russian theory of deep penetration or blitzkrieg through the use of highly mobile balanced combat teams that pressed on regardless of their open flanks, relying on the supporting infantry to move up before the Germans had time to react. The success of the White Russian offensive by the Red Army in June 1944 is shown in a net result of a 275-kilometer advance in 2 weeks through difficult terrain and on a limited road network. During this period the Russians experienced minimal losses and captured over

50,000 German prisoners. However, without the element of surprise and the time needed to concentrate an overwhelming force, future blitzkriegs against the German army were seldom possible. Given Stalin's desire to occupy as much territory as possible before the end of the war, the Red Army had few opportunities for deception and resorted to costly frontal attacks.

If one or more elements are missing in an attack, it quickly bogs down because the enemy will have time to move in more reserves to block the exploiting armored units before they make any significant progress. Logistics gave the Germans the needed time after 3 July 1944, when they reestablished a continuous front with reserves transferred from other sectors. Then the deadly process of grinding away with frontal attacks resumed and Soviet losses escalated. To advance the remaining 325 kilometers to Warsaw would take 8 more weeks and cost the Red Army most of the 180,000 permanent losses and 590,000 sick and wounded in the White Russian operation from 22 June to 29 August 1944.[5]

As the paths of the Red Army mobile columns are traced in the first phase of the White Russian operation, we will see ample evidence of the application of all elements of blitzkrieg. By 1944, with the output of the Soviet arms industry and Lend Lease imports of trucks, Stalin had the tools to implement the blitzkrieg theory to the fullest. The crushing victory in White Russia was possible because the Soviets had the men, weapons, training, and experience to execute the blitzkrieg.

Notes

1. *Fremde Heer Ost,* Captured German Records (Washington, D.C.: National Archives), Roll 549, Frame 217.

2. Ibid., Roll 549, Frame 201.

3. Ibid., 11 March, 1944, Roll 549, Frame 84.

4. Ibid., H3/811, Roll 578, Frame 346.

5. G. F. Krivosheev, *Grif Sekretnosti Snyat', Poteri Vooruzhenikh Sil SSSR v Voinakh, Boevikh Deistviyakh i Voennikh Konfliktakh* (Moscow: Voenizdat, 1993), p. 145.

CHAPTER 1

The Strategic Position

S oviet strategic planning in early 1944 was complicated because the end of the war was in sight and there was a limited amount of time to acquire territory before hostilities ended. Stalin and his advisers had more resources than in any previous year, but they had to use them wisely to obtain the maximum benefit in the minimum of time. Once White Russia had been selected as the most promising area for the major offensive in June, the Soviet planners had to consider many factors. The weather was crucial in penetrating the swamps and determined the timing. Other concerns were cleaning up the front with minor operations to set the stage, developing a complex operations plan for 2 million men, as well as developing new techniques for overcoming the German defenses, deceiving German intelligence as to the location of the offensive, moving in the additional troops without German knowledge, and finally transporting the thousands of tons of supplies—again, without being detected. All these factors would strain the available resources, and carefully detailed planning was essential to place every piece of the puzzle properly.

War on the Eastern Front was a seasonal event. The critical change in climate was the thaw, not the cold temperature associated with winter. The daily low temperature in most winters seldom dropped below –15 degrees Celsius (5 degrees above zero and 27 degrees below freezing Fahrenheit), and the highs for even those days were often above freezing. The critical factor was mud. During the late fall in Russia, the rain made most of the secondary dirt roads impassable except to tracked or four-wheel-drive vehicles. Once the ground froze in December movement began again. In the spring, the thaw reduced the roads to mud and heavy use of the dirt roads was delayed until April or May. The roads dried in the south earlier than in the north.

The year 1944 began with a series of Russian victories in the Ukraine, the center, and at Leningrad. While the ground was still frozen, Soviet offensives cleared the bend of the lower Dnieper River in January 1944, took Kovel south of the Pripyat Marshes in February, and cleared the area around Leningrad in March.

The cleanup of the Crimea began on 8 April 1944 with the Soviet Coastal Army at Kerch at the eastern tip of the peninsula, and the 51st and 2nd Guard Armies attacking across the narrow neck at Perekop. By 12 April the Russians had driven the German Seventeenth Army back to Simferopol well on the way to Sevastopol. The three armies joined under the command of the 4th Ukrainian Front. On 5 May the second phase of the operation began and Sevastopol was taken on the evening of 9 May 1944. The Germans lost about 110,000 in killed, wounded, and prisoners.[1]

As a prologue to the main operation in White Russia, an offensive against Finland began on 9 June 1944, and Vipuri (Vyborg), the Finnish stronghold (which had German troops among its defenders), was taken on 20 June. On 21 June another attack was begun in southern Karelia north of Lake Ladoga. Both offensives were successful, and in September 1944 the Finns asked for peace.[2] This distraction, along with the crisis situation in the west as the Allies landed in Normandy, occupied much of Hitler's attention and may have contributed to his reluctance to make decisions in a timely fashion in late June.

In April Stalin and the Soviet general staff (Stavka) began making plans for the summer. A basic consideration was how much territory the Soviet Union could occupy within the next 6 months, given the expected British and the United States invasion of France in May. With the opening of the second front the possibility of a German collapse was evident and the war would end by June. (Had the plot to kill Hitler succeeded in July 1944, the war might well have ended abruptly.) Stalin knew that the Western Allies would not willingly cede territory to him, so the Red Army would have to take it before the war ended.[3]

In early April 1944 the Western Allies informed the Soviets that a second front would be opened on 31 May 1944 and requested that the Soviet Union launch a major offensive to coincide with the landings and to prevent the Germans from transferring divisions from the Eastern Front to France. The Western Allies mistakenly were concerned that the Russians were too weak and would be unable to cooperate, indicating the West's lack of knowledge of Soviet reserves and capabilities. Nevertheless, the Russians assured the Americans on 23 April that an attack would be launched, but informed the

Americans and British that the time and place of the attack had not been decided, which was true.[4]

Not only did the United States and Britain underestimate the Red Army, they overestimated the political ability of the West to determine the shape of postwar Europe. In April 1944 a contretemps between Stalin and Churchill had erupted over the Polish government in exile in London that revealed the true interpretation of political power by Stalin and by Churchill. Stalin compared the Poles with the forces of Draza Mihajlovic in Yugoslavia, some of which were cooperating with the Germans in fighting the Partisan forces of the communist leader Tito. Churchill objected, but his futile protest merely strengthened the Soviet resolve to occupy Poland before peace talks and to prevent any possibility of a Polish state being established that would not be dominated by the Communists. Churchill's objections only reinforced Stalin's determination to attack White Russia for political and military reasons.

The Soviet Stavka proposed a number of options on 15 April 1944. Continuation of the offensives in the Ukraine would achieve immediate military and postwar political control of Germany's allies, Rumania, Bulgaria, Hungary, and Croatia. However, the Balkans presented logistical problems, and western Russia would still be in German hands if the war ended in the summer of 1944.[5]

A second option was a massive Russian drive from Lvov heading for East Prussia and the Baltic Sea. The scale of the drive would have been enormous, with over 3 million men and monumental logistical and administrative problems. This drive would play directly into the hands of the Germans for they could concentrate their armored reserves in a single area. Prior Soviet experience indicated that multiple drives had the advantage of forcing the Germans to move their reserves back and forth over long distances and reducing their ability to stop Soviet forces.[6]

A third option was to crush Finland, thus ensuring the safety of the rail line to Murmansk and the Lend Lease convoys. In addition, liberating the Baltic states would relieve Leningrad of any threat. Both options were minor operations and meant frontal assaults that would be necessary against well-prepared defenses. The goal of reaching the Baltic Sea was inconsequential because the Germans would continue to control the sea with submarines.[7]

The fourth Soviet option was to envelop the formidable German Army Group Center from the north and south. The salient in White Russia made concentric attacks possible, and victory would cripple this German army. The other advantages would be to cut the land supply route to Army Group North, ensuring political control of

Poland after the war, and to liberate White Russia, with the symbolic achievement of chasing the Germans from the last piece of Soviet territory. This offensive would set the stage for a final drive to Berlin if the war did not end immediately.[8]

The Stavka did not believe that it had sufficient resources to launch two major offensives at the same time: an attack at Kovel and a drive for the Baltic Sea in conjunction with a drive from the north, cutting off both Army Group Center and Army Group North.[9] The Stavka may have lacked the confidence to coordinate two major offensives simultaneously and also feared the German armored reserves that would remain on the left flank of the southern drive.[10]

A series of meetings was held from 20 April to 23 April that included Stalin, Marshal Georgiey Zhukov, coordinator for the 1st Baltic Front and the 3rd White Russian Fronts, and Marshal Alexander Vasilevsky, coordinator for the 1st and 2nd White Russian Fronts. Stalin selected the elimination of the salient in White Russia because it was only 470 kilometers from Moscow, placing the capital within easy range of German bombers. The salient also posed a threat to the northern flank of the 1st Ukrainian Front, tying down a half-dozen Soviet armies in defense positions. The planning centered around the capture of Vitebsk, Orsha, Mogilev, and Bobruysk, the entire eastern face of the salient.[11]

The first objective of the Soviet offensive was to reach a line from Molodechno in the north to Stolbtsy in the south by 15 July, an advance of 250 to 300 kilometers. A second objective was to reach a line from Daugavpils to Grodno by 15 August, a total of 500 to 600 kilometers in 51 days and well in excess of the distance of the June front line from Moscow. The offensive was to continue without pause after the first objective had been reached.[12]

The Stavka and Stalin showed their determination and confidence in deciding to launch the attack on the face of the White Russian salient despite previous unsuccessful attempts. Stalin believed he could provide sufficient reinforcements for an attack on the face to overwhelm the strong German defenses.[13] On 28 April 1944 Stalin and his immediate group of military advisers outlined the program for 1944. The grand strategy for the summer was to consist of five consecutive offensives: Finland in early June, a frontal attack on White Russia in mid-June, Lvov-Sandomir in southern Poland in early July, Lublin-Brest in southern Poland in late July, and Iasi-Kishinev in the south in August.[14] A key to unit symbols and an organization table of Red Army units to be used in White Russia are presented in Figures 1.1 and 1.2.

Stalin and his advisers also revised the plan for White Russia that called for the 1st Baltic Front to screen the northern shoulder

Figure 1.1   Key to Military Unit Symbols

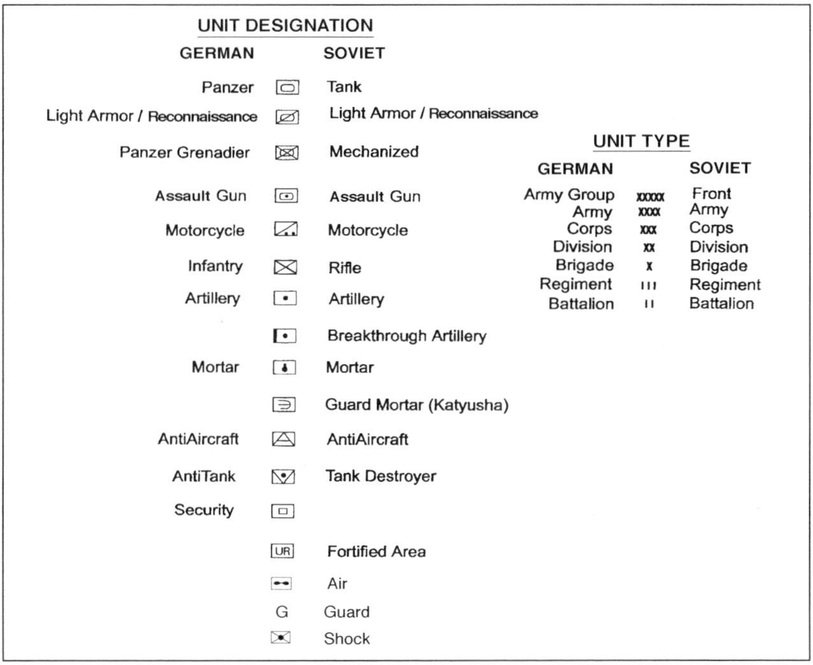

UNIT DESIGNATION		
GERMAN		**SOVIET**
Panzer	⬭	Tank
Light Armor / Reconnaissance	⬚	Light Armor / Reconnaissance
Panzer Grenadier	⬚	Mechanized
Assault Gun	⬚	Assault Gun
Motorcycle	⬚	Motorcycle
Infantry	⬚	Rifle
Artillery	⬚	Artillery
	⬚	Breakthrough Artillery
Mortar	⬚	Mortar
	⬚	Guard Mortar (Katyusha)
AntiAircraft	⬚	AntiAircraft
AntiTank	⬚	Tank Destroyer
Security	⬚	
	UR	Fortified Area
	⬚	Air
	G	Guard
	⬚	Shock

UNIT TYPE		
GERMAN		**SOVIET**
Army Group	xxxxx	Front
Army	xxxx	Army
Corps	xxx	Corps
Division	xx	Division
Brigade	x	Brigade
Regiment	iii	Regiment
Battalion	ii	Battalion

and the 1st White Russian Front the southern shoulder. The German defenses were to be pierced at six points, north and south of Vitebsk, north of Orsha, at Mogilev, and north and south of Bobruysk. The start date was set at 19 or 20 June.[15]

On 20 May 1944 an operational plan was presented calling for a first phase of two drives on Minsk from Vitebsk and Zhlobin to encircle Army Group Center. The northern attack would be by the 1st Baltic and 3rd White Russian Fronts and the southern attack by the 2nd White Russian and elements of the 1st White Russian Fronts. The second phase would be a frontal attack on a broad front to reach a line from Molodechno to Stolbtsy.[16]

The Stavka pinpointed flaws in an underestimation of German forces and a failure to provide the 2nd Baltic Front with enough forces to prevent Army Group North from reinforcing Army Group Center. The Stavka also feared that the marshlands would delay the advance and allow time for the Germans to bring in reserves. Therefore, Zhukov and Vasilevsky wanted more artillery to break through the German first defense zone and prevent the defenders from withdrawing to the second zone.[17]

From 22 and 23 May a second conference convened to amend

Figure 1.2   The Red Army in White Russia, June 1944

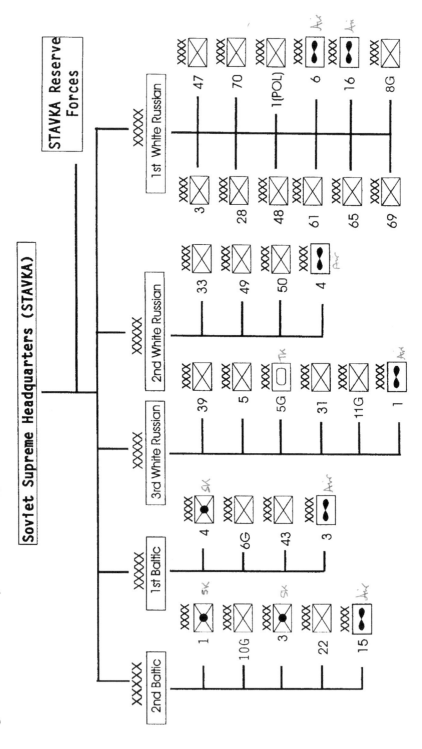

the operational plan. The 2nd Baltic Front would hold the German Army Group North at bay in the north with help from the 1st Baltic Front. The 1st Baltic Front would advance due west to Polotsk and Lepel after the breakthrough. The 3rd White Russian Front was to take Vitebsk and Orsha, then turn southwest to encircle the Germans east of Minsk. To accomplish this mammoth assignment the Stavka proposed adding the 5th Guard Tank Army to the thrust south of Vitebsk. The role of the 2nd White Russian Front, the weakest of the four, was to pin down the Germans at Mogilev.[18]

To ensure his southern flank the commander of the 1st White Russian Front, General Konstantin Rokossovsky, wanted to control the armies holding the long southern shoulder of the salient. In response the Stavka transferred three armies to Rokossovsky (61st, 70th, and 47th), but rejected an enlarged thrust in the south toward Baranovichi that would require an additional tank army. Instead, Rokossovsky was given Pliev's Horse-Mechanized Group and two tank corps for the drive toward Baranovichi.[19]

On 30 May the final plan, Operation Bagration, named for a general killed at the Battle of Borodino during Napoleon's invasion of Russia in 1812, was approved but included only the first objective, the Molodechno-to-Stolbtsy line. Circulation of the plan began with the front commanders on the next day, and by 15 June all the staff work on the operational details had been completed.[20]

With the strategy and objectives decided, the task of implementing the plan was next. Crucial to the execution was penetrating the three German defense zones in the first few days before the Germans had time to transfer panzer divisions from Kovel and other reinforcements from the north and from Germany. The plan required overwhelming superiority both in men and weapons in the sectors to be attacked.[21]

The plan called for six breakthroughs: the 1st Baltic Front northwest of Vitebsk, the 3rd White Russian Front southwest of Vitebsk and north of Orsha, the 2nd White Russian Front northeast of Mogilev, and the 1st White Russian Front north of Rogachev and south of Parichi. The final plan called for the 1st Baltic Front to break through a 20-kilometer-wide sector north of Vitebsk with the 6th Guard Army and the 43rd Army. Using the 1st Tank Corps as a spearhead, the first objective was to take Beshenkovichi and cross the Dvina River. The 1st Baltic Front would subsequently drive west to Lepel and hold the northern flank of the attack at Polotsk. The 3rd White Russian Front would attack Vitebsk from the north with the 43rd Army and the 39th Army.[22]

South of Vitebsk, the 3rd White Russian Front would break through a 15-kilometer sector with the southern flank of the 39th

Army, the 5th Army, and Oslikovskiy's Horse-Mechanized Group. The 39th Army would turn north to meet the 43rd Army and surround Vitebsk. The 5th Army would head due west, take Bogushevsk and Senno, and press on westward. The Horse-Mechanized Group would pass through the northern end of the breach in the German defenses and establish bridgeheads over the Berezina River north of Borisov and advance in full to the Berezina River.

The southern group of the 3rd White Russian Front was to break through north of Orsha with the 11th Guard Army and the 31st Army. A mobile column headed by the 2nd Guard Tank Corps would bypass Orsha and advance to the Berezina River south of Borisov. The 5th Guard Tank Army would support either the 5th Army at Bogushevsk or the 11th Guard Army's drive for Borisov.[23]

The fourth breakthrough would be made by the 2nd White Russian Front. The 49th Army would take Mogilev and then advance to the Berezina River, while the 33rd and 50th Armies contained the German forces.[24] The fifth breakthrough would be made by the 3rd and 48th Armies of the 1st White Russian Front north of Rogachev, which were to advance north of Bobruysk led by the 9th Tank Corps. The final breakthrough would be made by the 65th and 28th Armies at Parichi. The 65th Army would surround Bobruysk while the 1st Guard Tank Corps drove northwest toward Minsk. The 28th Army and the Pliev Horse-Mechanized Group would pass through the breach in the German defenses and drive west toward Slutsk. The left wing of the 1st White Russian Front would hold the German Second Army along the southern edge of the Pripyat Marshes to prevent the Germans from sending reinforcements to the north.[25]

At each breakthrough sector, the Soviet army concentrated divisions as densely as one per 1.5 kilometers, including the units in the second echelon behind the attacking divisions to sustain the attack. The front-line divisions usually had sectors from 2.5 to 3.0 kilometers wide or over 2,000 men per kilometer. Each rifle regiment in the front line had a sector of only 1 kilometer.[26] By contrast, the Germans in Army Group Center had much larger divisional sectors of 24 kilometers or more. In one instance, a Soviet division with 9 battalions with about 380 men each attacked a German battalion of about 350 men.[27]

In July 1943 at Kursk the Germans had obtained superiority at two breakthrough points north and south of the salient and pierced the first defense zones, but took too long to penetrate the second zone and failed to pierce the third. The Germans did not have enough reserves to sustain the weight of the attack, and in fact had to drain units from the spearhead to bolster the flanks. In White Russia, the Soviet army had almost as many units in the second echelon as the first and ample infantry to protect the flanks.

The theory of defense in depth used by both Germans and Russians was to withdraw from the first trench line in the first defense zone before an enemy artillery barrage began so that the shells would fall on empty trenches, and then return as soon as the barrage had lifted. To counter this defense technique the Red Army employed reconnaissance in force, sending rifle battalions forward before the barrage began. The probes were preceded by a brief 30-minute artillery barrage. If the Germans were still in the trenches, the Red Army battalion would halt and the main barrage would begin in 2 or 3 hours. If the Germans had withdrawn, then the Russians would occupy the German forward trenches and similarly probe toward the next line of trenches and repeat the process; if the Germans were still there the Russians would order up a barrage and then attack. If the Germans had abandoned the position, the Russians would occupy these trenches and then repeat the process. The 8th Guard Army used two battalions from each of the two front-line divisions and a fifth from the second-echelon division in this maneuver, a total of five battalions with tank support on a corps front.[28]

The defense-in-depth theory advocated giving up the first defense zone (usually with three successive lines of trenches) as soon as it had been penetrated and the attacker had begun to roll up the trenches from the flanks. Troops withdrawing from the first defense zone would then reinforce the troops in the second zone, while reserves would counterattack to slow the attacker. However, in White Russia the Germans had most of their troops in the first defense zone, and only a few infantry regiments and battalions were available to counterattack.[29] Therefore the second zone was not adequately manned and was penetrated quickly by the Russians. The same process was repeated at the third defense zone, at which point Red Army troops had passed through the entire defense system and Soviet armored columns would thrust through the gaps to make advances of 25 kilometers per day.

The breakthroughs were possible because the Russians concentrated infantry, independent tank brigades and regiments, and artillery at the six points indicated above. Most of the tank corps waited until the gap was opened, rather than being expended in the breakthrough process, which was left to the infantry, the artillery, and tank and assault gun regiments.[30] However, the 1st Guard Tank Corps did participate in the breakthrough, probably because so few armored units were available to the 65th Army. One assault force composed of the 16th Guard Tank Brigade, the 345th Assault Gun Regiment, a battery of the 1296th Assault Gun Regiment, and the 167th Engineer Battalion supported the attack of the 44th Guard Rifle Division of the 65th Army.[31] At Rakovichi the 1st Guard Motorized Brigade with one battalion mounted on tanks, the 1001st Assault Gun Regiment, and the 455th Mortar Regiment supported the attack of the 18th Corps of the 65th Army. Northwest of Petrovichei, the 17th Guard Tank Brigade, the 354th Heavy Assault Gun Regiment, the 3rd Guard Tank Destroyer Brigade, and two companies of the 121st Engineer Battalion supported the infantry.[32]

At Kursk the Germans had had to deal with vigorous counterattacks after breaching the main line of resistance. This allowed most of the Soviet troops in the forward zone to move back and reinforce the second defense zone. Breaching the second zone took more than a day, and counterattacks again slowed the German advance. By the time the Germans had reached the third zone, the defenders had been reinforced by units from the first and second zones plus reserves from the rear, making the third zone by far the strongest and thus impenetrable by the Germans. In White Russia few Germans escaped to their third zone, and there were few if any additional reserves from the rear. The third zone was the quickest to fall rather than being the final wall of resistance.

Major Soviet reinforcements of men and material were needed to implement the plan, and all had to be moved without alerting the Germans. Deception was a major ingredient of the logistical plan, which called for moving about 400,000 men plus supplies for over 2 million men without arousing German suspicions. In favor of the Soviet deceptive measures was air supremacy in the area that curtailed German air force reconnaissance flights. Second, German agents could not cross the front line as freely as in the past.[33]

The German army OKH was reluctant to believe the corps and division intelligence reports that were based on local patrols and observation. This reluctance helped the Russians in their planned deception. Dire consequences often follow refusal to believe bad news. Local German intelligence officers had detected a major buildup at Rogachev on 30 May, but the information was considered a trick by the OKH, which was not convinced that a major offensive was in progress until 25 June, 3 days after the attack had begun! Fremde Heer Ost (FHO), the German military intelligence group, had identified the units on the front line and expected some form of attack in the six sectors, but it had no knowledge of Soviet strategic reserves in the area and was completely surprised by the appearance of the 6th Guard Army west of Vitebsk.[34]

Major General Reinhard Gehlen, head of the FHO, was convinced that the major attack would come at Kovel.[35] The Germans were so convinced that the main offensive in the summer of 1944 would come at the Kovel-Lvov area that fresh German divisions were sent to that area in May and early June, increasing the strength of Army Group North Ukraine to 27 German infantry divisions, 8 panzer divisions, and 10 Hungarian divisions on a front less than half the length than that of the Army Group Center sector. The LVI Panzer Corps was transferred from Army Group Center to Army Group North Ukraine and positioned at Kovel. On 22 June the armies of Army Group Center had very few reserve divisions.[36]

As part of the deception plan, the Red Army stopped all offensive action in White Russia in mid-April and began the construction of defensive fortifications to convince the Germans that it was planning a defense of the area. Strict control over scouting operations was necessary to avoid arousing German suspicions, and circulation of all orders pertaining to the coming offensive was limited. Army commanders received their orders on 20 June, 3 days before the attack.[37]

The operation involved one-third of the Soviet troops on the Eastern Front, some of whom had been gathered from as far away as the Crimea. Some divisions had had to move 500 to 2,500 kilometers. If the loading of a few tank regiments was delayed for some trivial cause, the ripple effect could take days to unravel. For example, to improve the flexibility of the logistics plan, 12,000 trucks moved in 25,000-ton lots daily.[38]

Rail traffic was strictly monitored. Some units were unloaded south of the Pripyat Marshes behind the 1st White Russian Front and marched north by night to their assault positions. Loaded trains moved troops and supplies to the attack area, also by night, where they were unloaded at many stations along the rail line as far as 100 kilometers from the front. These same trains, emptied of their cargoes, moved away from the attack areas by day.[39] Movement by road was confined to the few hours of darkness available in June and to times of bad weather to conceal the movements from German aircraft. New units were held at least 50 kilometers from the front until 5 to 7 days before the attack, when they moved to assembly areas 12 to 20 kilometers from the front. The final move forward was made one or two nights before the attack.[40]

Within 25 kilometers of the front, all reserve units were concealed and Soviet officers were specifically charged with seeing that camouflage was effective. Radio silence was imposed on new units, antiaircraft fire was limited, and artillery was allowed only a few registration shots.[41]

A determined effort was made by the 3rd Ukrainian Front in the south to convince the Germans that a major attack was being planned there. Intensive antiaircraft fire and abundant Red Air Force fighter cover prevented the Germans from having too close a look at fake Red Army installations.[42]

Troop movements began with the transport of the two armies from the Crimea and the armored units from the Stavka reserve and the military districts on 21 May 1944. The two major movements were those of the 5th Guard Tank Army from the Ukraine to the rear of the 3rd White Russian Front and the transfer of the 2nd Guard Army and the 51st Army from the Crimea to provide strategic reserves for the offensive even though they were not to be employed in the first phase. The 51st Army moved to Gomel and the 2nd Guard Army to Yartsevo.[43] The movement of the 5th Guard Tank Army was made even more difficult by the insistence of the Stavka that the army be at full strength before it moved. The usual technique in preparation for a move was to slough off inferior equipment and delay manpower replacements. When the move was complete, the tank army would remain behind the front for several weeks while men and equipment arrived directly from the factories and training regiments. The Russians believed that they could not keep the presence of the 5th Tank Army secret for 2 or more weeks and so insisted on the rebuilding before the move.[44]

Additional reinforcements included the 1st Tank Corps for the 1st Baltic Front, the 11th Guard Army and the 2nd Guard Tank Corps for the 3rd White Russian Front, and the 81st Rifle Corps for the 2nd White Russian Front. The 28th Army, the 9th Tank Corps, the 1st Guard Tank Corps, and the two corps of the Pliev Horse-Mechanized Group moved to the right flank of the 1st White Russian Front.[45]

On 5 June the rail movements were behind schedule. The most serious problem was the need to have the 5th Guard Tank Army delivered to the 3rd White Russian Front by 18 June. By 9 June problems were emerging. The 3rd Guard Mechanized Corps was delayed and the matter was referred to Stalin. Stalin assumed that the railroads were clogged and therefore delayed the date of the attack from 14 June to 23 June.[46] The delay was caused not by the capacity of the rail lines, but by the concern for secrecy that dictated that unusual rail traffic move by night. However, the short 6-hour June nights did not allow sufficient time, and delay was inevitable.[47] The delay would have serious consequences because it moved the opening of the offensive into a period often marked by heavy rain, which did indeed fall.

Because the Germans tracked the whereabouts of the five tank armies with great care as an indicator of the location of the next major offensive, the movement of the 5th Guard Tank Army had to be especially guarded. On 21 June German intelligence did not know the location of the 5th Guard Tank Army and still placed it in the south where it was last identified. None of the other tank armies were used in White Russia for fear of triggering a similar movement of German panzer reserves. Instead, two horse-mechanized groups were assembled to act as small tank armies.[48]

From the beginning the White Russian offensive was planned for surprise; the buildup was to be done in secret to catch the Germans with their reserves in the wrong place. The deception was successful. The Germans believed that the 5th Guard Tank Army was in Romania and had no knowledge of the presence of the 2nd Guard Army and the 51st Army up from the Crimea. Nor was the movement of the 28th Army 200 kilometers to its new sector detected. The move of the 6th Guard Army to Vitebsk was also missed. On 22 June German intelligence mistakenly estimated that there were 400 to 1,100 tanks and assault guns opposite Army Group Center, whereas the actual number was 5,000.[49]

As usual, Soviet offensive plans revolved largely around the rail capacity in the area. In this regard, White Russia was well served in contrast to the extreme difficulties imposed by the lack of railroads in the battles at Stalingrad and Kursk. Four major east-west double-track lines led to Polotsk, Vitebsk, Mogilev, and Gomel. There were two major north-south lines east of the front for lateral movement of troops. A double-track line could accommodate forty-eight trains per day, one every half-hour. A single-track line could handle only twenty-four because of the delays in switching other trains to sidings to allow trains to pass in the opposite direction. (Anyone who has traveled on a low-priority troop train knows the frustration of moving for an hour, switching to a siding to allow an oncoming train to pass, moving off the siding for an hour, and then being switched back to a siding.) The four double-track lines had a total capacity of 200 trains per day. The need for secrecy dictated that most of the trains arrive by night, reducing the capacity by half. On average, 90 to 100 trains, each with about 45 cars, arrived in the sector every 24 hours with men and supplies, about 7,000 trains in 10 weeks.[50]

The rail capacity was divided between daily supplies required by the troops, new units being moved into the sector, and reserves of supplies being stockpiled for the offensive. Although the Red Army man lived on far less than his German counterpart, the authorized allotment for an actively engaged rifle division in December 1943 was 311 tons of munitions, 19 tons of rations, 15 tons of fodder for the horses, and 13 tons of fuel, for a total of 358 tons.[51] While a division was in reserve the quantity of munitions was greatly reduced, resulting in 275 tons per day for an inactive division. With the equivalent of more than 150 divisions in the four fronts, the daily requirement was at least 41,250 tons or about 20 trains per day each with about 2,000 tons of supplies. A car usually carried from 40 to 50 tons with about 45 cars per train for a total of 2,000 tons per train. Therefore, daily maintenance for active units required nearly one-fifth of the 100 trains that arrived each day.[52]

The Red Army delivered 5,718,916 tons of supplies in 126,589 freight cars (2,800 trains) in the last 6 weeks before 22 June.[53] This amount would have required 67 trains per day or two-thirds of the incoming trains. Presumably the 5.7 million tons included both daily supplies and buildup. The four fronts were required to stockpile 1.2 million tons, including 400,000 tons of munitions, 300,000 tons of fuel, and 500,000 tons of rations. The remaining 4.5 million tons were daily supplies and allowances for incoming units.[54]

Therefore supplies (daily requirements and stockpile) required roughly 67 trains per day, leaving 20 to 30 for troop movements, a total of up to 2,100 trains for troops. A Soviet army rifle division required up to 16 trains, a tank corps 20 trains, a mechanized corps 33 trains, and a cavalry corps 57 trains because of the many horses. A tank brigade needed 3 trains, a tank regiment 2, and an assault gun regiment 1 train.[55] The Russians moved in 56 rifle divisions (896 trains), 4 cavalry corps (228 trains), 10 tank corps (200 trains), 2 mechanized corps (66 trains), 1 tank brigade (3 trains), 18 tank regiments (36 trains), and 31 assault gun regiments (31 trains). These major units required 1,433 trains spread over 10 weeks or 21 trains per day. Artillery and other units required the remaining 10 trains per day.[56]

The computation validates the Soviet statistics and spells out the the buildup operation's magnitude, which can be easily overlooked when reading seven-digit numbers. To conceal the movement, the Russians were using only half the capacity of the four rail lines to bring in a hundred trains per day, so there was some flexibility to delivering more trains on one day and fewer on another. However, the complexity of scheduling that number of special trains (quite unlike a normal train schedule that remains unchanged for months at a time) and the friction that was certain to occur made the undertaking phenomenal.

By 20 June 1944 the Red Army had completed the concentration of troops for the offensive. On the north shoulder, the 1st Baltic Front under General I. K. Bagramyan included the 4th Shock Army, the 6th Guard Army (Chistyakov), the 43rd Army (A. P. Beloborodov), and the 1st Tank Corps (Butkov), which had been added to the front and would spearhead the drive to surround Vitebsk from the north along with the 43rd Army. In addition the front had five armored brigades and nine armored regiments. The front had 359,500 men, 561 tanks, 126 assault guns, 778 antitank guns, 2,133 guns, 2,213 mortars, 604 *katyusha* rockets, 420 antiaircraft guns, 902 aircraft, and 19,537 trucks.[57]

The 3rd White Russian Front under General I. Cherniakhovsky was divided into two groups. The northern group with the 39th Army holding the garrison of Vitebsk would send the 5th Army and the Oslikovskiy Horse-Mechanized Group around the south of Vitebsk to join up with the 43rd Army from the north. The southern group of the front was assigned the task of breaking through the German defenses south of Vitebsk and striking due west to Bogushevsk spearheaded by the 2nd Guard Tank Corps followed by the 11th Guard Army and 31st Army. The 5th Guard Tank Army was in reserve to reinforce the deep penetration. The 11th Guard Army, the 5th Guard Tank Army, and the 2nd Guard Tank Corps had been added to the front as part of the buildup. In addition the front had five armored brigades and twenty-three armored regiments. The front (not including the 5th Guard Tank Army) had 579,300 men, 1,169 tanks, 641 assault guns, 1,175 antitank guns, 2,893 guns, 3,552 mortars, 689 *katyushas*, 329 antiaircraft guns, 1,864 aircraft, and 16,208 trucks.[58]

The 2nd White Russian Front under General M. V. Zakharov had three armies, the 49th, 33rd, and 50th, assigned to envelop Mogilev from the north and south and maintain the link with the 1st White Russian Front. In addition the 2nd White Russian Front had four armored brigades and ten armored regiments. The front had 319,500 men, 102 tanks, 174 assault guns, 833 antitank guns, 1,768 guns, 1,957 mortars, 264 *katyushas*, 329 antiaircraft guns, 528 aircraft, and 7,727 trucks.[59]

The left wing of the 1st White Russian Front with the 61st, 8th Guard, 70th, 47th, 69th, and 1st Polish Army took but a small part in the offensive, holding the south shoulder of the salient. These armies made some effort by demonstrations to hold the divisions of the German Second Army from being sent to the assistance of the other armies in Army Group Center.[60]

The right wing of the 1st White Russian Front was divided into the northern and southern groups. The northern group with the 3rd and 48th Armies spearheaded by the 9th Tank Corps would drive north of Bobruysk and cut the town off from the north. The southern group with the 65th Army spearheaded by the 1st Guard Tank ‾ would drive northwest to cut off Bobruysk from the south, wh 28th Army and the Pliev Horse-Mechanized Group would straight west for Slutsk. All of the armored units were new arrivals, along with the 28th Army. The right wing also had one independent armored brigade and twenty-two armored regiments. The right wing of the front had 883 tanks, 414 assault guns, 1,444 antitank guns, 3,769 guns, 3,792 mortars, 749 *katyushas*, 762 antiaircraft guns, 2,033 aircraft, and 17,177 trucks. The entire 1st White Russian Front had 1,071,100 men.[61]

Including the Dnieper flotilla, 2,331,700 men were involved in the operation, one-third of all the Soviet military manpower on the Eastern Front. During the operation, 178,507 were killed, were missing, or did not return to duty after wounds, and 587,308 were wounded. One out of three Russians in this operation became a casualty by 29 August 1944.[62]

The Germans had 2,242,649 men on the Eastern Front in the spring of 1944, with 792,196 in Army Group Center, 540,965 in Army Group North, 400,542 in Army Group North Ukraine, and 508,946 in Army Group South Ukraine. Stronger by far than the other three, Army Group Center had more than one-third of all the troops.[63]

The stage was set and the cast was in place for the beginning of an operation that would rip the heart out of the German army in the Soviet Union within 2 weeks, leaving the entire front weak and fragile as the other German Army Groups were denuded to provide reserves to plug the gaping hole in White Russia. Through concentration of forces, deception, training, and a massive logistical operation, the Red Army was able to take advantage of the weather and the versatility of American-built trucks to surprise the German Army Group Center and destroy it.

Notes

1. *Geschichte des Grossen Vaterlandischen Krieges der Sowjetunion*, IV (Berlin: Deutscher Militärverlag, 1964), pp. 104–109; John Erickson, *The Road to Berlin* (Boulder, Colo.: Westview Press, 1983), pp. 193–196.

2. Erickson, pp. 205, 210; David M. Glantz and Jonathan M. House, *When Titans Clashed, How the Red Army Stopped Hitler* (Lawrence: The University Press of Kansas, 1995), pp. 195, 202.

3. Glantz and House, p. 195; Erickson, pp. 197–198.

4. Erickson, p. 191.

5. Glantz and House, p. 195.

6. Ibid.

7. Ibid., p. 195; Erickson, p. 197.

8. Glantz and House, p. 196.

9. G. Niepold, *The Battle for White Russia: The Destruction of Army Group Centre, June 1944* (London: Brassey's, 1987), p. 38.

10. Ibid.

11. Ibid., p. 36.

12. Ibid., pp. 37–39.
13. Erickson, p. 196.
14. Glantz and House, p. 196; David M. Glantz, *Soviet Military Deception in the Second World War* (London: Frank Cass, 1989), p. 351; Erickson, pp. 197–198.
15. Niepold, p. 39; Erickson, pp. 196–197.
16. *Geschichte*, IV, p. 180; Niepold, pp. 38–39; Erickson, p. 200.
17. *Geschichte*, IV, p. 201; Niepold, p. 39.
18. Erickson, pp. 202–203, 207; Glantz and House, pp. 189–199; Earl F. Ziemke, *Stalingrad to Berlin: The German Campaign in Russia, 1942–1945* (New York: Dorset Press, 1968), pp. 316–318.
19. Erickson, pp. 202–203; Glantz and House, p. 199.
20. Niepold, pp. 42, 44; Erickson, pp. 199, 207.
21. Niepold, p. 42.
22. Erickson, p. 213; *Geschichte*, IV, p. 183.
23. Erickson, p. 213; *Geschichte*, IV, p. 183.
24. Erickson, p. 214; *Geschichte*, IV, p. 185.
25. *Geschichte*, IV, p. 185; Erickson, pp. 213–214.
26. Niepold, pp. 53–54; *Geschichte*, VI, p. 296.
27. Niepold, pp. 58–69.
28. V. I. Chuikov, *The End of the Third Reich* (Moscow: Progress Publishers, 1978), p. 25; Niepold, pp. 61–62.
29. Niepold, p. 58.
30. Ziemke, p. 321; Erickson, p. 217.
31. A. M. Samsanov, ed., *Osvobozhdenie Belorussii, 1944* (Moscow: Nauka, 1974), pp. 625–626.
32. Ibid., p. 626.
33. Glantz, p. 362; Glantz and House, p. 203; Niepold, p. 49.
34. Niepold, p. 27.
35. Erickson, p. 200; Glantz and House, p. 203; Ziemke, p. 315; Glantz, p. 371.
36. Ziemke, p. 319; Erickson, pp. 206, 211.
37. Niepold, p. 49; Ziemke, pp. 311, 314.
38. Samsanov, pp. 730–731; Erickson, p. 214.
39. Glantz, p. 357; Niepold, p. 49.
40. Niepold, p. 49; Glantz, p. 357.
41. Niepold, p. 50; Erickson, p. 198; Ziemke, p. 311.
42. Glantz, p. 355.
43. Erickson, p. 201; *Geschichte*, IV, p. 182.
44. Samsanov, p. 729; Erickson, p. 204.
45. Erickson, p. 204; Samsanov, p. 729; *Geschichte*, IV, p. 182; Glantz, p. 365.
46. Erickson, p. 208; Niepold, p. 52.
47. Glantz and House, p. 201.
48. Niepold, p. 27.
49. Glantz, pp. 370–371.
50. Samsanov, pp. 730–731; Walter S. Dunn, Jr., *The Soviet Economy and the Red Army, 1930–1945* (Westport, Conn.: Praeger, 1995), pp. 199–201.
51. *Fremde Heer Ost (FHO), Captured German Records (CGR)* (Washington, D.C.: National Archives, 1982), Roll 556, Frame 360.
52. Ibid., Roll 562, Frame 1055; Dunn, pp. 60–63; Niepold, p. 51.
53. Samsanov, p. 730.
54. Ibid., pp. 729, 658.

55. *FHO*, CGR, 11 March 1944, Roll 562, Frame 1055.
56. Niepold, p. 51.
57. G. F. Krivosheev, *Grif Sekretnosti Snyat', Poteri Vooruzhenikh Sil SSSR v Voinakh, Boevikh Deistviyakh i Voennikh Konfliktakh* (Moscow: Voenizdat, 1993), p. 203; Samsanov, p. 54; Erickson, p. 213.
58. Krivosheev, p. 203; Samsanov, p. 54; Erickson, p. 213.
59. Samsanov, p. 54; Krivosheev, p. 203.
60. Samsanov, p. 54; Erickson, p. 214.
61. Samsanov, p. 54; Erickson, p. 214; Krivosheev, p. 203.
62. Krivosheev, p. 203.
63. Ziemke, p. 311.

CHAPTER 2

Comparison of German and Soviet Units

To comprehend the relative significance of units and to under-
stand the operations, a working knowledge is needed of the
comparative strength of units. The German and Soviet units differed
in force even though they had similar designations. For example, a
German panzer corps was at least twice as strong as a Soviet tank
corps, and a Soviet tank company consisted of only ten tanks,
whereas the German tank company had about seventeen tanks. On
the other hand, a Soviet assault gun brigade included more than
sixty assault guns, in contrast to as few as thirty-six in a German
assault gun brigade.

The largest Red Army organization was the front, which consisted of three or more field and tank armies. The field army usually
included three or four corps, each with two to four rifle divisions
and possibly some tank formations.

Soviet tanks were organized into tank armies that controlled two
tank corps and a mechanized corps. A tank corps had three tank
brigades, a mechanized rifle brigade, several assault gun regiments,
and a generous number of artillery and mortar units. The strength of
a tank corps in June 1944 was about 180 tanks and 60 assault guns,
contrasted to about 100 tanks and assault guns in a German panzer
division. The Soviet tank corps had six battalions of motorized
infantry and a motorcycle battalion, compared with only four in a
German panzer division.

The Soviet mechanized corps had three brigades of mechanized
infantry and a brigade of tanks. Each mechanized brigade had a tank
regiment used to transport one of the battalions into battle. The
corps had about 200 tanks and ten battalions of motorized infantry.

Independent Soviet tank and assault gun brigades had about
sixty tanks. Independent tank and assault gun regiments had about
twenty tanks or assault guns. Unlike the German units that were

chronically short of their authorized armored vehicles, by June 1944 the Russians had large reserves of tanks and assault guns and began operations at full strength. An efficient evacuation and repair organization salvaged and restored damaged tanks to combat condition during operations. The Soviets had thousands of tanks in depots, more than enough to replace total losses. Soviet tank armies often held about a hundred tanks complete with crews in replacement units to bring the tank brigades up to strength quickly, rather than waiting for damaged tanks to be repaired.

The Soviet field army had an established organization of support and service troops. From 1943 on the field army usually had three or four rifle corps each with three rifle divisions, but in certain circumstances would have considerably fewer rifle formations or additional units. As in all other armies, the field army was a flexible organization, but because the Soviet field army service units delivered supplies rather than the division picking them up in army depots as was done in the German army, the tie between a Soviet division and its field army was much closer. Unlike its counterpart in the German army, the Soviet division would remain assigned to a field army for many months or even years. Supporting troops (artillery, tank destroyer, antiaircraft, engineer, assault gun, and tank units) were assigned to the field army. As dictated by operations the field army would attach the supporting troops to its corps and divisions.

By 1944 a Soviet field army usually included an antiaircraft regiment, one or more artillery regiments, a mortar regiment, a tank destroyer regiment, plus from time to time tank regiments, engineer units, and guard mortar regiments. The field army in 1944 would have from 2,034 to 3,250 guns and mortars.[1]

Both German and Soviet armies used the division to denote a self-contained formation made up of infantry and appropriate supporting arms. The Soviet rifle division contained three rifle regiments, an artillery regiment, and other supporting units. In June 1944 the Red Army had built the strength of a division in White Russia to 6,500 men or more, in contrast to 10,000 or more in a German division. However, the Soviet division had far fewer service troops because the field army delivered supplies to the division. By 1944 the Germans still called the unit an infantry division, but infantry regiments and battalions were designated as either grenadier or fusilier. The German division consisted of either two regiments with three battalions each or three regiments with two battalions each and a fusilier battalion, for a total of seven battalions in most divisions. Some German infantry divisions had only four or five battalions. German battalions had an authorized strength of about 700 with about 150 men in the rifle companies, but usually the battalions had only 500 men with 100 men each in the three rifle companies and the machine gun company.[2]

In the fall of 1943, the German army revised the table of organization of an infantry division with the designation "infantry division, n. a. (new type)" with 13,656 men. Facing a severe shortage of replacements and the increasing dependence on heavy weapons rather than riflemen to provide firepower, on 10 January 1944 the table of organization of the infantry division was reduced. The new division, "infantry division, new type (reduced)," still had six infantry battalions and a fusilier battalion. The objective was to maintain the number of infantrymen, as well as increase the number of weapons, reduce the service components, replace light trucks with vehicles suited to the Eastern Front, and improve the ratio between support troops and combat troops.[3]

Among the savings in German manpower was the substitution of trucks and small tracked vehicles for the horses that pulled the artillery and wagons. Another saving in the reduced division was the decrease by 60 percent in the amount of ammunition held by the division as a basic reserve, eliminating 231 men, 336 horses, and 20 trucks. The rationale for the cut in munitions was that attacking divisions would receive assistance in supplying munitions from army troops, while divisions in defensive sectors would have ample opportunity to obtain the reduced amount of munitions from army depots. The total saving in the smaller division was 1,261 men, reducing the total German division to an authorized strength of 12,395, including 1,455 Russian volunteer service troops and 9,652 combat soldiers.[4]

The reduced German infantry division of 1944 included 3 grenadier regiments each with a headquarters company, an infantry gun company (2 heavy 105mm howitzers and 6 light 75mm infantry guns), an antitank company with three 75mm antitank guns and 36 antitank rocket launchers, and 2 grenadier battalions each with 4 companies with 6 heavy machine guns, 4 heavy mortars, and 6 medium mortars.[5]

The former German organization of three regiments with three battalions had usually resulted in two regiments each with two battalions in the first line and a third in the second, the third regiment being held in reserve in a third line. To do otherwise would disrupt the chain of command. With seven battalions, two regiments each with two battalions were in the first line, a third regiment with two battalions was in the second line, and the fusilier battalion could either form the third line or be used to reinforce the other two lines. The result was the same with four battalions in the front, but the overstrong reserve was reduced from five battalions to three. An added benefit was that the regimental artillery and antitank companies supported two battalions rather than three.

The division also included an artillery regiment with thirty-six 105mm howitzers and nine (later twelve) 150mm howitzers, a fusilier battalion, an engineer battalion, and an antitank battalion with either twelve 75mm or twelve 50mm antitank guns. Some divisions had in addition ten assault guns and either nine 37mm antiaircraft guns or twelve 20mm antiaircraft guns. The infantry regiment had an authorized strength of 1,987 men and the fusilier battalion 708. The division was authorized 8,598 rifles, 1,595 machine pistols, 614 light machine guns, and 102 heavy machine guns. Division transport included 536 cars and trucks, 1,866 horsedrawn vehicles, and 154 motorcycles plus some specialized vehicles, including 58 of the tracked towing vehicle, the Raupenschlepper-Ost, to replace horses. Remaining were 3,979 riding and draft horses.[6]

The actual strength of the German divisions in June 1944 in Army Group Center was close to the authorized strength. The Germans had reduced the number of riflemen in the new organization to a bare minimum and placed much more reliance on heavy weapons and artillery. Because the Germans had suffered few casualties in the first 6 months of 1944, replacements were sufficient to bring most divisions up to full strength. The average number of men in the infantry and engineer units of the eleven divisions in the 4th German Army was less than 3,000. The divisional sectors averaged about 24 kilometers with about 119 infantry and engineers per kilometer.[7]

In the German IX Corps on 19 June, the 252nd Infantry Division and Corps Detachment D had a total of eleven infantry battalions on the front line, each with an average strength of 350 infantrymen, thus about equal to a Soviet rifle battalion. The Germans had only 50 to 80 men per kilometer, a very slender hold on a crucial sector.[8] Soon after the offensive began this number of riflemen was reduced by casualties. The security units and combat groups drawn into the battle were usually very short of heavy weapons and seldom had adequate artillery support, making them substantially weaker than the heavily armed Soviet divisions.[9]

The Red Army rifle divisions averaged 6,900 to 7,200 men, weaker than full-strength German divisions. (Although many Soviet divisions were designated as guard rifle divisions, thereby increasing the troop's pay, guard divisions had in reality only a few more men and better weapons.) The organization of the Soviet rifle division had changed considerably during the war, reducing the number of riflemen and increasing the number of heavy weapons. However, even though rifle divisions were often below strength, they usually had the authorized number of heavy weapons and artillery pieces because most of the "missing" men had been in the rifle companies. The Soviet division was authorized forty-four 76mm guns, twenty 122mm howitzers, 127 mortars, 12 antiaircraft guns (37mm or 76mm), 54 antitank guns (37mm, 45mm, or 57mm), 6,330 rifles, 3,594 machine pistols, 337 light machine guns, 166 heavy machine guns, 342 motor vehicles, and 1,200 horses. Compared with a German division the Soviet division had 2,200 fewer rifles, 2,000 additional machine pistols, 200 fewer machine guns, 2,800 fewer horses, and 200 fewer trucks.[10]

The division organization included 3 rifle regiments each with 3 rifle battalions, an antitank company with 45mm guns, an artillery company with 76mm guns, and a mortar company with 120mm mortars. The rifle battalion had 3 rifle companies, a machine gun company, and a mortar company. The divisional artillery regiment had 3 light battalions with 76mm guns, a medium battalion with 122mm howitzers, an antiaircraft battalion with 37mm guns, and an antitank battalion with 45mm or 57mm guns.[11] In 1944 the artillery regiments of guard rifle divisions were reorganized as brigades with a regiment of twenty 76mm guns, a regiment of twenty 122mm howitzers, and a regiment of twenty 160mm mortars.[12]

A critical factor was the actual number of men in a Soviet division in June 1944, the table of organization of a rifle division having been increased to 11,706 men from a low of 9,435 in 1943. However, the new table was not implemented and there were no completely full divisions. A Soviet document dated 28 December 1943 reduced some divisions to 6,000 men as a result of heavy losses, eliminated the third battalion of the rifle regiments, and cut the rifle battalion to 424 men, with three rifle companies of 113 men.[13] In 1944 only a quarter of the divisions had up to 8,000 men, and the others ranged from 5,000 to 7,000, with a few as low as 3,000.[14] Soviet estimates of the strength of divisions in the Battle for White Russia ranged from 6,500 men to 7,000 men.[15] It was assumed that during an operation a division of 8,000 men would dwindle to 5,000 or 6,000, according to the Red Army philosophy of not adding replacements during combat.[16]

A German intelligence report of 6 March 1944 based on captured documents stated that the Soviet 212th Rifle Division had only 5,200 men rather than the authorized strength of 8,200 in December 1943.[17] A German intelligence summary of 20 March 1944 listed the Soviet rifle division as having 5,400 men, with 367 men in the rifle battalions. Soviet divisions had 166 light and 54 heavy machine guns, forty 50mm mortars, forty 80mm mortars, eighteen 120mm mortars,

26 antitank guns, 12 infantry guns, twenty 76mm guns, and twelve 150mm howitzers.[18]

A captured document described the 864th Regiment of the 189th Rifle Division of the Red Army on 1 March 1944 (the 189th Rifle Division was in the Leningrad area and had probably suffered heavy casualties during the January 1944 offensive). The regiment had only 2 rifle battalions with 158 men in the first and 200 in the second battalion. The headquarters and service units had 250 men, and there were an additional 113 men in the 45mm antitank battery, the 76mm gun battery, and the 120mm mortar battery. Nearly 200 of the 727 men in the regiment operated heavy weapons, and only 204 were riflemen and light machine gun crew members. The ratio of heavy weapons to riflemen was greater than in German units.[19]

These totals are about half the authorized unit strength, but the German report was probably based on intelligence gathered before the massive buildup program initiated by the Red Army in the spring of 1944. A Soviet document of 27 April 1944 noted that all available men in newly liberated territory were to be mobilized, and, with these reinforcements, rifle divisions would be increased to 6,000 men or more.[20] Another Soviet document stated that the rifle company was to be reduced to seventy men or even sixty with only six light machine guns. The rifle regiment was reduced to 1,468 men.[21]

A German report based on captured documents gave the strength of two rifle divisions and two rifle brigades in May 1944, as shown Table 2.1, and reveal that Soviet rifle divisions may have been smaller than Soviet sources indicated.

Table 2.1   Strength of Soviet Rifle Divisions

	227th Rifle Division	383rd Rifle Division	255th Rifle Brigade	83rd Rifle Brigade
Men	5,505	4,225	1,928	1,876
Machine Guns	160	204	69	74
82mm Mortars	38	36	13	20
120mm Mortars	11	10	8	8
Total Mortars	49	46	21	28
45mm Guns	19	15	11	9
76mm Guns	35	22	13	17
122mm Howitzers	9	4	–	–
Total Artillery	63	41	24	26

Source: Militärakademie M. W. Frunse, Der Durchbruch der Schutzenverbände Durch eine Vorbereitete Verteidigung (Berlin: Ministerium für Nationale Verteidigung, 1959), p. 129.

However, the German sources relate to different times and areas. Even though the average Soviet division in the summer of 1944 had only 5,000 men, while the rifle company had only sixty or seventy men, and rifle regiments had been cut to two battalions, a special effort had been made to raise to a higher standard the divisions taking part in the White Russian offensive.[22] Therefore the Soviet average of 6,500 men, which would include a high proportion of guard divisions, may indeed be accurate.

The cavalry played an important role in the Red Army, especially when joined with a mechanized corps to form a horse-mechanized group. The cavalry corps had two divisions, each with a total of 9,240 men, 16,000 horses, 128 light tanks, 44 armored cars, 32 antitank guns, 40 antiaircraft guns, and 128 mortars.[23]

A Russian cavalry division in 1943 had three cavalry regiments and a tank regiment, a horsedrawn artillery-mortar regiment, and an antiaircraft battalion. The cavalry regiments had four squadrons, a 76mm gun battery, a 45mm antitank battery, and an 82mm mortar battery. The division had twenty-three T34s and 16 light T70 tanks, forty-four 76mm guns, twelve 45mm antitank guns, 28 antiaircraft guns, and 54 mortars.[24]

The artillery division was a powerful component of the Red Army. In August 1944 the artillery division included seven brigades: a light brigade with forty-eight 76mm guns, a howitzer brigade with eighty-four 122mm howitzers, another howitzer brigade with 32 long-range 152mm howitzers, a heavy howitzer brigade with twenty-four 203mm howitzers, a mortar brigade with one hundred six 120mm mortars, a heavy mortar brigade with thirty-two 160mm mortars, and a guard mortar brigade with thirty-six M31 rocket launchers.[25] Usually employed as a unit, rather than being parceled out, the artillery divisions could deliver a punishing barrage on German defenses. With the seven brigades under a single command, the artillery division had unit integrity and could be moved from sector to sector with a minimum of command decisions. The brigades were trained to work together, and the artillery division commander had a flexible instrument to deliver an enormous volume of fire with a minimum of preparation, in contrast to the lengthy process of integrating separate battalions for a mission.

The German equivalent was the numbered artillery command headquarters assigned to armies and corps that would have a varying number of artillery battalions. The artillery command tended to be permanently assigned to an army, for example Artillery Command 101 was assigned to the Ninth Army throughout the war. The German method of organization lacked flexibility and unit cohesion, because when additional artillery was needed, independent artillery battalions would be attached and a command relationship established. When operations no longer required a large artillery contingent, individual artillery battalions would be transferred elsewhere, but the headquarters remained with the army to which it was assigned.

The difficulty in comparing armored units is compounded because the Russians had substantial reserves of tanks with crews that flowed steadily from the tank depots, while the German panzer divisions were often below authorized strength. The panzer division was the basic armored unit of the German army with an authorized strength of 180 tanks and four *panzergrenadier* battalions. The panzer division in 1944 had a tank regiment with two battalions and two *panzergrenadier* regiments each with two battalions of infantry. One of the four *panzergrenadier* battalions was equipped with lightly armored halftracks that could accompany tanks; the remainder of the infantrymen rode in trucks and dismounted when fighting commenced.[26] In 1944 the Germans often used tank companies with twenty tanks to support operations, for example by being attached to a *panzergrenadier* battalion. Even more often tank battalions were used as components of mixed battle groups.

The German panzer division, type 43, table of organization included a Pzkw IV battalion with 86 tanks and a Panther battalion with 73 tanks. In addition there were 11 command tanks and 4 reconnaissance tanks. The artillery regiment included 12 Wasps (self-propelled 105mm howitzers) and 6 Hummels (self-propelled 150mm howitzers). The division had thirteen 75mm antitank guns, thirteen 105mm howitzers, eight 150mm howitzers, and four 100mm guns. Assigned to the four panzergrenadier battalions were twelve self-propelled infantry guns. The panzer division's antiaircraft guns included thirty-four 20mm, seventeen quadruple 20mm, nine 37mm, and twelve 88mm.[27]

German tank production could not match the heavy attrition in France and Russia in the summer of 1944, and panzer divisions were rarely at full strength once a battle began. Despite the miraculous performance by German repair crews that returned damaged tanks to action within a few days, tank battalions were often reduced to only forty tanks.

The basic Soviet tank unit was the tank corps with 200 tanks and sixty assault guns. In 1944 a tank corps contained three tank brigades, a motorized infantry brigade with three battalions, three assault gun regiments, a mortar regiment, an antiaircraft regiment, a guard mortar battalion, an armored car battalion, and an engineer battalion. The tank brigades had about sixty tanks divided into three battalions, each with two companies of ten tanks. In addition each tank brigade had a motorized infantry battalion, giving the corps a total of six motorized infantry battalions. A light tank regiment (twenty tanks) was assigned to the motorized brigade, and one of the infantry battalions rode on the tanks into battle. When firing commenced, the men, called "jumpers" and armed with machine pistols, leaped off the tanks and cleaned up after the tanks had broken through a German defensive position. The jumpers also protected the tanks from *faustniki*, Germans with *panzerfaust* rocket launchers who would emerge from cover and fire when Soviet tanks were at close range. The Soviet tank corps had 12,010 men, 207 medium tanks, sixty-three assault guns, forty-four 76mm, twenty-four 45mm antitank, and sixteen 37mm antiaircraft guns, forty-eight 82mm and forty-two 120mm mortars, and eight rocket launchers.[28]

The Red Army motorized rifle battalion usually had 3 companies of about 100 men with 12 light machine guns, 2 heavy machine guns, and 44 machine pistols. In addition the battalion had a heavy machine gun company with 9 to 12 heavy machine guns, a mortar company with six 82mm mortars, an antitank battery with four 45mm antitank guns, an antitank rifle company with 18 antitank rifles, and a truck company with 40 trucks.[29]

The Russians seldom used tanks in company strength (a Soviet tank company had only ten tanks and no administrative structure). Tanks were employed most often in brigade strength of sixty tanks. German reports usually referred to attacks by fifty or sixty tank units. Soviet descriptions often described a tank corps assigning missions to each of the four brigades.

The Soviet mechanized corps in 1944 had three mechanized brigades, one tank brigade, three tank regiments, three assault gun regiments, a mortar regiment, an antiaircraft regiment, a guard mortar battalion, an armored car battalion, and an engineer battalion. In February 1944 the light tanks in the mechanized brigade were replaced with regiments of thirty-five medium tanks. Handles were welded to the tanks so that 175 men of each mechanized brigade could ride into battle on the tanks. The replacement of the light T70 tanks with the medium T34s was a significant step forward in 1944, increasing the number of jumpers from 100 to 175. Five jumpers armed with machine pistols could ride on a T34 rather than just three on a T70.

The Soviet mechanized corps had 3 tank battalions in the tank brigade and 3 tank regiments in the mechanized brigades. The corps had 10 motorized infantry battalions as opposed to only 4 in a German panzer division. The authorized strength of a Red Army mechanized corps was 16,442 men, 183 medium tanks, 63 assault guns, 234 guns and mortars, and 8 rocket launchers. With 40 more tanks and 4 additional battalions of infantry, the mechanized corps was considerably stronger than the Soviet tank corps.[30]

The Soviet 3rd Guard Mechanized Corps on 27 May 1944 had 3 mechanized brigades each with 3 battalions and a tank regiment, a tank brigade, and 2 assault gun regiments. The corps had 16,090 men, 240 tanks, 42 assault guns, 99 armored vehicles, 255 guns and mortars, eighteen 37mm antiaircraft guns, and 1,223 trucks. The corps was over strength in tanks, but short 1 assault gun regiment.[31]

The authorized strength of a Red Army mechanized brigade was three motorized battalions, an artillery battalion with twelve 76mm guns, a mortar battalion with twelve 82mm mortars and six 120mm mortars, a reconnaissance company with armored cars and scout cars, a machine pistol company, an antitank company with thirty-six antitank rifles, a service company, an antiaircraft battery with eight to twelve 12.7mm machine guns or eight 37mm antiaircraft guns, a truck company with 100 or more trucks, and engineer, medical, and signal units.[32]

The Soviet 20th Guard Mechanized Brigade in August 1944 had three battalions each with 400 men, a tank regiment with thirty T34s, an artillery battalion with ten 76mm guns, a truck company with 120 trucks sufficient to carry the entire brigade, an engineer company, a reconnaissance company, and a signal platoon. The brigade had from 1,500 to 1,700 men.[33] The brigade was very near to authorized strength.

Red Army independent tank brigades were widely used to spearhead attacks in association with a rifle corps, which provided sufficient motorized infantry to create a balanced combat team. In 1943 the authorized strength of a tank brigade was 1,354 men in 3 tank battalions, a motorized rifle battalion, an antiaircraft company, and an antitank company, The brigade was armed with sixty-five T34 tanks, 20 light machine guns, 4 heavy machine guns, 9 antiaircraft .50-caliber machine guns, six 82mm mortars, four 57mm antitank guns, and 350 machine pistols. The brigade had 120 trucks.[34]

In July 1944 the Soviet 29th Tank Brigade had one battalion with 20 new T34 tanks and two battalions, each with 20 old T70 light tanks that had been repaired in Moscow. Each tank battalion had 2 companies of 10 tanks. The companies had 3 platoons of 3 tanks and a command tank. A supply platoon had 10 trucks. Attached to the 29th Tank Brigade was an assault gun regiment with fifteen SU152 self-propelled guns. The extra heavy assault guns made up for the light tanks in 2 of the battalions.[35]

The 41st Soviet Guard Tank Brigade on 2 May 1944 had 3 battalions numbered 203, 204, and 206. Each battalion had 2 companies each with 3 platoons. On 25 April the brigade received 21 new T34s from Nishnij-Tagil and had 6 tanks in repair. The new tanks were picked up at Nishnij-Tagil by new crews that spent 5 to 10 days equipping the tanks with radios, machine guns, and other accessories while they familiarized themselves with the tanks.[36]

Tank regiments were widely used for infantry support, eliminating the need to split up the larger armored formations. The tank regiment was authorized forty-one tanks and sixty trucks.[37] In all the examples of actual units provided above, the Soviet armored units were very near to authorized strength. No examples were found of armored units seriously below strength in mid-1944.

In 1944 the Soviets were expanding the number of tank and assault gun regiments to support the rifle divisions in keeping with the overall policy of providing more weapons per man. The assembly lines in the Urals and Lend Lease shipments provided an ample supply of tanks and assault guns. For example, the 12th Tank Training Regiment was formed at Toksova in early 1944 with cadres from abolished tank units. The 12th Tank Training Regiment provided tank and tractor drivers for the 27th Tank Regiment, which had been formed in Narofominsk near Moscow in the winter of 1943–1944. The trainees came from disbanded units and recruits from the classes of 1924 and 1925 (19- and 20-year-olds). The 27th Tank Regiment was sent by rail to Leningrad and on 15 June 1944 took part in the attack on Vipuri.[38]

An increasing number of Lend Lease tanks was being assigned to tank regiments. The 259th Tank Regiment was formed in Kharkov in early March 1944 and equipped with ten U.S. Sherman M4A2 medium tanks and ten British Valentines, plus twenty trucks and three passenger vehicles, probably jeeps. The tanks had been delivered via the Persian Gulf and Baku to Kharkov on 10 March 1944. The regiment was transported by rail via Kiev and Sarny to the Kovel area and moved on its own tracks and wheels to Kovel from the railhead on 12 April 1944. The crews were fresh from tank schools, and although the Russians considered the British tank engines superior to those made in the Soviet Union, they believed that the Soviet tanks had better armor.[39]

The British tanks were mechanically more reliable than the Soviet tanks. The 260th Breakthrough Tank Regiment in July 1944 had ten tanks operational, including five British Churchills. The remainder were being repaired. The Soviet philosophy of producing weapons of minimum quality to perform their tasks and the 6-month life expectancy of a tank dictated that little effort was made to produce a long-lasting tank engine.[40]

The Red Army 230th Tank Regiment at Kovel on 19 March 1944

had 10 Sherman M4A2s, 10 Valentines, 3 armored cars, and 10 trucks. The regiment had been formed at Baku in February 1944 with new Lend Lease tanks, and had a company of men armed with machine pistols and a total strength of 300 to 350 men. The men had been trained for 9 months in British tanks in the 27th and 28th Tank Training Regiments at Baku and the Tank School at Kazan. On 7 March 1944 the regiment was unloaded at Kharkov and was in action on 16 March.[41]

All of these examples indicated that the Lend Lease tanks were being used to form tank regiments for infantry support, an increasingly crucial factor as the number of riflemen in the Red Army division declined.

A completely different program was the formation of guard heavy tank regiments to break through German defense lines and destroy Tiger tanks. The Soviet heavy tank regiments were equipped with twenty-one JS2 heavy tanks along with a supporting infantry company and engineers.[42] In 1944 three of the heavy tank regiments were joined to form a heavy tank brigade with sixty-five JS2 tanks, three SU76s, nineteen armored personnel carriers, and three armored cars.[43]

Whereas the Germans continued to concentrate their tanks in panzer divisions, the Russians had tank armies and corps for spearheading deep-penetration and independent brigades and regiments for infantry support. Assault gun units in both the German army and Red Army were used for infantry support and to support tank units. Both the German panzer divisions and the Soviet tank corps had organic assault gun units. The German division had a *panzerjäger* battalion with about forty assault guns, while the Soviet corps had three assault gun regiments each with twenty-one assault guns.

The German assault gun brigade designed for infantry support received its nomenclature from the artillery and contained batteries rather than companies. In 1944 the assault gun brigade consisted of a staff with three assault guns, three combat batteries, and an infantry battery armed with assault rifles. The gun batteries had fourteen assault guns with either Hetzers with L48 75mm guns on a Czechoslovak T38 chassis or Jagdpanzer IVs with long-barrel L70 75mm guns, for a total of forty-five assault guns in the brigade.[44]

The Germans also formed heavy tank destroyer battalions with Ferdinands armed with L71 88mm guns (more powerful than those on the Tiger tanks), the Jagdpanther armed with an L71 88mm gun on a Panther chassis, and the Jagdtiger armed with an L55 128mm gun on a Tiger chassis.[45] The German assault gun brigades and tank destroyer battalions were attached to army corps to act as tank destroyers and to closely support counterattacks against Soviet armored spearheads.

The Russians used the light assault gun regiments as escort artillery for the infantry to attack field fortifications in the second and third defense lines once the artillery had cleared the way through the first line. By 1944 the 76mm gun on the SU76 self-propelled gun was relatively ineffective against the newer German tanks. The medium and heavy assault guns were used primarily as tank destroyers. The medium and heavy regiments worked mostly with armored units, while the light regiments were attached to rifle corps.[46]

The Soviet light SU76 had a 76mm gun mounted on a T70 light tank chassis with minimal armor and no top. The SU76i used captured German Pzkw III chassis. Over 1,200 German tanks were converted at the restored tank plant at Stalingrad. In contrast to the SU76 the SU76i had an armored top. The SU85 was a tank destroyer built on a T34 chassis as a means to place on a tracked vehicle a gun comparable with the German 88mm gun. Production ceased in June 1944 when the T34/85 came into use. Manufacture began on the SU100 in September 1944 at Sverdlovsk. The SU152 and the ISU152 with heavy howitzers that could blow the turret off a Tiger tank were in use in early 1944.[47]

In 1943 Soviet assault gun regiments had various numbers of guns, depending on the caliber. There were three types of assault gun regiments: the light regiment had four batteries each with five SU76s and a total of twenty-one SU76s in the regiment; the medium regiments had four batteries, each with four SU122s, with sixteen SU122s and a T34 tank in the regiment; and the heavy regiments had four batteries, each with three SU152s, with twelve SU152s and a KV tank in the regiment.[48]

At the beginning of 1944, all three types of Red Army assault gun regiments were increased to twenty-one guns, and a company of infantry armed with machine pistols was added. Later in the year a few brigades with three regiments of assault guns were formed. During 1944 the JSU152, the SU100, and the SU85 were produced in significant numbers to upgrade the power of the medium and heavy regiments.[49] The regiments were generally at full strength. In July 1944 the 1228th Assault Gun Regiment had twenty-one SU76s, 1 light truck, 18 heavy trucks, 4 special trucks, and 42 machine pistols.[50]

The Russians relied more heavily on towed antitank weapons to destroy tanks rather than assault guns. In 1944 the independent tank destroyer regiment was given a fifth battery of 4 guns, increasing the total to 20 guns. Two regiments of 76mm guns and 1 regiment of 45mm guns were joined to form tank destroyer brigades, a powerful force of 60 guns that could stop a panzer division under most conditions. In 1944 there were 50 tank destroyer brigades plus 21 independent regiments.[51]

In January 1944 the Russians formed light assault gun brigades using Lend Lease halftracks mounting 57mm guns. The brigades were used primarily to concentrate a large number of antitank guns quickly in a small area to withstand an expected German counterattack. The brigades had sixty-three halftracks each with the effective U.S. 57mm antitank gun that had greater range and penetration power than some of the heavier caliber guns. The brigades were formed using experienced cadres from abolished tank brigades. The first combat was in August 1944 with the 8th Guard Mechanized Corps.[52]

As the story of the White Russian operation unfolds in the succeeding chapters, one should keep in mind some basic comparisons between the Soviet and German units. To start with, a fresh German infantry division coming to reinforce Army Group Center was equal to two Soviet rifle divisions depleted after hard fighting in the early days of July.

A significant comparison is the number of heavy weapons possessed by each division. The German divisional artillery regiment had twelve 150mm howitzers and thirty-six 105mm howitzers, whereas the Russian artillery regiment had twelve 152mm howitzers and thirty-six 76mm guns, the latter much less effective as long-range artillery but far better as antitank guns than the German 105mm howitzers. The German howitzers were positioned well to the rear, whereas the Soviet 76mm guns often were placed near the front and fired directly on German positions. The Germans had very few artillery units at the corps and army level, but the Red Army had huge numbers and grouped them in artillery corps, divisions, and brigades.

Both the German army and the Red Army increased the ratio of heavy weapons to riflemen. The Russians also increased the number of machine pistols and light machine guns in the rifle company, increasing the firepower while reducing the number of men. The Soviet division had more heavy weapons, along with the machine pistols, than did the German division.

German divisions had more service units as they operated individually and moved from army to army. Red Army divisions usually remained within the same corps and field armies. The Soviet division relied on the field army service units to deliver supplies rather than fetching the supplies from army depots the way the Germans did. The Soviet division was closely linked administratively to the field army, whereas the frequent moving of a German division from one army to another was of little consequence. In the Red Army such a move happened infrequently in battle, and more often an army corps along with supporting units was transferred rather than individual divisions.

The comparable strength of fresh German and Soviet divisions was in the range of 1.00 : 0.75. However, given the nature of the combat in the summer of 1944 with the Red Army attacking well-entrenched Germans, the Soviet divisions tended to dwindle more rapidly, and new personnel from field army replacement units came at a slower pace (usually during a lull in the fighting) than in the German army with replacement battalions in each division.

A Red Army tank corps was slightly stronger than a panzer division. The panzer division and the Soviet tank corps were about equal in authorized tank and assault gun strength, but the Soviet corps had six motorized battalions compared with only four in the panzer division. The German assault gun brigades were equal to two Soviet assault gun regiments.

Although Red Army rifle divisions were not as strong as the German equivalents, the number of divisions and tank corps was far greater than the German infantry and tank units in June 1944. German reinforcements by 3 July 1944 were relatively insignificant in contrast to the strength of the Soviet juggernaut even though the Soviets units were gradually weakened by combat losses and extended supply lines.

Notes

1. P. Babich and A. G. Baier, *Razvitie Vooruzheniia i Organizatsii Sovetskikh Sukhoputnikh Voisk v Godakh Velikoy Otechestvennoy Voiny* (Moscow: Izdanie Akademii, 1990), p. 32.

2. G. Niepold, *The Battle for White Russia: The Destruction of Army Group Centre, June 1944* (London: Brassey's, 1987), p. 28.

3. Wolf Keilig, *Das Deutsche Heer, 1939–1945*, III (Bad Nauheim: Podzun, 1956–1972), sec. 101, V, p. 51.

4. Ibid., sec. 101, V, pp. 52–56; Burkhart Mueller-Hillebrand, *Das Heer, 1933–1945*, III (Frankfurt-am-Main: E. S. Mittler & Sohn, 1959–1969), p. 138.

5. Keilig, sec. 101, V, p. 62
6. Ibid., sec. 101, V, pp. 62–68.
7. Niepold, p. 33.
8. Ibid., pp. 34–35.
9. Ibid., pp. 28–32.
10. Babich and Baier, p. 34.
11. Ibid., p. 37.

12. Ibid., p. 54.
13. *Fremde Heer Ost (FHO)*, Captured German Records (CGR) (Washington, D.C.: National Archives, 1982), 11 March, 1944, Roll 460, Frame 6438547.
14. *Geschichte des Grossen Vaterlandischen Krieges der Sowjetunion*, VI (Berlin: Deutscher Militarverlag, 1964), p. 282.
15. Ibid., IV, p. 26; A. M. Samsanov, ed., *Osvobozhdenie Belorussii, 1944* (Moscow: Nauka, 1974), p. 144.
16. *Geschichte*, VI, p. 282.
17. *FHO*, CGR, Roll 460, Frame 6438493.
18. Ibid., Roll 460, Frame 6438439.
19. Ibid., Roll 460, Frame 6438502.
20. Ibid., Roll 460, Frame 6438386.
21. Ibid., Roll 460, Frame 6438388.
22. Samsanov, p. 130.
23. Babich and Baier, p. 61.
24. Ibid., p. 62.
25. Ibid., pp. 53, 56.
26. Mueller-Hillebrand, III, p. 227.
27. Keilig, sec. 103, V, p. 11.
28. Babich and Baier, p. 43; O. A. Losik, *Stroitelstvo i Boevoe Primenenie Sovetskikh Tankovykh Voisk v Godakh Velikoy Otechestvennoy Voiny* (Moscow: Voenizdat, 1979), p. 69; *FHO*, CGR, Roll 460, Frame 6438276.
29. *FHO*, CGR, Roll 460, Frame 6438961.
30. Babich and Baier, p. 45; Losik, pp. 68–70; Andrei I. Eremenko, *Gody Vozeddiia* (Moscow: Nauka, 1969), p. 111.
31. Samsanov, p. 588.
32. *FHO*, CGR, Roll 460, Frame 6438922.
33. Ibid., Roll 460, Frame 6438934.
34. Ibid., Roll 460, Frame 6438280; Roll 562, Frame 1050; Babich and Baier, p. 41; Pavel A. Kurochkina, *Obshchevoiskovaya Armiya v Nastuplenii* (Moscow: Voyenizdat, 1966), p. 206.
35. *FHO*, CGR, Roll 585, Frame 362.
36. Ibid., Roll 585, Frame 152.
37. Ibid., Roll 562, Frame 1050.
38. Ibid., Roll 585, Frame 366.
39. Ibid., Roll 585, Frame 122.
40. Ibid., Roll 585, Frame 348.
41. Ibid., Roll 585, Frame 122.
42. Babich and Baier, p. 47.
43. Ibid., pp. 45–46; Stepan A. Tiushkevich, ed., *Sovetskie Vooruzhennye Sily* (Moscow: Voenizdat, 1978), p. 391; Losik, pp. 62–63; K. Malanin, "Razvitie Organizatsionnikh Form Sukhoputnikh Voisk v Velikoy Otechestvennoy Voine," *VIZH* 8 (August 1967), p. 37.
44. Franz Kurowski Tornau, *Sturmartillerie: Fels in der Brandung* (Herford and Bonn: Maximilian, 1965), pp. 24, 281.
45. Ibid., pp. 27, 281.
46. *FHO*, CGR, Roll 551, Frame 236.
47. Steven J. Zaloga and James Grandsen, *Soviet Tanks and Combat Vehicles of World War Two* (London: Arms and Armour Press, 1984), pp. 172–183.

48. Babich and Baier, pp. 48–49.
49. Ibid., p. 49; Losik, p. 62.
50. *FHO,* CGR, Roll 550, Frame 274.
51. Babich and Baier, p. 54.
52. *FHO,* CGR, Roll 550, Frame 274.

CHAPTER 3

Rebuilding the Red Army and the German Army

B ad weather imposed a delay on operations on the Russian Front in spring 1944 and gave both the Germans and the Russians an opportunity to rebuild and prepare for the summer offensives. The German effort was divided because of the certainty of a second front in the summer of 1944. In the west the Germans had to reinforce and make two army groups combat worthy after their 3 years of occupation duty. In the east the Germans had to restore their divisions after heavy losses in late 1943 and early 1944. In the west the Germans achieved a remarkable expansion of the number of units and in the east rebuilt many divisions, but these accomplishments would not be adequate because the summer of 1944 was marked by an endless series of disasters.

The Russians took advantage of the lull to expand and improve their armies in the first half of 1944. While the German army concentrated on creating new divisions to defend the additional front expected in the west and to replace divisions destroyed in the east, the Red Army replaced losses in existing rifle divisions and invested more of its resources in creating new support units—mechanized corps, tank brigades, heavy tank regiments, and assault gun regiments, as well as all types of artillery units. By June 1944 the Red Army had increased the ratio of heavy weapons to riflemen significantly to counter the ever increasing strength of German defensive positions. The Eastern Front in World War II was a bloodbath of gigantic proportions for soldiers and civilians. Over 28 million Soviet citizens died, most of them civilians. Over 6 million soldiers were killed in action or died of wounds, another 4.5 million were missing or prisoners of war, and another half million died of sickness or accidents, for a total of 11 million military dead or missing. In addition 22 were wounded or sick, and among those 1.4 million died and 3.8 million were permanently disabled. These totals are beyond comprehension when one compares them with the losses suffered by other nations. The Germans and their allies lost about 4 million killed during the war.

With this steady drain of killed, wounded, and missing, both the Germans and Soviets had to find millions of replacements every year. Both countries developed a sophisticated system that churned out millions of replacements. While the Russians were able to maintain about 6.0 million on the front with Germany and an additional 5.0 million on other fronts and behind the lines, the Germans reached a peak of 12.0 million men in 1944 but dropped to 9.7 million in 1945. While the Germans had 3.1 million on the Eastern Front in July 1943, by February 1944 the total had dropped to 2.4 million as the demands of other fronts drew strength away from the east.

The Soviet routine of inducting and training new men each year had a major impact on the timing of Soviet offensives, even though the condition of the roads dictated where and when operations would take place. Each spring and fall about half of the annual class, young men who had reached the age of 18, were inducted and trained in schools in the various military districts. Riflemen received up to 4 months' training, while tank crew members were trained for as long as a year. Beginning in January and again in June of each year, up to 1 million new replacements were available to the Red Army to fill divisions depleted in the prior 6 months. Of course there was a flow of replacements during the intervening months too, primarily from men returning from hospitals, but the biggest bumps in manpower came around January and June.

The German replacement system was based on experience in World War I when infantry divisions required a steady stream of new men to fill the vacancies created by the crushing toll of trench warfare. The limited losses of the first 2 years of World War II had produced a surplus of replacements. Therefore, in the spring of 1941, in Germany's preparation for the invasion of the Soviet Union, many new divisions were created from both newly trained men and cadres taken from existing divisions.

The German replacement system was altered by the new divisions. Instead of a replacement battalion providing men for only a regiment, the battalions were supporting an entire division. In 1942 the Germans rebuilt battered divisions in France and created new ones from newly trained men and cadres of old divisions. In the spring of 1943 twenty divisions to replace those lost at Stalingrad drained the replacement system. From then on the German army was perpetually short of replacements.

The German corps detachments constituted a makeshift program to utilize the surviving units of badly mauled divisions. The detachments were first formed during November 1943 from remnants of divisions that had suffered heavy losses in the summer and fall of 1943. These divisions could not be rebuilt as usual with replacements from the training battalions, because all available personnel were being used to fill the new "Stalingrad" divisions bearing the same numbers as the divisions lost at Stalingrad.[1]

Six of the German corps detachments were formed, A through F, the first five by Army Groups South and Center and the last in March 1944 by Army Group South Ukraine. The typical organization included three regiment-sized groups, each representing a former division and receiving replacements from the replacement battalion that served the former division. The regiment groups consisted of two or three battalions, each representing a regiment of the former division. In this way, the normal course of replacement continued with men from a military district and replacement battalion going to a unit representing the division. The intent was that once the crisis had passed, the normal flow of replacements would permit the regimental groups to be reinforced to full divisions.[2]

Corps Detachment D was formed by the Ninth German Army in December 1943 from the 56th and 262nd Infantry Divisions. The corps detachment was assigned to the IX Corps of the Third Panzer Army on 23 June 1944. Corps Detachment D had the 171st and 234th Regiments from the 56th Division and Division Group 262 representing the 262nd Division with the 462nd and 482nd Regiment Groups' battalion-sized units representing two regiments of the former 262nd Division.[3] Corps Detachment D was abolished in July 1944, after suffering heavy losses in the Battle for White Russia. The 56th Infantry Division was re-formed from some of the survivors, and the remainder was used in the creation of the 277th Infantry Division.[4]

In addition to division groups in the German corps detachments, from September 1943 to May 1944, infantry remnants of sixteen divisions were reduced to division groups and attached to other infantry divisions in place of infantry regiments. In this way, a division that had enough replacements to create only two infantry regiments would receive the equivalent of a third regiment in the form of a division group and therefore have the authorized seven-battalion organization.

Men were inducted annually, but the date of induction was pushed forward in 1943 to provide replacements sooner. New draftees received 4 to 6 months' training in the Replacement Army. The time of training varied with the gravity of the situation. The class of 1924 (men born in 1924 reaching the age of 18 in 1942) received about 6 months' training and entered combat in the winter of 1942–1943. The class of 1925 (age 18 in 1943) drafted in May 1943 had only 4 months of training before being sent to the front as early as September 1943.

From August 1943 to May 1944, the Germans suffered a series of disasters on the Eastern Front. From August 1943 to January 1944, the German army lost forty-one divisions in the Soviet Union. The class of 1926 was drafted in the late fall of 1943 before its members reached 18 and were given 4 months of training before being sent to units beginning in March 1944, 9 months earlier than the class of 1924. After training in Germany, the inductees were formed into march battalions and sent to the Soviet Union or to new divisions being formed in Germany or France. New men sent to the Soviet Union went either to field training divisions or to infantry division replacement battalions. There the young Germans received further training under combat-experienced noncommissioned officers (NCOs). The men of the class of 1926 were assigned to combat units by June 1944, also ahead of schedule by at least 5 months.[5]

During the period from August 1943 to May 1944, 54 new German divisions were formed, 37 army, 3 parachute, and 12 SS divisions. Included in the army total were 8 occupation divisions, 22 infantry divisions, 3 divisions of non-Germans, 3 panzer divisions, and 3 special divisions. The SS divisions included 5 panzergrenadier, 6 divisions of non-Germans, and 2 panzergrenadier brigades (equal to a division). The three parachute divisions were elite infantry divisions raised by the Luftwaffe, but they were not trained parachutists. These divisions were not similar to the small air force divisions formed in 1942 from airfield defense units. The three special divisions were the 1st Ski Jäger Division, the Rhodes Assault Division, and the 18th Artillery Division.[6]

New German divisions were formed in a series of waves, a group of new divisions created under similar circumstances and with similar tables of organization in a given time. In November 1943 the Germans formed the 21st Wave with nine divisions. The divisions of the 21st Wave were formed from the remnants of burned-out divisions from the Soviet Union with men previously classified as unfit for combat from the classes of 1901 through 1922 (ages 21 through 42 years). Three of the divisions were formed in France, two in Denmark, two in Poland, one in Italy, and one in Croatia. The formations were complete by February 1944.[7]

The six divisions of the 22nd Wave were created from January to June 1944. Five were formed in France and one in Italy. The division cadres came from burned-out divisions from the Eastern Front and reserve divisions.[8]

In January 1944 the 23rd Wave consisted of four field training divisions formed January to June 1944 from the remnants of four training divisions of the same number.[9]

The 24th Wave consisted of three *schatten* divisions bearing the names of training camps formed in January 1944 by the staffs of reserve divisions. *Schatten* divisions were skeleton divisions with three rifle regiments and a few support units used to flesh out the remnant of a burned-out division that usually had sustained heavy losses in riflemen but few losses in headquarters, service, and artillery units.

The six German infantry divisions of the 25th Wave were assembled in January 1944 from reinforced grenadier regiments formed by the Replacement Army to supplement the forces in the west. The organization was completed by May 1944.[10] These divisions were combat ready with two regiments of three battalions each, a fusilier battalion, three artillery battalions, an engineer battalion, and a field replacement battalion. Two of the divisions had an 88mm gun battalion in place of one of the light howitzer battalions. The divisions had only an antitank company rather than a battalion. Three of the divisions were formed in France, one in Norway, one in Italy, and one in Germany.[11]

The 26th Wave included four new *schatten* divisions created in April 1944. The new divisions had two infantry regiments each of three battalions, a single artillery battalion with eight light and four heavy howitzers, a motorized antitank company, and an engineer battalion with two companies. The *schatten* divisions had few service elements because few casualties occurred in those units. The rebuilding process was completed by August 1944.[12]

Five more German occupation divisions were formed in June 1944 in France and Italy as the 27th Wave. The divisions had three regiments with two battalions, an artillery regiment with three battalions with nine rather than twelve guns in each, and an antitank company rather than a battalion. The service units were reduced. The divisions had 11,246 men, including 588 Russian volunteers.[13]

Three panzer divisions were formed, the 116th from the remnant of the 16th Panzergrenadier Division in France, the Panzer Lehr Division in France from school troops, and the weak Norway Panzer Division from tank units stationed in Norway. The Rhodes Assault Division was simply a new title for the occupation forces on the island of Rhodes in the Mediterranean. The 1st Ski Jäger Division was created from the Ski Jäger Brigade in Russia in January 1944. The 18th Artillery Division, created from the 18th Panzer Division survivors, included nine artillery battalions, an antiaircraft battalion, and an assault gun battery with ten guns. However, the experimental artillery division was abolished in April 1944.[14]

An example of the impact of the rebuilding program was provided by the 134th Infantry Division. The division received the 1003rd March Battalion in late February 1944 to replace losses in defensive battles in January and February. At the same time, the service elements of the division were forced to sacrifice more men, and, together with the new replacements, the division was able to reform the 445th Infantry Regiment and restore the division to seven battalions.[15] The 134th Division received more replacements and returning wounded in April, as well as new weapons. As a result the division not only filled its units to authorized strength, but was overstrength because of the wounded returning to the division. In view of the surplus of manpower, from four to six soldiers from each battalion were sent home to Germany on leave.[16] The division was further reinforced by the attachment of ten assault guns from the 244th Assault Gun Brigade. At the beginning of June 1944, all of the infantry battalions were at full strength, and the divisional commander was able to rotate rifle companies from the front line for rest periods in the rear.[17]

A similar situation of plentiful replacements existed in the 260th German Division, also in Army Group Center. On 20 June 1944 the 260/22 March Company arrived from Stuttgart, with 227 wounded men returning to the division. Returning wounded were sent in companies, while new recruits came in battalions at longer intervals. Because all of the units of the 260th Division were overstrength, the returning wounded were distributed evenly to the seven battalions.[18] A training school for NCOs was established in the field replacement battalion. Along with all of the other divisions in the Fourth Army, the divisional antitank battalion received new 75mm antitank guns and 20mm antiaircraft guns. The 1st Company of the antitank battalion was sent back to Mielau in Germany in mid-June for training with new assault guns. Also in June, the 14th Company of each infantry regiment received a platoon of three 75mm antitank guns and two platoons armed with hand-held antitank rocket launchers.[19]

The surplus of Germans over authorized strength probably prevailed among most of the divisions in Army Group Center in June. The improvements in both divisions reflected a plentiful supply of men and weapons for the Eastern Front, rather than a shortage because of the diversion of men and material to France.

The impact of Germany's need to reinforce the west from the fall of 1943 until June 1944 is clearly indicated by Table 3.1.[20]

Table 3.1   Allocation of German Divisions

Theater	July 1943	June 1944
Soviet Union	187	157
Finland	7	7
Norway	14	12
Denmark	3	3
West (France and Low Countries)	44	54
Italy	7	27
Balkans	15	25
Total	277	285

Table 3.1 does not reveal the relative quality of the German divisions. Whereas most of the divisions on the Eastern Front were fit for combat, many of the divisions in France, in both 1943 and 1944, were occupation divisions with low-grade personnel and very little transport. The net loss of the thirty German divisions abolished in the Soviet Union was matched by a similar gain in France and Italy where they were rebuilt and given new numbers. The enormous effort in rebuilding the German army in 1943–1944 was primarily to form a defensive position in the west, while the divisions in the Soviet Union, which did not receive sufficient replacements to maintain existing divisions, were combined into corps detachments or sent to the West where they were rebuilt and added to the forces there. In contrast to previous years, no new fresh divisions were sent to the Eastern Front in the spring to provide the Germans with an offensive reserve.

The favorable situation was a result of the "One Million Men for the Front" program. Given the certainty of a second front in 1944 and the disasters occurring in the east, Hitler on 27 November 1943 announced a plan for the army and the SS to produce a million new combat soldiers. Part of the plan was to reduce the service elements in the table of organization of divisions by a 25 percent cut in all command and service units, and by abolishing noncombat organizations. The saving of 560,000 men was the goal, 120,000 from 150 infantry divisions, 20,000 from panzer and panzergrenadier divisions, 120,000 from service units, 260,000 through substituting Russian volunteers for German troops in service units, 20,000 from headquarters, and an additional 20,000 from miscellaneous sources. To enforce these orders, special control commissions were formed to visit units to ensure that the cuts were made. The heavy German losses in the winter of 1943–1944 led to a further search for replacements by substituting limited-service men for combat-fit men in service, communications, and headquarters units.[21]

An unprofitable German exercise was the use of Russian volunteers both as service troops and in infantry battalions added to German infantry divisions in France to replace battalions sent to the Eastern Front. Desertion and surrender to the enemy were common among Soviet prisoners of war in the Ost battalions and service units. When the Western Allies invaded in June, some of the Russians fighting for the Germans shot their Nazi cadres and gave themselves up.[22] The number of *Hiwis*, Russians who volunteered to assist the German army in service units, increased steadily in the first half of 1944. The new type division of late 1943 increased the authorized strength of *Hiwis* from 700 to 2,005, although not all divisions had a full allotment. The German defeats that began at Kursk had reduced the enthusiasm of the Russian volunteers when German victory seemed more remote as the months passed.[23]

The Ost battalions used Soviet prisoners of war (POWs) in combat units. The number of battalions increased rapidly in 1944 as aggressive recruiting in the POW camps was initiated, and by June 1944 200 Ost battalions had been formed. Given the option of dying of starvation and ill treatment as large numbers had faced before, many Soviet POWs volunteered, especially members of dissident minorities. The Ost battalions were not used in the Soviet Union, but were sent to France and Italy in exchange for German battalions to reinforce divisions on the Eastern Front. In June 1944 sixty battalions of Ost troops were part of the German divisions defending the French coast and seven battalions were in the Balkans.[24]

An additional source of men was found among the Volksdeutsch, those born outside Germany of one or two German parents. These men were classified according to their degree of loyalty to Germany. Those considered unreliable were classified as Volksdeutsch IV and were exempted from military service. In 1944 many of these same men were reclassified as Volksdeutsch III and drafted.[25]

During 1944 the German armed forces reached their peak strength of 12,070,000, including the army, replacement army, air force, navy, SS, foreign forces, and armed forces' civilian workers. An important factor in the reconditioning of German divisions on the Russian front in the first 6 months of 1944 was the reduction in the rate of losses. In the 3 months from March 1944 and May 1944, only 342,000 German soldiers were lost in the east, while 357,000 replacements arrived, a net gain of 16,000.[26] In the first 6 months of 1944, the Replacement Army provided 449,500 new replacements for combat divisions, returned 356,500 wounded to their divisions, used

63,000 men to refit burned-out divisions, and sent 261,000 men to newly organized divisions, a total of 1,130,000 men.[27] Despite the diversion of one-fourth of the men to new divisions, the vast majority became replacements for existing divisions. The result of the replacement effort in Russia in the month of May is shown in Table 3.2.

Table 3.2   Increase in Strength of Army Groups in Russia

Army Group	1 May 1944	1 June 1944
South Ukraine	360,984	418,197
North Ukraine	423,579	475,347
Center	499,450	578,225
North	340,958	376,268
Total	1,624,971	1,848,037

Army Group Center increased by nearly 80,000 men in May, more than any other army group during the same period.[28] However, the increase in the German army was no match for the increase on the other side of the line. While the Germans were frantically piecing together new divisions to meet the challenge of the second front, the Soviet Union concentrated on building up existing infantry organizations and creating new armored and artillery brigades and regiments. In sharp contrast to the explosive creation of new divisions by the Germans, the Russians formed only eleven new divisions in 1944 and reorganized rifle brigades to create five more. The divisions were given the numbers of divisions that had been designated as guards and renumbered. By 1 June 1944 there were only seventeen independent rifle brigades in the Red Army. In December 1943 the Red Army had 480 divisions and gave priority to providing replacements rather than creating additional divisions. By 1 June 1944 the Red Army had 476 divisions rather than 480 on 1 January. The number of other major formations remained stable as well. Tank and mechanized corps increased from 35 to 37, independent tank brigades declined from 46 to 37, and artillery divisions increased from 80 to 83.[29] On 1 July 1944 there were 6.4 million Soviet troops in operational units on the Eastern Front opposed by nearly 2.0 million Germans and 1.1 million Finns, Rumanians, and Hungarians.[30] Soviet statistics show that there was little change in the number of men in operational units. The low level of Red losses permitted it to increase the size of the rifle divisions period. In January 1944 the strength of rifle divisions varie

6,000 to 7,000; by June 1944 the divisions assigned to the White Russian offensive were increased to a range of 6,900 to 7,200.[31] An increase of 500 men per division times 476 divisions would have required 238,000 men, so not all rifle divisions were reinforced.

The Soviet Union was able to sustain this high level, despite the severe losses in the first 3 years of the war, by inducting up to 2 million men per year into the military. The class of 1926, those reaching age 18 during 1944, included at least 2.2 million men as a result of a birth rate of 43.6 children per thousand in 1926. Prior to 1942 the annual class had provided only 1.6 million men because of the low birth rate in the Soviet Union caused by World War I and the Civil War. The New Economic Policy in the Soviet Union in 1924 had led to better living conditions that were reflected in a higher birth rate beginning in 1924. The addition of a half-million men to the annual class of recruits in 1942 and subsequent years was a determining factor in keeping the Red Army up to strength.[32]

Because the Soviets were able to replace men in the armaments industry and on the farms with women and teenagers, most 18-year-olds were available for the army. Over 1.4 million Soviet women were in war production by 1942.[33] Few men were excused from military service on the basis of physical disability.[34] The Germans estimated that up to 1.7 million of the 2.2 million Soviet men drafted in 1943 were judged fit for service.[35] In contrast only 550,000 Germans fit for service reached military age each year.[36]

An additional factor was the recruitment of men in the newly liberated Soviet territory in 1943. Despite the efforts of the Germans to evacuate Russians of military age before surrendering territory, the Red Army recruited hundreds of thousands of Soviet citizens, called "booty troops" by the Germans, as the Red Army advanced. In 2 months the 2nd Ukrainian Front absorbed 265,000 men and the 3rd Ukrainian Front 79,000 from 1 March 1944 to 20 May 1944. In some units more than half of the men were booty troops.[37] The 54th and 55th Rifle Corps increased their rifle company strength to over 120 men by drafting civilians in reoccupied territory in the first half of 1944.[38] Some of the men were former Partisans, and most had prior military service. After a few days training the booty troops were sent to the rifle companies.

Comparing two Soviet units provides an insight into the distribution of manpower by the Red Army. The 261st Heavy Antitank Battalion was a front-line unit performing an essential role. The battalion had 268 men, 15 18-year-olds, 17 19-year-olds, 13 20-year-olds, 40 aged from 21 to 25, 139 aged 26 to 35, 30 aged 36 to 45, and 4 men over 45. Of all the men in the unit, only 34 were over age 36, an acceptable age spread in the U.S. Army. The high proportion of younger men indicated a heavy casualty rate, as would be expected in a front-line unit with dangerous missions.

The 615th Artillery Regiment, positioned well behind the line, made fewer physical demands on the troops. One battery of the regiment had 71 men of which 2 were 19, 9 were 20, 44 were between 21 and 29, 8 were between 30 and 35, and 8 were over 35. In the artillery battery, 35 had only elementary schooling; 21 had attended but not graduated from elementary school; 9 were high school graduates; and 6 had attended but not graduated. Given the age structure of the Red Army, the age spread of the battery was surprisingly low, as was the level of education. However the high number of men in the age group of 21 to 35 (52 out of 71) indicated that the battery had more experienced soldiers, probably because the casualty rate in the artillery was far less than in the infantry.[39]

Additional Soviet manpower was required for the formation of support units. During the first half of 1944, the Red Army rapidly formed numerous assault gun regiments, providing three for each tank corps and a plentiful supply to support attacking rifle divisions. The new units were formed by the Moscow Military District, which along with the Stavka Reserve commanded the enormous pool of units that could be assigned to assault armies.

The Moscow Military District included the major share of the camps and schools that formed and rehabilitated new units. The new units, held by the district until their training was complete, were then sent to the Stavka Reserve or directly to the front. On 1 June 1944 the Moscow Military District held a large number of units, many of which would be transferred to the fronts involved in the White Russian offensive during June, July, and August. The Moscow Military District had 5 tank brigades, all of which remained in reserve; 23 tank regiments, 13 of which were sent to the battle by the end of August; 14 artillery brigades, 5 of which were sent to the front; 24 assault gun regiments, 10 of which went to White Russia; 6 guard mortar regiments, 4 of which went to White Russia; 4 tank destroyer brigades, 2 of which went to the front; and 6 antiaircraft divisions, 2 of which went to White Russia.

The Stavka Reserve was the holding command for the strategic reserve and for armies employed in subsidiary operations, for example, the Coastal Army in the Crimea after the Germans surrendered. The Stavka Reserve included the 2nd Guard Army, which was transferred to the 1st Baltic Front in July, and the 51st Army, which went to the 1st Baltic Front in June. Both these armies had been with the 4th Ukrainian Front in the Crimea in April. The 5th Guard Tank Army was added to the 3rd White Russian Front in June. The Coastal Army remained in the Crimea as part of the Stavka Reserve.

The movements of these reserve units were very difficult for German intelligence to track. Located far from the front and in areas that were not easily photographed from the air, Soviet units being re-formed would disappear from the German intelligence unit cards for weeks. New units would not be identified until they appeared at the front. As a result, German intelligence consistently underestimated the number of Soviet reserves. Even the unit numbers that were identified were often challenged by Hitler as being the product of negative thinking. Historians also have been confused by the process in which a mass of relatively small units was concentrated to create an overwhelmingly powerful striking force in June 1944. One historian noted that the buildup in White Russia came in the form of reinforcements to existing units rather than the addition of new units. The creation of the two horse-mechanized groups that substituted for tank armies in spearheading two of the major thrusts was difficult to track because the groups were not formally part of the table of organization, but rather an unofficial grouping of units assigned to front reserves.

Even after these many transfers had been made, the Moscow Military District and the Stavka Reserve had substantial numbers of armored units available to support ensuing operations. The cupboard was far from bare. For example, seven armored corps still remained in the Stavka Reserve on 1 August 1944. New units were continuously being formed, many with experienced cadres that quickly assembled the men from training schools into combat-ready units. Other military districts, Kharkov and Stalingrad, for example, were also cranking out tank and assault gun regiments. The Red Army had staying power based on the steady flow of new units that it would need in the face of stubborn German defense in the last year of the war.

Countering the enormous intake of new men each year were the horrendous losses suffered at the hands of the Germans. In 1943 the Russians lost 1,977,000 killed, permanently disabled, or missing and 5,500,000 wounded or sick who would later return to duty. In comparison with permanent losses of nearly 3 million in both 1941 and 1942, the year 1943 experienced an improvement, but still left little opportunity to expand the Red Army. Even in 1944 the Soviet infantry suffered heavy losses. One regiment from 1 December 1943 to 23 February 1944 had 222 killed, 967 wounded, 71 sick, 373 missing and 5 lost due to other causes. Total losses in the regiment for eks were 1,638 from a unit of about 2,000 men.[40]

ver, in the first half of 1944, only 721,000 Soviet soldiers nanently lost. On 31 December 1943 there were 6,387,000 women in operational units of the Red Army. That number

ɔd to 6,447,000 by 30 June 1944.[41] The difference between t
h on 31 December 1943 and 30 June 1944 (60,000) plus the
erable losses (721,000) indicated 781,000 additions. The ebb
ɔw of wounded and sick who would later return to duty
the total gain slightly if the wounded were transferred from
ɾational forces. Remarkably few new additions were made in
months (781,000 compared to an average of over 1 million), a
le result of sending large numbers of men to armored and
y regiments forming in the military districts and possibly the
ɔn of trainees in replacement regiments in anticipation of
ɛasualties in the summer.
ɛ temporary respite from heavy losses allowed the Soviets to
ɾ existing rifle divisions just prior to the White Russian offen-
ɾith an annual intake of nearly 2 million recruits and acquisi-
 booty troops from the reconquered territory, the Red Army
an excellent position to build its forces.[42]
ɛ replacement system began with the induction of new
ɛ who were sent to one of over 300 (and perhaps as many as
ɛplacement regiments. By comparison the German replace-
ɾmy had 560 replacement battalions. In each Soviet regiment
vere about 3,000 trainees and 500 cadre, although some regi-
ranged from 4,000 to 6,000 trainees.
d Army commissioned officers were trained in forty to sixty
 replacement regiments, each with about 500 to 1,000 trainees;
ɾont had at least one regiment and most had two such regi-
 The regiments gave a short course to qualified NCOs and
eturned them to their divisions as officers.[43] Other officer-
ɡ regiments were in the rear. An officer school at Omsk had
ɾainees who received 12 months of training to become tank
s. The cadre members were older men or the severely wound-
h extensive combat experience.[44]
ɛ Red Army embarked on a major program to upgrade its
ɔns in the first half of 1944. Because of a policy not adding
ements to a unit actively engaged in operations, the usual
ɛe was to withdraw a division into reserve, fill the vacancies
eplacements and supply new weapons, provide a period of
training, and then return the division to active duty.[45]

The new Soviet recruit received considerable training. A Private
Baranov was an example. He was born in 1925 and drafted on 30
August 1943 at the age of 18. He was trained in the 72nd Replacement Regiment and on 24 December 1943 (just 4 months after being
drafted) was assigned to the machine pistol company of the 508th
Regiment of the 174th Rifle Division. After 6 months, the average
period of survival, he was captured on 5 April 1944, becoming a per-

manent loss to the Red Army.[46] From this example one can comprehend the incredible turnover in Soviet manpower experienced on
the Eastern Front. In 1943 and 1944 one-third of the total strength of
the operational units on this front were permanent losses and had to
be replaced by 2 million new men.

The 2nd Guard Army, which took part in the White Russian
offensive, was ordered to bring all of its divisions up to 7,000 men
and rifle companies up to 104 men. Men over 40 years of age were to
be transferred out of the rifle companies, although exceptional soldiers over 40 could be retained. In each of the divisions of the 2nd
Guard Army, at least 400 men in service units were to be exchanged
for the overage riflemen. All men over 50 years of age were formed
in a special company and sent to the 9th Army Replacement
Regiment, presumably for assignment to noncombat duty.[47]

The 8th Guard Army, another army that would play a part in the
offensive, was moved secretly from the Ukraine to a position behind
the 1st White Russian Front. The divisions were brought up to a
strength of 6,700 men while in the south and began moving on 12
June 1944. When it arrived the army was concealed in a forest. More
replacements came in and were trained by the veterans before the
army moved to the front.[48]

The Red Army divisions used in the Battle for White Russia
were probably in better condition than those that had endured
almost continual fighting in the Ukraine since July 1943. The
Germans in Army Group Center discovered that the Soviet infantry
was more aggressive in offense and more tenacious in defense, often
holding a position rather than withdrawing from a hopeless situation. The Germans believed that the morale of the Soviet divisions
was higher because the latter had sustained fewer casualties in a
comparatively quiet sector. The Soviet divisions had more cohesion
because the turnover had been lower and leaders were experienced
in their positions of command.[49]

The Red Army had ceased to create many rifle divisions in 1944
and concentrated instead on the formation of new tank, assault gun,
and artillery units. The replacement statistics indicate that the Soviet
Union rather than exhausting its resources was controlling the flow
of manpower into the operational forces to balance losses. The
Russians used their temporary surplus to increase the number of
men in the 476 rifle divisions and to create additional artillery and
armored units to support the rifle divisions. In the second quarter of
1944, the Soviets directed about 25 percent of the new men to
artillery and armored units being formed in the military districts.
The result was that Soviet rifle divisions in 1944 were supported by

far more tanks and artillery pieces than were German divisions. This growing disparity would have a profound impact on the Battle for White Russia.

The Germans used their surplus replacements in the first half of 1944 to build new infantry divisions to defend France and bring most of the divisions on the Eastern Front up to the numbers in the new tables of organization. Still, many remnants of divisions were left at the regiment level and combined to form corps detachments.

The German army was frantically creating new divisions to replace those destroyed on the Eastern Front and to reinforce the army groups in France. While the Russians continued to suffer heavy casualties at the hand of the Germans in 1943 and 1944, the enormous reserve of Soviet manpower made possible the continual replacement of losses in the divisions. The Germans were forced to keep their divisions in action until they were on the verge of extinction and then rebuild them completely. While the Red Army obligations were being reduced by the shortening of the front and the launching of the second front by the Western Allies, the demands on the German army were increasing with the need to form an army to defend France and to fight for every inch of ground in the east to delay the Soviet onslaught.

The German rebuilding effort in the summer of 1944 was not enough to stop the combined efforts of the Allies in the east and west. As 1944 progressed, the Germans resorted to ever more desperate measures to create divisions to delay the inevitable end of the war.

An essential difference between the German army and the Red Army in 1944 was the existence of a large Soviet strategic reserve. The German garrison of France had served as a strategic reserve from 1941 to 1943 available in the event of a crisis. However, with the second front certain to come in the summer of 1944, there was no possibility of removing German divisions from France for duty elsewhere. Therefore the German armies in Russia had to create their own reserves by withdrawing divisions from quiet sectors of the front line.

In contrast, the Red Army had enough divisions to allow the withdrawal of entire armies from the front for rehabilitation. Uncommitted divisions by the dozens—a strategic reserve—were available to reinforce any sector selected for an offensive operation. In the summer of 1944, the strategic reserve was at a high point because of a relatively low casualty rate in the spring as well as a contraction of the front resulting from successful operations south of Leningrad and in the Crimea that freed entire armies for deployment elsewhere.

Notes

1. Wolf Keilig, *Das Deutsche Heer, 1939–1945*, III (Bad Nauheim: Podzun, 1956–1972), sec. 96, p. 1.

2. Ibid., sec. 96, p. 2; Burkhart Mueller-Hillebrand, *Das Heer, 1933–1945*, III (Frankfurt-am-Main: E. S. Mittler & Sohn, 1959–1969), p. 223.

3. Keilig, sec. 96, pp. 3, 6; Mueller-Hillebrand, III, p. 223.

4. Mueller-Hillebrand, III, p. 223.

5. Ibid., pp. 136–137.

6. Ibid., pp. 139, 231.

7. Ibid., p. 230; Keilig, sec. 101, p. 6.

8. Mueller-Hillebrand, III, p. 230; Keilig, sec. 101, p. 6.

9. Keilig, sec. 101, p. 6.

10. Ibid., sec. 101, p. 7.

11. Ibid., sec. 101, V, pp. 4–6; Mueller-Hillebrand, III, pp. 230–231.

12. Keilig, sec. 101, p. 7; V, pp. 7–8; Mueller-Hillebrand, III, p. 228.

13. Keilig, sec. 101, p. 7; V, pp. 9–12.

14. Mueller-Hillebrand, III, p. 231.

15. Werner von Haupt, *Geschichte der 134. Infanterie-Division* (Weinsberg: Herausgegeben vom Kamaradenkreis der Ehemaligen, 134. Inf.-Division, 1971), p. 214.

16. Ibid., pp. 216-217.

17. Ibid., p. 219.

18. Werner von Haupt, *Die 260. Infanterie-Division, 1939–1944* (Bad Nauheim and Dorheim: Verlag Hans-Henning Podzun, 1970), p. 221.

19. Ibid., p. 220.

20. Mueller-Hillebrand, III, p. 152.

21. Ibid., pp. 134, 136–137.

22. Ibid., p. 184.

23. Ibid., pp. 140–141.

24. Ibid., p. 141.

25. Ibid., p. 136.

26. Ibid., p. 133.

27. Ibid., p. 173.

28. Keilig, sec. 204/1944, p. 7.

29. *Geschichte des Grossen Vaterlandischen Krieges der Sowjetunion*, IV (Berlin: Deutscher Militärverlag, 1964), pp. 20, 143; Walter S. Dunn Jr., *Hitler's Nemesis: The Red Army, 1930–1945* (Westport, Conn.: Praeger, 1994), pp. 42–43.

30. David M. Glantz and Jonathan M. House, *When Titans Clashed, How the Red Army Stopped Hitler* (Lawrence: The University Press of Kansas, 1995), p. 304.

31. *Geschichte*, IV, p. 25.

32. B. Urlanis, *Wars and Population* (Moscow: Progress Publishers, 1971), p. 255; *Fremde Heer Ost (FHO)*, Captured German Records (CGR), (Washington, D.C.: National Archives, 1982), Roll 551, Frame 207; Roll 580, Frame 855.

33. *FHO*, CGR, Roll 580, Frames 855–857.

34. Ibid., Roll 551, Frame 207.

35. Ibid., Roll 587, Frame 14.

36. Ibid.

37. *Geschichte*, IV, p. 298.

38. *FHO,* CGR, Roll 460, Frame 6438424.

39. Ibid., Roll 549, Frame 87.

40. Ibid., Roll 460, Frame 6438736.

41. G. F. Krivosheev, *Grif Sekretnosti Snyat', Poteri Vooruzhenikh Sil SSSR v Voinakh, Boevikh Deistviyakh i Voennikh Konfliktakh* (Moscow: Voenizdat, 1993), p. 101.

42. Ibid., p. 101.

43. *FHO,* CGR, Roll 552, Frames 504–505.

44. Ibid., Roll 585, Frame 152.

45. *Geschichte,* VI, p. 253.

46. *FHO,* CGR, Roll 460, Frame 6438464.

47. Ibid., Roll 460, Frame 6438389.

48. V. I. Chuikov, *The End of the Third Reich* (Moscow: Progress Publishers, 1978), pp. 7, 15–17, 26.

49. Albert Seaton, *The Russo-German War, 1941–45* (New York: Praeger, 1970), p. 432.

CHAPTER 4

The Production Battle

On 22 June 1944 Army Group Center had far fewer tanks, assault guns, artillery pieces, heavy weapons, and even machine pistols than the attacking Russians. By June 1944 Germany had lost the production battle, and as the White Russian operation unfolded and the Germans lost many of their armored vehicles and weapons, there were few replacements. German division-sized battle groups had only a single artillery battalion and a handful of anti-tank guns to fend off Soviet armored corps equipped with new T34/85 tanks with guns equal to the 88mm gun on the German Tigers.

With the opening of the second front in France in June, Germany experienced the full impact of the loss of the production battle. The Germans were faced with high rates of attrition in practically every division in the army. The toll in loss of weapons in the summer of 1944 was as serious as the loss of men, despite record amounts being produced under Albert Speer's armaments program.

From 1939 to 1941 the Germans had enjoyed the luxury of having superior weapons in greater quantities than their opponents. The blitzkrieg concept of a short but intense campaign achieved by marshaling overwhelming superiority at the crucial points and breaking through the enemy defenses while spreading panic in the rear area had resulted in very few losses of men or weapons to Germany until the winter of 1941–1942.

In that winter the combined resources of the Soviet Union, the United States, and Great Britain reversed Germany's superior position. Given the heavy losses of equipment during the Soviet winter offensive of 1941–1942, Hitler ordered massive increases in German armament production. He realized that the cheap victories in France, Scandinavia, and the Balkans would not continue. On 6 February 1942 the first meeting of a new commission to implement the dra-

71

matic new program took place under the leadership of Fritz Todt, who was killed 2 days later in an air crash. Albert Speer was named to replace Todt and carry forward the new policies.[1]

The new program resulted in steep increases in munitions production in the second quarter of 1942. The additional military productive capacity was made available through the transfer of civilian production to the occupied countries and a reduction of nonmilitary production in Germany at the expense of the formerly comfortable German civilian economy. Before 1944 Germans had enjoyed a high standard of living. Based on an index of 100 for 1939, the civilian production index dropped only slightly to 96 in 1941 and to 86 in 1942 and then rose to 91 in 1943.[2]

The German military production index rose gradually from 103 in January 1942 to 133 in April 1942. By January 1943 arms production had increased to 182 after a year of intensive effort and continued to climb. The military index increased sharply from 241 in January 1944 to 322 in June. After June 1944 German arms production began to drop gradually as British and U.S. air attacks mounted. The major increase in military production was in armored vehicles. The armored vehicle index rose from 95 in January 1942 to 154 in January 1943 and 438 in 1944, and this index continued to rise, despite the air raids, to 598 in December 1944.[3] Production numbers are shown in Table 4.1.

Table 4.1   German Production of Weapons in 1943 and 1944

	1943	1944
Rifles and Machine Pistols	2,508,000	3,144,000
Machine Guns	169,000	290,000
80mm and 120mm Mortars	22,956	31,812
75mm Antitank Guns	8,760	11,700
Infantry Guns	2,736	10,836
Light Howitzers	4,224	10,392
Heavy Howitzers	1,320	3,180
Trucks	76,800	70,980

Source: Keilig, Das Deutsche Heer, 1939–1945, III, p. 3. Totals were obtained by multiplying monthly averages to make the table comparable to the Soviet table.

The production battle was not lost because of lack of German effort or as a result of air attacks until after June 1944. The primary cause was the escalating rate of attrition on the Eastern Front and the ever increasing Allied armies. To oppose these armies demanded far greater numbers of weapons than the German economy could provide.

Of major concern in the land battles was the availability of heavy weapons to equip the German infantry divisions. As the number of men in the divisions and rifle companies dwindled, the reliance on heavy weapons increased.

The increases in German production were neutralized by heavy losses on the Eastern Front. In June 1941 the German army had 203,000 machine guns and in October 1944, 211,000, a slight increase despite a production level of 290,000 per year. The number of infantry guns declined from 5,000 in June 1941 to only 3,752 in October 1944, even though 10,836 were produced in 1944, thus indicating a staggering rate of loss. The stock of light howitzers dropped to 6,529 and heavy howitzers to 2,521 in October 1944 despite sharp increases in production.[4] By comparison, the Russians had 15,300 76mm guns in June 1941, and 41,100 at the end of 1944, producing 17,300 and losing 10,800 in 1944.[5] Light artillery was often the infantryman's best friend, and the disparity was of major significance on the battlefield. In addition, the smaller German stock had to be divided among fronts in France, Italy, and the Soviet Union.

Because of the lull on the Eastern Front in the second quarter of 1944, the Germans made significant increases in their stock of available heavy weapons by June 1944, but that temporary gain was eradicated during the catastrophes in both the east and west in the summer of 1944.

German tank production actually surpassed losses through 1944. Heavy and medium tank production increased sharply from 1943 to 1944, as can be seen in Table 4.2, while production of light tanks ceased. In the summer of 1944 the German army was using two versions of the Tiger with an 88mm gun as heavy tanks. The Panther, with a high-velocity 75mm gun, and the Panzer IV, with a 75mm

Table 4.2   German Tank Production in 1943 and 1944

Tank Type	1943	1944
Heavy	644	999
Medium	4,868	7,675
Light	315	0
Other (antiaircraft, command)	182	487
Total	6,009	9,161

Source: Mueller-Hillebrand, Das Heer, III, p. 180.

gun, were the most common medium tanks. Some Panzer III light tanks with 37mm guns were used for reconnaissance. The Germans had 5,648 tanks on 1 January 1943 and were down to 5,266 by 1 January 1944. With increased production and fewer losses in the second quarter of 1944, the total increased to 7,447 on 1 July 1944. However, only 5,807 of the tanks were considered combat worthy: the Panzer IIs, Panzer IIIs with 37mm guns, and Czechoslovak T38s were useful only for training and interior security work. The most significant increase on 1 July 1944 was in heavy tanks, with 686 on hand versus only 395 on 1 January, and the production of Panthers, which increased the total from 1,084 on 1 January 1944 to 2,105 on 1 July 1944.

The increase in stock by 1 July 1944 was the result of greater production and fewer losses in the first 6 months of the year. Total German losses on all fronts in 1943 were 6,362 compared with only 1,997 in the first 5 months of 1944. Heavy losses during the second half of 1944 in both east and west reduced the total stock from 7,447 on 1 July 1944 to 6,284 by 1 January 1945, a decline of over a thousand despite a 50 percent increase in production. During the full year 1944 a total of 6,434 tanks were lost, including 2,617 Panzer IVs and 2,297 Panthers.[6]

Given the growing shortage of tanks in 1944, the Germans turned to assault guns to fill the void (see Table 4.3). Assault guns, cheaper to build and easier to maintain, were assuming the role of tanks. Some panzer divisions had a battalion of tanks and a brigade (equal to a battalion) of assault guns rather than two tank battalions in 1944.

Table 4.3   German Production of Assault Guns in 1943 and 1944

Assault Gun	1943	1944
Heavy	91	276
Medium	3,315	8,405
Self-Propelled Guns	1,375	441
Total	4,781	9,122

Source: Mueller-Hillebrand, III, p. 274.

A wide variety of assault guns were used; the most common was a 75mm gun mounted on either a Czechoslovak T38 chassis or a Panzer IV chassis. The Germans differentiated between assault guns that were completely armored and self-propelled guns that had a minimum of armor and open tops. Self-propelled guns were used in the panzer divisions for indirect fire rather than for assault gun duties. The Soviet SU76 was more like the German self-propelled gun, but was used as an assault gun. The Germans lost 1,705 assault guns and 925 self-propelled guns in 1943, including 39 of the original 90 Ferdinands in the Orel operation that followed Kursk. By the end of 1944 another 35 Ferdinands were lost. The remaining Ferdinands were written off in October 1944 because of parts and maintenance difficulties, with only twelve left in active service in September. The greatest German losses occurred in July 1944 when 1,056 assault guns and 335 self-propelled guns were lost. The losses in 1944 of 4,490 assault guns and 1,155 self-propelled guns were more than compensated by increased production. The German stock of assault guns and self-propelled guns increased dramatically from 2,279 on 1 January 1943 to 3,882 on 1 January 1944 and 6,891 on 1 January 1945.[7]

Soviet production far exceeded German production in 1943 and 1944 (see Table 4.4). By January 1944 Soviet stocks of most weapons were so great that production was cut back during that year. Production of rifles and carbines declined from 3,850,000 in 1943 to 2,060,000 in 1944, while machine pistols declined from 2,060,000 to 1,780,000.

Table 4.4   Soviet Annual Receipt of Weapons

Weapon	1943	1944
Rifles and Machine Pistols	5,910,000	3,840,000
Machine Guns	355,100	284,400
82mm, 120mm, and 160mm Mortars	67,900	2,000
76mm Guns	16,600	17,300
Medium and Heavy Artillery	5,500	4,300
Trucks	158,500	157,900

Sources: Krivosheev, Grif, pp. 244, 246–258; Harrison, Soviet Planning, p. 250.

The number of weapons received by the Red Army includes both Soviet production and Lend Lease deliveries. In 1944 Lend Lease provided 151,700 small arms, 9,400 guns and mortars, 11,900 tanks and assault guns, over 5,000 halftrack personnel carriers, and 18,300 aircraft.[8] Lend Lease made major contributions to other needs of the Red Army. American-produced canned meat became a common part of the army ration. About half of the men in some units were issued British or American Lend Lease boots, which the

Russian troops did not favor because the boots were not water-proof.[9]

The Russians used 76mm guns instead of 105mm howitzers as light artillery in the rifle divisions. The 76mm gun was also used in tank destroyer brigades as a heavy antitank weapon. Losses of 76mm guns in 1943 were only 5,000 in contrast to production of 16,600, so no sizable increase in production was made in 1944 even though losses increased to 10,800.

As can readily be seen by a comparison of the German and Soviet tables, Soviet stocks and production far exceeded even the dramatically increased German production in 1944 in spite of their trade-off of military production for civilian goods. While all Soviet production could be concentrated on the Eastern Front, operations in France and Italy made demands on German production even before the Normandy landings in June 1944, as the Germans attempted to create a viable defense.

Trucks had a major influence on the conduct of the war. The German estimate of Soviet monthly truck production in mid-1944 was 2,700 1.5-ton GAZ trucks, 4,350 3-ton SIS trucks, 1,100 5-ton JaS trucks, 800 cross-country SIS trucks, and 550 small cars, for a total of 9,500 vehicles per month or 114,000 per year.[10] Given the large number of Lend Lease trucks, the Soviet production estimate seems unusually high unless many were diverted to the civilian economy and not included in the deliveries to the army. The Soviet tables indicate that 158,500 trucks were "received by the armed forces" (not produced) in 1943, and 157,900 trucks were received in 1944. There is no mention of the number of trucks from Lend Lease in the Soviet source.[11]

The United States had promised to send 159,000 motor vehicles to the Soviet Union between July 1943 and June 1944. A total of 427,386 trucks were shipped under Lend Lease, and more than half of these shipments were made in 1943 and 1944. Therefore, the assumption is that at least 100,000 trucks were delivered to the Soviet Union in 1943 and a similar number in 1944. Deliveries after January 1945 were much higher than average because the ships could unload in the Black Sea ports, and many trucks were sent to the Far East in preparation for the Manchurian campaign. A reasonable estimate would be that 50,000 were sent in 1942, 100,000 in 1943, 125,000 in 1944, and 150,000 after January 1945. Either Soviet production was less than the Germans assumed or it included the assembly of American-made components in Soviet truck factories. The truck factory at Gorkiy had ceased production of Soviet vehicles in 1944 and switched to assembling American-model trucks from subassemblies sent in crates to save shipping space, a very practical solution to the shortage of cargo ships.[12]

The Red Army soldiers liked the 2.5-ton trucks and the Jeeps, which were considered much better than Soviet trucks because of their ability to navigate cross-country. Therefore American-model vehicles became an integral part of many Soviet units. In 1944 the motorcycle regiment attached to a tank army consisted of three battalions of infantry on motorcycles, an armored car battalion, and a battalion of six 45mm guns and six 76mm guns, all towed by Jeeps.[13] The 615th Howitzer Regiment on 11 March 1944 had seven GAZ-AA Russian trucks, a Jeep, twenty-one International Harvester 2.5-ton trucks, and fourteen Studebaker 2.5-ton trucks.[14] Other German reports and photographs indicate a similar dependence on American-made trucks.

Soviet tank and assault gun production continued at a high level in 1944 because of previous enormous losses. Perhaps a third of the stock on hand consisted of obsolete tanks and ones that required extensive repair, while another third was assigned to training units in the military districts and the armies in the Far East. Only a third to a half of the armored vehicle stock was available to fight the Germans, but still enough to maintain a decided advantage. For Soviet tank production in 1943 and 1944, see Table 4.5.

The number of Soviet tanks and assault guns in the theater of operations was only 5,800 of the 24,400 at the end of 1943 and 8,300 of 35,400 at the end of 1944. The remaining tanks were in the Stavka Reserve, the military districts, the Far East, training units, or in

Table 4.5   Soviet Tank Production in 1943 and 1944

Tank Type	Available 1 January 1943	Received 1943	Lost 1943	Available 1 January 1944
Heavy	2,000	900	1,300	1,600
Medium	7,600	16,300	14,700	9,200
Light	11,000	5,700	6,400	10,300
Total	20,600	22,900	22,400	21,100

Tank Type	Available 1 January 1944	Received 1944	Lost 1944	Available 1 January 1945
Heavy	1,600	4,000	900	4,700
Medium	9,200	17,000	13,800	12,400
Light	10,300	200	2,200	8,300
Total	21,100	21,200	16,900	25,400

depots in various states of repair.[15] About 10 percent of the tanks were usually in transit from depots to the front or being returned for repair. The low figure of tanks in combat units for January 1944 is directly related to the large number of tank units being rehabilitated in the rear.

Beginning with a total of 20,600 tanks on 1 January 1943, the Red Army increased its holdings to 21,100 tanks and 3,300 assault guns by the end of the year. Of those in stock on 1 January 1944, about 12,000 were available to fight the Germans, including those in combat units, the Stavka Reserve, and depots in the military districts. Most of the 9,148 German tanks and assault guns available on 1 January 1944 were on the Eastern Front. By the end of 1944, the Russians had 35,400 in stock in contrast to 13,175 German tanks and assault guns, of which 12,336 were suitable for combat. Although the Soviet total includes obsolete tanks, tanks under long-term repair, or even abandoned heavily damaged tanks, still 35,400 was an impressive number of armored vehicles, even if over half were not combat ready.

The new T34/85s were armed with an 85mm gun that was the equal of the 88mm gun on the early German Tigers, giving the Russians an even greater superiority in tanks with 85mm guns. The new Soviet JS tanks mounted an 85mm gun that outranged the Tiger gun; the 11th Guard Heavy Tank Brigade took on the 503rd Tiger Battalion at Korsun and was able to hit the Tigers from beyond the effective range of the German 88mm guns.[16]

The "received" columns in Tables 4.5 and 4.6 (27,300 in 1943 and 34,700 in 1944) includes tanks and assault guns received from Britain and the United States. Armored vehicle production in the Soviet Union in 1943 was 24,100 tanks and assault guns, and in 1944 29,000.[17] The remaining receipts, 3,200 in 1943 and 5,700 in 1944, represented the Lend Lease tanks and assault guns. German estimates of both Soviet production and Lend Lease arrivals were lower than the actual numbers.[18] In 1944 the Germans identified 2 brigades with British tanks, 4 with U.S. tanks, 5 with a combination of British and Russian tanks, and 8 with U.S. and Russian tanks, for a total of 19 out of 119 tank brigades identified.[19]

The United States sent the medium Grant M3, the light Stuart M3, and the medium Sherman M4A2. The British sent Valentines, Matildas, and Churchills, plus obsolescent U.S. tanks from depots in Egypt. Many Valentines were produced in Canada specifically for export to the Soviet Union after the British army had canceled its orders. The British sent a total of 5,218 tanks, including 1,388 from Canada, during the war. The United States sent 7,056 tanks (5,797 mediums) and 4,158 miscellaneous armored vehicles.[20]

Although the Russians liked the Jeeps and 2.5-ton trucks, their opinions of Lend Lease tanks were generally unfavorable. According to German intelligence reports, the Soviet tank drivers thought the Valentine was the best British tank but that it could not compete with a Panther or Tiger. The Matilda could not move in bad weather because the tracks were too narrow, and the armor was too thin and the gun too small. The Soviets replaced the British 2-pounder (40mm) gun on the Matilda with their 76mm gun but could not replace the armor. Nevertheless the engine was better than those in Russian tanks. The Matilda was used as an infantry support tank rather than against German tanks. The Russians did not like the Churchill either, although it was used widely in heavy-tank regiments.

Red Army tank crews hated the Grant and the Stuart, one crewman stating, "When I sit in a Grant or Stuart it is like I am in a coffin." Both tanks used high-octane gasoline for their engines that would explode if hit by German guns, unlike the diesel fuel used by British tanks and the special versions of the Sherman. The nickname for the Grant was "a coffin for seven comrades," referring to the large crew and its tendency to burn. However, the Russians did like the later version of the Sherman with its diesel engine, improved armor, and capacity for a smaller crew.[21]

In 1944 the Soviets had a wide range of assault gun types. In the heavy category were the JSU152 with a 152mm gun howitzer on a JS chassis, the JSU122S with a high-velocity 122mm gun on a JS chassis,

Table 4.6   Soviet Assault Gun Production in 1943 and 1944

Assault Gun Type	Available 1 January 1943	Received 1943	Lost 1943	Available 1 January 1944
Heavy	0	1,300	500	800
Medium	0	800	100	700
Light	0	2,300	500	1,800
Total	0	4,400	1,100	3,300

	Available 1 January 1944	Received 1944	Lost 1944	Available 1 January 1944
Heavy	800	2,500	900	2,400
Medium	700	2,400	1,000	2,100
Light	1,800	8,600	4,900	5,500
Total	3,300	13,500	6,800	10,000

Source: Krivosheev, *Grif*, pp. 252–253.

and the JSU122 with a standard 122mm gun on a JS chassis. In the medium class the Russians had the SU152 with a 152mm gun howitzer on a T34 chassis, the SU122 with a standard 122m gun, and the SU85 with an 85mm gun. The SU76 was the primary light assault gun. (See Table 4.6 for production figures.) The U.S. SU57s with 57mm guns mounted on half-tracks did not enter combat until August 1944.

The impact of Soviet production was reflected in the status of armaments of the 3rd Guard Tank Army on 28 January 1945. The army had 2,000 rifles in storage, an indication that fewer men were armed with rifles. More riflemen were given machine pistols, so that there were 1,236 extra machine pistols in use. Other indications of the reduced number of infantry were the seventy-five machine guns in storage and fewer handheld antitank rocket launchers than authorized. The lack of thirty-five 57mm antitank guns was more than compensated by a surplus of sixty-one 76mm guns and eleven 85mm guns, clearly identifying a decision to upgrade the quality of antitank defense. The light assault gun brigade equipped with U.S. 57mm guns on halftracks was short thirteen vehicles, suggesting that the stock provided by the Americans was running low and replacements were no longer available. The United States had sent the entire stock to the Russians in 1943 and was no longer manufacturing the vehicle. All other assault gun units were at full strength.[22]

Soviet arms production was providing the Red Army with an ample supply of weapons, in fact so many that production was cut back in 1944. In contrast, although German arms production increased sharply in 1943 and the first half of 1944, the German army was short of weapons. On 1 June 1944 the new divisions in the west and most of the combat-weary divisions in the east were at authorized strength, but the Germans did not have sufficient men or weapons to restore nearly twenty battered divisions in the east that were joined together in the corps detachments.

After the catastrophic losses of June and July 1944, and the loss of productive capacity from air raids, the German army dwindled rapidly during the following months. The Red Army on the other hand had a declining rate of loss and therefore a surplus of weapons. Arms production was curtailed in the final year of the war. At the same time, Lend Lease deliveries increased sharply and bottlenecks in the supply line were eliminated by the construction of railroads in Iran and the removal of the German threat to the conoys in the north. After the defeat in White Russia, the Germans uld only prolong their own agony as they became more heavily gunned in both the east and west.

Notes

1. Alan S. Milward, *War Economy and Society 1939–1945* (London: Lane, 1977), p. 509.

2. Ibid., pp. 501–504, 506–507.

3. Burkhart Mueller-Hillebrand, *Das Heer, 1933–1945*, III (Frankfurt-am-Main: E. S. Mittler & Sohn, 1959–1969), p. 182.

4. Ibid., III, p. 180.

5. G. F. Krivosheev, *Grif Sekretnosti Snyat', Poteri Vooruzhenikh Sil SSSR v Voinakh, Boevikh Deistviyakh i Voennikh Konfliktakh* (Moscow: Voenizdat, 1993), p. 251.

6. Mueller-Hillebrand, III, p. 274.

7. Ibid.

8. Krivosheev, p. 258.

9. *Fremde Heer Ost (FHO)*, Captured German Records (CGR), (Washington, D.C.: National Archives, 1982), Roll 578, Frame 1142.

10. Ibid., Roll 578, Frame 274.

11. Krivosheev, p. 257.

12. Joan Beaumont, *Comrades in Arms: British Aid to Russia, 1941–1945* (London: Davis-Poynter, 1980), pp. 154, 191; *FHO*, CGR, Roll 578, Frame 1142.

13. Ibid., Roll 549, Frame 646.

14. Ibid., Frame 84.

15. Krivosheev, p. 245.

16. Steven J. Zaloga and James Grandsen, *Soviet Tanks and Combat Vehicles of World War Two* (London: Arms and Armour Press, 1984), p. 28.

17. Krivosheev, p. 244.

18. *FHO*, CGR, Roll 552, Frame 572.

19. Ibid., Roll 578, Frame 1131.

20. Beaumont, pp. 204, 141; Mark Harrison, *Soviet Planning in Peace and War, 1938–1945* (Cambridge: Cambridge University Press, 1985), p. 258; Hubert Van Tuyll, *Feeding the Bear: American Aid to the Soviet Union, 1941–1945* (Westport, Conn.: Greenwood Press, 1989), p. 157; Brian B. Schofield, *The Russian Convoys* (London: B. T. Batsford, 1964), p. 213.

21. *FHO*, CGR, Roll 578, Frame 1140.

22. *FHO*, CGR, Roll 549, Frame 594.

CHAPTER 5

The Northern Shoulder

G eneral A. I. Eremenko's 2nd Baltic Front was the northernmost front involved in the offensive with the mission of keeping pressure on the German Sixteenth Army. The limited Soviet attacks reduced the number of German divisions that could be shifted south to counter the other Soviet attacking fronts. The second mission of the 2nd Baltic Front was to secure the northern flank of the break-through to the south. Once the 1st Baltic Front had broken through the German lines, the 2nd Baltic Front would provide coverage of the northern flank as the 1st Baltic Front drove deeper into the German defenses. To do so, the 2nd Baltic Front's forces were arranged to allow the main strength to be applied along the south-ern portion of the front's sector. Thus the 1st Shock Army was on the north, then to the south were the 10th Guard, 3rd Shock, and 22nd Armies. The 3rd Shock Army and the 22nd Army were to attack, ensuring that they pivoted while keeping contact with the 4th Shock Army of the 1st Baltic Front to the left. The 1st Baltic Front's 4th Shock Army commanded by General P. F. Malyshev and the 6th Guard Army under General I. M. Chistyakov were charged with driving to the west on the line Polotsk to Kaunas, in Lithuania The two armies were to ensure that the northern arm of the trap for the Germans was formed quickly and efficiently.

After 4 July the 2nd Baltic Front would attack and drive back the German Sixteenth Army when the Germans weakened the army to provide reserves for Army Group Center. The disposition of the German army and its allied large units, as well as Soviet fronts, and the northern sector are shown in Map 5.1. See Figures 5.1 and 5.2 for the tables of organization of the 2nd Baltic Front and Army Group Center. The Soviet 1st Shock Army (90th, 12th Guard, and 14th Guard Rifle Corps) had been assigned to the 2nd Baltic Front since 1943. The 90th Rifle Corps was transferred to the 1st Shock

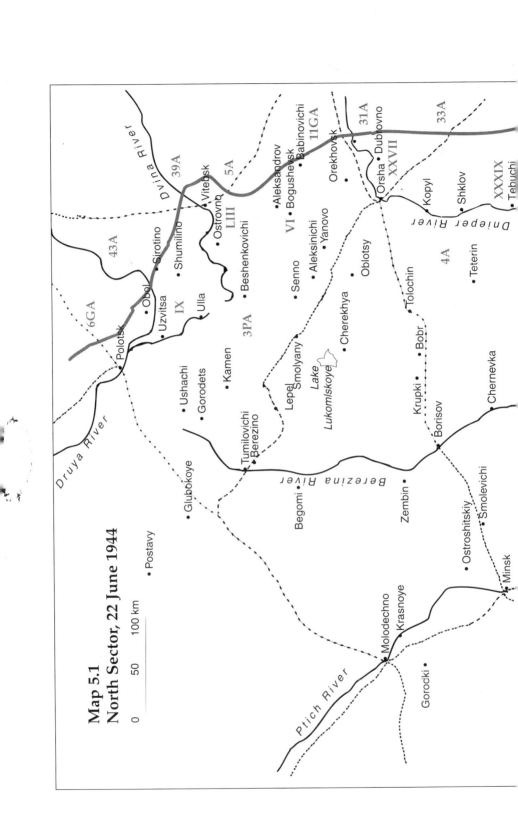

Map 5.1
North Sector, 22 June 1944

0   50   100 km

Figure 5.1   The 2nd Baltic Front

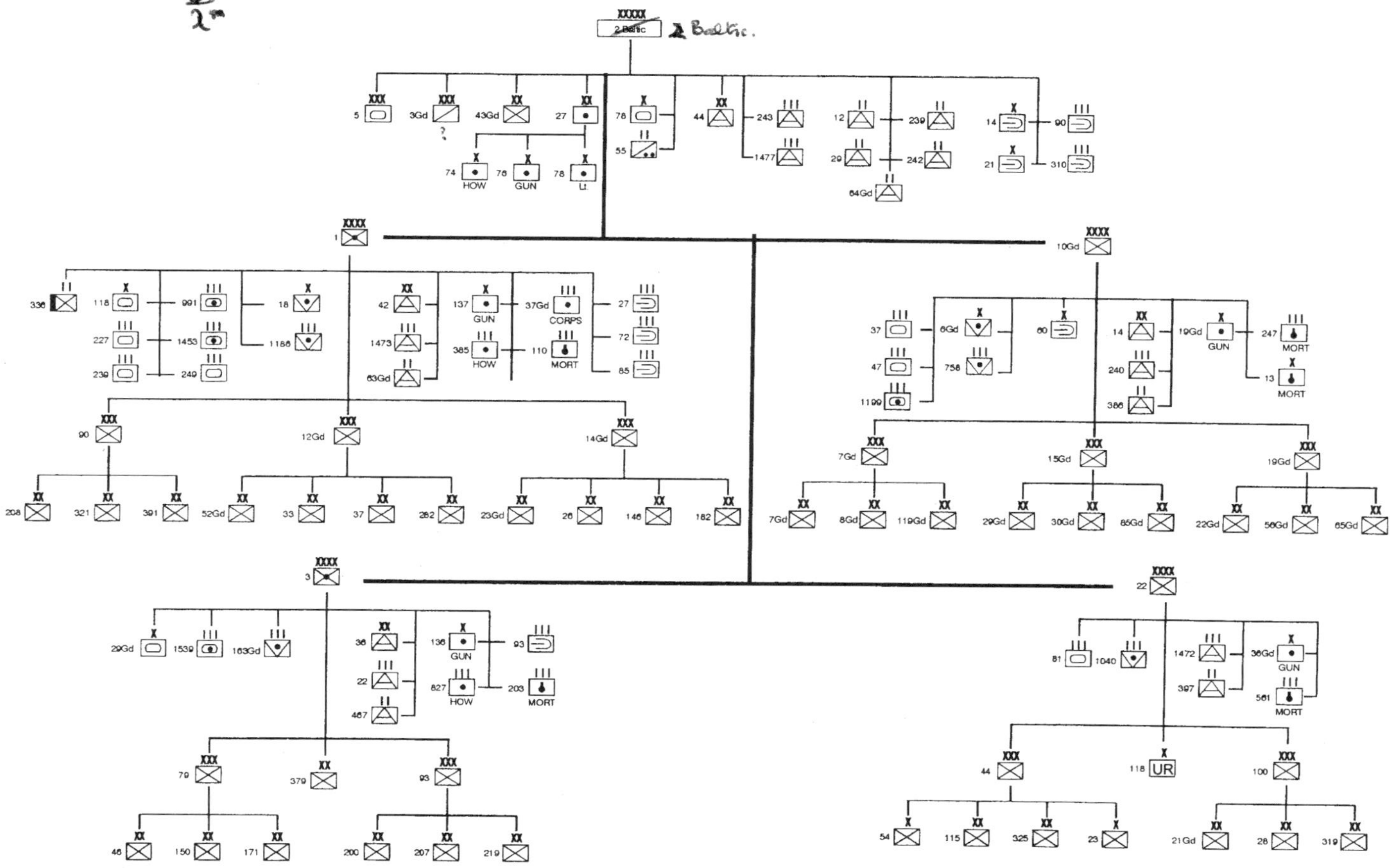

Figure 5.2 Army Group Center

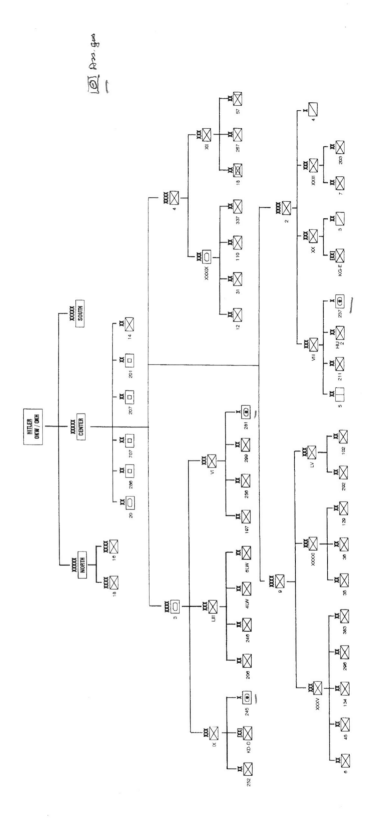

Army in April from the 3rd Shock Army. The divisions of the 90th Rifle Corps included the 208th Rifle Division, moved to the 90th Corps in April; the 321st Rifle Division, formed in April from the 137th Rifle Brigade and probably still in the process of absorbing new men and assimilating new units in June; and the 391st Rifle Division, assigned to the 90th Rifle Corps in May. Because of these many changes, the corps units were not accustomed to working together, so, appropriately, the corps was not given a difficult assignment.

The 12th Guard Rifle Corps (52nd Guard and 33rd, 37th, and 282nd Rifle Divisions) joined the 1st Shock Army in April. Three of the rifle divisions had been with the 12th Guard Rifle Corps since March. The 33rd Rifle Division joined the 12th Guard Rifle Corps in April. The corps was a well established unit and, with the extra rifle division, a more powerful entity.

Two of the Soviet 14th Guard Rifle Corps divisions (23rd Guard and 26th, 146th, and 182nd Rifle Divisions) had been with the 1st Shock Army since March. The 26th and 146th Rifle Divisions had come to the corps in April. With four divisions, the corps was able to occupy a broader sector, and all its divisions were familiar with the area.

The 1st Shock Army support troops received the 18th Tank Destroyer Brigade from the front reserve in April, while the 42nd Antiaircraft Division had been with the army since 1943. The army had a strong armored component, the 118th Tank Brigade, and the 227th, 239th, and 249th Tank Regiments, all of which had been with the 2nd Baltic Front since March. The artillery component was also strong. The 137th Gun Brigade had been formed in May from existing regiments in the 3rd Shock and 10th Guard Armies. The 385th Howitzer Regiment, the 37th Guard Corps Artillery Regiment, the 110th Mortar Regiment, the 1186th Tank Destroyer Regiment, and the 1473rd Antiaircraft Regiment had been with the 1st Shock Army since March. The 991st Assault Gun Regiment was transferred from the 4th Tank Army of the 1st Ukrainian Front in April, and the 1453rd Assault Gun Regiment had come from the front reserve, also in April. The 27th, 72nd, and 85th Guard Mortar Regiments had arrived from the front reserve in April and May. In June the 27th Artillery Division, with the 74th Howitzer Brigade, the 76th Gun Brigade, and the 78th Light Artillery Brigade, was added to the 1st Shock Army from the front reserve.

The Soviet 1st Shock Army had received sizable increments of support troops in April and May, mostly from the 2nd Baltic Front reserve, but some from as far away as the 1st Ukrainian Front. However, during June the army received no reinforcements, other than the artillery division, unlike most of the other armies engaged in the Battle for White Russia, and lost two divisions, the 391st Rifle Division and the 182nd Rifle Division, an indication that the 1st Shock Army was to have a subordinate role. In addition, the army transferred the 249th Tank Regiment and the 1453rd Assault Gun Regiment to the 10th Guard Army, a further indication that the latter army would play a more active role in the coming months.

The Soviet 10th Guard Army, positioned south of the 1st Shock Army, included the 7th Guard Rifle Corps (7th, 8th, and 119th Guard Rifle Divisions), the 15th Guard Rifle Corps (29th, 30th, and 85th Guard Rifle Divisions), and 19th Guard Rifle Corps (22nd, 56th, and 65th Guard Rifle Divisions). The liberal allotment of guard formations to this army was an indication of better quality manpower and additional weapons. All of the divisions had been with the 10th Guard Army since March, except the 8th Guard Rifle Division, which came from the 22nd Army, and the 65th Guard Rifle Division from the 3rd Shock Army. Both divisions had arrived in April, indicating that the 2nd Baltic Front was concentrating its best divisions in the 10th Guard Army. To screen the less active portion of the army sector, the 118th Fortified Area was transferred from the 22nd Army in June.

The supporting troops of the Soviet 10th Guard Army were reinforced to ensure its having ample strength to strike west against the German Sixteenth Army. The supporting armor units included two tank regiments as of 1 June: the 37th Tank Regiment had come from the front reserve, and the 47th Tank Regiment had been transferred in from the 3rd Shock Army in April, but was sent to the 6th Guard Army in June to take part in the main assault and was replaced by the 78th Tank Brigade from the 22nd Army. The 249th Tank Regiment was added from the 1st Shock Army in June. The 1199th Assault Gun Regiment came from the front reserve in May and the 1453rd Assault Gun Regiment in June. By the end of June, the 10th Guard Army had a sizable force of nearly 200 tanks and assault guns, giving it ample armored forces to provide a strong northern shoulder for the other armies advancing to the south.

The Soviet 10th Guard Army artillery was reinforced heavily as the 2nd Baltic Front concentrated its assets in the 10th Guard Army. The front reserve sent the 60th Guard Mortar Regiment in April and the 19th Guard Gun Brigade in May. These units joined the 240th Antiaircraft Regiment, the 13th Mortar Brigade, and the 758th Tank Destroyer Regiment, all of which had been with the 10th Guard Army since March. The assignment of a full mortar brigade of four regiments was unusual and added a great deal to the weight of explosives in the artillery barrage. Along with the 3rd Shock Army to the south, the 10th Guard Army had ample strength to strike due west against the German Sixteenth Army to shield the northern flank of the main offensive.

The Soviet 3rd Shock Army had the mission of striking west toward Dvinsk to protect the northern flank of the assault group that would cut off Vitebsk from the north. It was a strong force with experienced units that had been together for many months. Although the army had only two rifle corps (79th and 93rd), an additional division was assigned to the army on 1 June. The 379th Rifle Division was assigned to the 93rd Rifle Corps in early June. The 79th Corps and its divisions had been part of the 3rd Shock Army since 1943. The 93rd Corps and its divisions had also been part of the 3rd Shock Army since March. During June the 391st Rifle Division was added from the 1st Shock Army, but both corps gave up a rifle division during the same month: the 46th Guard Rifle Division was sent to the 6th Guard Army and the 200th Rifle Division to the 4th Shock Army, leaving the 3rd Shock Army with only six rifle divisions. However, the army units were well integrated and combat ready.

The support troops were quite numerous for a smaller army. The two artillery brigades were new, part of the overall expansion of artillery in the Red Army in the spring of 1944. The 136th Gun Brigade had been formed in May from the 136th Howitzer Regiment from the Moscow Military District, the 701st Gun Regiment, and the 1190th Gun Regiment, both from the 1st Shock Army. The 225th Gun Brigade was formed by the 3rd Shock Army in June. All the other support units, the 827th Howitzer Regiment, the 1539th Assault Gun Regiment, the 36th Antiaircraft Division, the 1622nd Antiaircraft Regiment, the 163rd Guard Tank Destroyer Regiment, and the 203rd Mortar Regiment (Guard), had been with the 3rd Shock Army since March. Much of the additional artillery came from the 1st Shock Army, reinforcing this assault army, the 3rd Shock, at the expense of the screening force. An unusual transfer from the main assault sector in May was the 93rd Guard Mortar Regiment from the 6th Guard Army of the 1st Baltic Front. These moves were probably dictated by a need to assist the breakthrough effort of the 3rd Shock Army during the second phase of the offensive. Another katyusha unit, the 310th Guard Mortar Regiment, came to this army in June from the front reserve.

The only armor in the 3rd Shock Army was the 29th Guard Tank Brigade, which had been with the army since March, a noticeable surprise given the army's pivotal mission of striking directly west toward Dvinsk to protect the offensive's northern flank.

At the southern flank of the 2nd Baltic Front was the 22nd Army.

It had been part of this front since January. Even though it had the mission of providing a screen, the 22nd Army was very small by Soviet standards, with only two rifle corps (44th and 100th) that included five rifle divisions and two rifle brigades. The 44th Rifle Corps had two divisions and two rifle brigades. One of the divisions, the 325th, had been formed in May 1944 from the 54th Rifle Brigade. The 44th Corps was without question a limited-service unit with about half the value of a standard rifle corps.

The Soviet 100th Rifle Corps was a more viable formation with three divisions, all three of which had been together in the corps since March and were well integrated. However, the 100th Rifle Corps headquarters, the 21st Guard Rifle Division, and the 28th Rifle Division were transferred to the 4th Shock Army, one of the main assault armies, in June, substantially weakening the 22nd Army. Also in June the 118th Fortified Region, typically used to screen inactive fronts, was sent to the 10th Guard Army. The 130th Rifle Corps ⚡ headquarters was formed in June but had no divisions assigned as of 1 July. On that date the 22nd Army had only three rifle divisions and a rifle brigade.

The 22nd Army support troops were very sparse: for example, there was no antiaircraft division, guard mortar regiment, assault gun regiment, or tank destroyer brigade, units usually assigned to field armies on a permanent basis. The 36th Guard Gun Brigade, as part of the expansion program, had been formed in May, probably as a combination of existing regiments. The other units, 81st Tank Regiment, 1040th Tank Destroyer Regiment, 1472nd Antiaircraft Regiment, and 561st Mortar Regiment, had been with the army since March. The only other new unit assigned to the 22nd Army since March was the 395th Howitzer Regiment from the 5th Army in June. The 22nd Army was obviously organized to provide a screen in a quiet sector before the offensive. The one strong corps was transferred when the attack began and the screening requirement decreased.

The 2nd Baltic Front reserves were not very strong, the front having dealt out many of its units to the 10th Guard Army and the 3rd Shock Army. The artillery component included the 27th Artillery Division with three brigades, two guard mortar brigades, two guard mortar regiments, the 44th Antiaircraft Division, two antiaircraft regiments, and five antiaircraft battalions. Most of these units had been with the 2nd Baltic Front since March.

The Soviet armored reserve included the 5th Tank Corps sent from the 1st Baltic Front in April. The corps had probably been refitted with 195 new T34/85 tanks during its respite in the spring, along with 42 new assault guns. The 78th Tank Brigade had been with the front since March. The 3rd Guard Cavalry Corps was sent to the 3rd White Russian Front reserve to form part of a horse-mechanized group in June, and the 27th Artillery Division was sent to the 1st Shock Army.

The 4th Shock Army of the 1st Baltic Front had taken part in the offensive against Army Group North in January, but by 23 June 1944 the army had been reduced to a very weak force composed of the 83rd Rifle Corps, a rifle division, and a rifle brigade. The 332nd Rifle Division and 101st Rifle Brigade had been with the army for 3 months, while the 119th and 360th Rifle Divisions came from the 6th Guard Army in April. The 16th Lithuanian Rifle Division also joined the 4th Shock Army in June. This latter division was of limited value because of its political importance: the lack of trained Lithuanian replacements dictated that the division could not be exposed to heavy losses in the summer of 1944.

Prior to 23 June the Soviet 4th Shock Army had lost the 60th Corps headquarters and two rifle divisions. After 23 June the 100th Rifle Corps with the 21st Guard Rifle Division and the 28th Rifle Division came from the 22nd Army. The 200th Rifle Division was transferred from the 3rd Shock Army and the 155th Fortified Sector from the 43rd Army. These moves were designed to shift the best units closer to the assault area.

The 4th Shock Army troops included the 138th Gun Brigade formed from artillery regiments that had been with the 1st Baltic Front for over 3 months. The 587th Tank Destroyer Regiment, the 556th Mortar Regiment, and the 1624th Antiaircraft Regiment had been with this army for 3 months. The 1714th Antiaircraft Regiment had come from the front reserve after 23 June. The only armor assigned to the 4th Shock Army was the 171st Tank Battalion, which had been with the army for 3 months.

As did the 22nd Army, the 4th Shock Army had limited offensive capability because of its designated role of simply protecting the northern flank of the major operation from whatever threat the German Army Group North could offer.

The German forces defending the line against the 4th Shock Army were units of the I Corps of the Sixteenth Army of German Army Group North, including the 205th, 24th, and 290th Infantry Divisions. The 205th Infantry Division had been part of the Sixteenth Army since October 1943 and part of the I Corps since January 1944. The division had three infantry regiments, each of two battalions, plus a fusilier battalion, for a total of seven infantry battalions. The division held a 20-kilometer sector defending the approach to Polotsk just north of the IX Corps of the Third Panzer Army. Elements of the 281st Security Division were in Polotsk.

Immediately north of the 205th Division was the 24th Infantry Division, which had been with the Sixteenth Army since April 1944. The German division had three regiments each with two battalions and a fusilier battalion for a total of seven. In support of the division was the 909th Assault Gun Brigade with an authorized strength of forty-five assault guns. The brigade had lost heavily in the Ukraine in the fall of 1943, and in January 1944 was sent to the Ninth Army in the Parichi area with only twenty-four assault guns. By the end of March, the brigade was equipped with thirty-four assault guns and sent by rail via Minsk to Polotsk, where it received new equipment.[1]

The 290th Infantry Division had been with the German Sixteenth Army since August 1941 and had the same organization as the previous two divisions. In addition, the I Corps had the 909th Assault Gun Brigade north of Polotsk and elements of the 281st Security Division at Polotsk.[2] All three German divisions had been in the Polotsk area for months and were well established in their defensive areas. The German I Corps was more than adequate to defend its sector against the Soviet 4th Shock Army and was able to release some of its units to protect the flank of Army Group North.

Since Malyshev's 4th Shock Army had the limited objective of preventing units of the Sixteenth German Army from attacking the northern flank of the Soviet offensive, when the offensive opened on 22 June, his army applied some pressure on the German 205th and 24th Infantry Divisions of the Sixteenth German Army screening the rail junction of Polotsk. The 4th Shock Army continued these attacks through 25 June.[3]

On 22 June Army Group North was ordered to commit the 24th German Infantry Division to the fight at Obol, and the division with an assault gun brigade was ordered to assist the 252nd German Division of the IX Corps.[4] On 23 June Army Group North ordered the 290th Division to Obol and the 212th Division to Polotsk to protect the army group's flank. On 24 June the Soviet 4th Shock Army made little headway toward Polotsk, but applied pressure to hold the German I Corps in place.[5]

On 27 June the 4th Shock Army continued to advance toward Polotsk, forcing the Germans to move the 81st and 290th Infantry Divisions to defend the city. A wide gap had opened between the Sixteenth German Army to the north and IX Corps of the Third Panzer Army to the south. This split at the boundary between the two German army groups was most serious. Armored columns of Chistyakov's 6th Guard Army were pouring through and threatening the flanks of both army groups. The Soviet armored columns consisted of a brigade of tanks, an infantry battalion, artillery, and engineers. The pressure on the Sixteenth Army made Army Group North reluctant to transfer divisions to help Army Group Center. This concern with their own forces by individual army groups was a natural part of an assault directed against the boundaries of forces, and each group tended to look inward rather than outward, thus increasing the chances that the penetration would succeed.

On 28 June Malyshev's 4th Shock Army created an assault group for the attack on Polotsk. The Soviet 100th Corps was added to the 48th Army to increase its punch. On 29 June Field Marshal Model requested that Army Group North withdraw to Polotsk and free two divisions for use elsewhere. Hitler agreed but demanded that Polotsk itself must be held.[6]

The Germans continued to feed divisions into the engulfing battle at Polotsk and desperately attempted to maintain a solid front to the south. On 30 June matters were getting out of hand for German Army Group Center. General Chistyakov ordered the 103rd Corps under General I. F. Fedyunkin and the 23rd Guard Corps under General A. N. Yermakov led by an armored column of General V. V. Butkov's 1st Tank Corps to bypass Polotsk. The 6th Guard Army advanced 30 kilometers by the evening of 30 June, bypassing Polotsk on the south, pushing back remnants of General R. Wuthmann's IX Corps, and opening a gap between the 3rd Panzer Army under General G. H. Reinhardt and the Sixteenth Army.

Also on 30 June General A. P. Beloborodov's 43rd Army was catching up after clearing Vitebsk and was pursuing Wuthmann's IX Corps, which was unable to offer any serious resistance.[7] To alleviate the situation, on 30 June the German Sixteenth Army extended its line south and restored contact with the Third Panzer Army. However, Butkov's 1st Tank Corps had crossed the Ulla River and driven west, cutting the rail line between Polotsk and Molodechno.[8]

The Germans poured reinforcements into the Polotsk area on 30 June: the 205th and 24th Infantry Divisions and the 201st and 221st Security Divisions reinforced the 290th and 81st German Divisions. The 212th Infantry Division was sent to Lepel south of the gap to help the remnants of the 252nd and 95th Divisions.[9]

However, a huge gap still remained between the units that had retreated to the north and the scattered units of the Third Panzer Army. On 1 July Malyshev's 4th Shock Army attacked Polotsk from three sides with the 83rd and 100th Corps. The 4th Shock Army advanced 20 kilometers and reached the outskirts of the town. General A. I. Ruchkin's 22nd Guard Corps of Chistyakov's 6th Guard Army reached the eastern edge of the town.[10] By 2 July the 4th Shock Army and the 6th Guard Army had broken into Polotsk, cleared the southern part of the city, and crossed the western Dvina River into the northern part. On 3 July the Soviet forces entered the city center, but street fighting continued through 4 July.

Hitler insisted that an attack be launched by two German divisions of the Sixteenth Army from the Polotsk area, while Model, then commanding Army Group Center, urged that the divisions be used to the southwest at Molodechno to blunt the Soviet attack. The Sixteenth Army was never able to react freely to the offensive and could only maintain contact with Wuthmann's IX Corps units at Molodechno through hard fighting as the Soviet juggernaut slowed.

General Eremenko's 2nd Baltic Front had accomplished its mission of screening the northern flank and effectively preventing the German Sixteenth Army from meaningful intervention in the battle. Army Group North was forced to look to its own problems, and could spare little for its southern neighbor. On 24 June, at a meeting at the headquarters of Army Group Center, the chief of staff of Army Group North stated that he had nothing to give to Center.

The role of the 2nd Baltic Front would expand greatly in the second phase of the offensive as the Red Army resumed the traditional process of grinding its way through the German defenses, and General Malyshev's army went on to perform well in the second phase of the great summer offensive.[11]

Notes

1. Franz Kurowski Tornau, *Sturmartillerie: Fels in der Brandung* (Herford and Bonn: Maximilian, 1965), pp. 226–228.

2. Wolf Keilig, *Das Deutsche Heer, 1939–1945,* III (Bad Nauheim: Podzun, 1956–1972), sec. 82.

3. A. M. Samsanov, ed., *Osvobozhdenie Belorussii, 1944* (Moscow: Nauka, 1974), p. 130.

4. G. Niepold, *The Battle for White Russia: The Destruction of Army Group Centre, June 1944* (London: Brassey's, 1987), pp. 78.

5. Ibid., pp. 85, 97.

6. David M. Glantz and Harold S. Orenstein, eds., *Belorussia 1944: The Soviet General Staff Study* (Carlisle, Pa.: David M. Glantz, 1998), pp. 85, 126; Niepold, p. 162.

7. Glantz and Orenstein, p. 126.

8. Ibid., p. 127; Earl F. Ziemke, *Stalingrad to Berlin: The German Campaign in Russia, 1942–1945* (New York: Dorset Press, 1968), p. 324.

9. Glantz and Orenstein, p. 127.

10. Ibid., pp. 128–129; Samsanov, p. 84; Niepold, p. 182.

11. Niepold, p. 182.

CHAPTER 6

Vitebsk

The attack north of Vitebsk on 22 June by the 1st Baltic Front took the Germans completely by surprise according to the Army Group Center war diary.[1] At 0400, after a very heavy artillery barrage lasting 20 minutes, as well as air attacks, two to three rifle companies of each of the seven Soviet divisions of the 6th Guard and 43rd Armies supported by four tank brigades, three tank regiments, and four assault gun regiments (a total of nearly 400 armored vehicles) attacked the 252nd German Division and Corps Detachment D on a 20-kilometer front. By 1000 assault battalions from each of the Soviet front-line regiments attacking with artillery and air support broke through the German main line of resistance, the front-line defense zone. By noon the three Red Army assault corps (23rd Guard, 1st, and 60th) and another division had advanced to the Obol River, breaking through the second defense line. By evening a Soviet armored group consisting of the 10th and 39th Guard Tank Brigades, the 179th and 306th Divisions of the 1st Corps, and the 145th Division of the 92nd Corps crossed the Obol with help from the 5th Assault Engineer Brigade and 28th Engineer Brigade. (See Figure 6.1 for the 1st Baltic Front table of organization.) The Russians pressed southwest to Sirotino on the Vitebsk-Polotsk rail line, having advanced 7 kilometers on a 12-kilometer front.[2]

The Germans moved a regiment of the 95th Division from the area south of Vitebsk to fill the gap opened between the 252nd Infantry Division and Corps Detachment D. In addition the German Army High Command (Oberkommando des Heeres–OKH) gave the Third Panzer Army, the 24th Infantry Division, and the 909th Assault Gun Brigade from the Sixteenth Army to the north to counterattack the Soviet penetration between Polotsk and Sirotino.[3]

The first day, 22 June, had been very successful for the Soviet 6th Guard Army and the 43rd Army. They had badly damaged the

Figure 6.1   The 1st Baltic Front

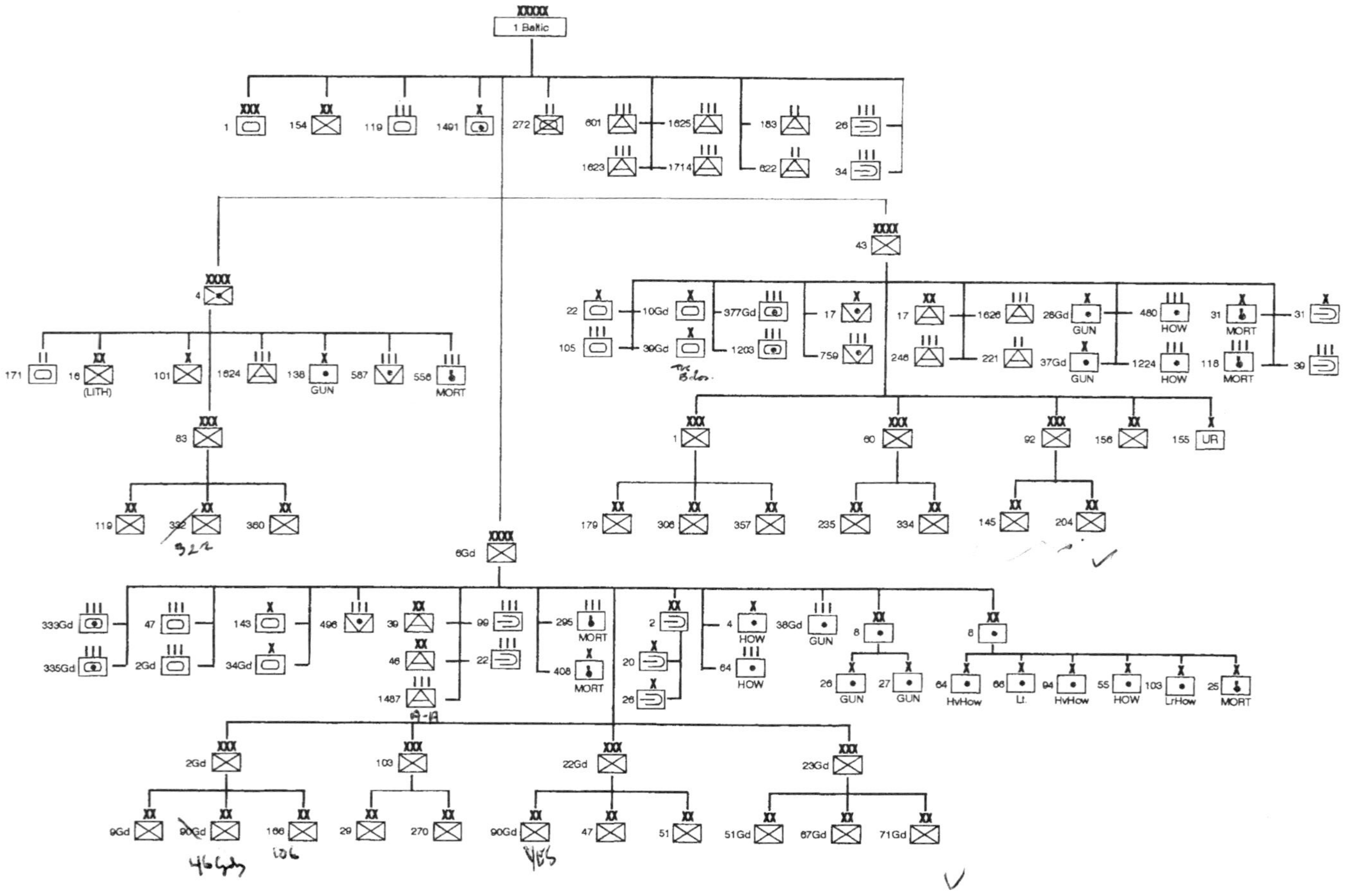

German 252nd Division and Corps Detachment D and forced the Germans to move in the 24th Division from the north and the 280th Regiment from the 95th Division in the south, while advancing 7 kilometers. The Red Air Force was also very active, with 381 sorties in support of the Soviet attack reported by the Germans.[4]

The perimeter around Vitebsk was comparatively quiet on 22 June, with the 92nd Corps of the Soviet 43rd Army and the 84th Corps of the 39th Army content to contain the four German divisions of the LIII Corps. A heavy artillery barrage in the north and northwest was accompanied by minor attacks to hold the Germans in position.[5] During the evening Field Marshal Busch requested a lengthy withdrawal to shorten the line and create reserves, but Hitler would not agree.[6]

Hitler and the German General Staff believed that the poor road network in White Russia precluded any large-scale armored operations. In the previous months the Germans had successfully defended the area by concentrating their defenses on the main highways and had improved their defenses since then. Without control of the few hard-surfaced roads, the German generals did not believe that the Russians could sustain an offensive in White Russia.

The key to the entire White Russian offensive was opening the road from Vitebsk to Minsk. General I. K. Bagramyan's 1st Baltic Front was assigned the task of breaking through north of Vitebsk and driving the surviving units of the German Third Panzer Army west to Molodechno. In the past many Russian efforts to take Vitebsk by frontal attack had failed because the Germans had constructed elaborate defenses held by four divisions in a relatively small sector. However, the Russians had whittled away at the German defenses, leaving Vitebsk in a salient surrounded on three sides by the Red Army.

The major surprise element was the introduction of General I. M. Chistyakov's 6th Guard Army whose presence was not detected by the Germans until the battle began. To achieve this surprise, the troops of the Soviet 43rd Army sidestepped to the right, concentrating two corps in a narrow 15-kilometer front, while the 6th Guard Army filled in the remaining 30 kilometers of the front. The 6th Guard Army, with nearly 100,000 men in twelve divisions plus a tank corps, made an approach march of 110 kilometers during the three nights preceding the attack.[7]

The 1st Baltic Front consisted of the 4th Shock, 6th Guard, and 43rd Armies. The 4th Shock Army under General P. F. Malyshev was assigned to protect the northern shoulder. Chistyakov's army and the 43rd Army commanded by General Beloborodov held a 150-kilometer sector north of Vitebsk with the objective of encircling Vitebsk from the north. General I. I. Lyudnikov's 39th Army of General I. D. Chernyakovskiy's 3rd White Russian Front held the face and south side of the salient and formed the spearhead that swept around Vitebsk from the south.

To ensure the rapid conquest of the city in June 1944, the Soviet plan of attack on Vitebsk called for Beloborodov's 43rd Army and Chistyakov's 6th Guard Army (2nd Guard, 103rd, 22nd Guard, and 23rd Guard Corps) of the 1st Baltic Front to strike the northern shoulder of the Vitebsk salient, while the 5th Guard Corps under General I. S. Bezugliy of the 39th Army swept around from the south. The three divisions of General A. S. Ksenofontov's 2nd Guard Corps, which had been with the 6th Guard Army for 3 months, was in the second echelon on 22 June to reinforce units after they broke through the German line.

The three divisions of Yermakov's 23rd Guard Corps had been with the army for more than 3 months. The corps was compressed into a 10-kilometer front, with all three divisions in line working with the two assault corps of Beloborodov's 43rd Army. Ruchkin's 22nd Guard Corps, transferred from the 43rd Army, held a large sector north of the 23rd Guard Corps and protected the western flank as the remainder of the army drove south to the Dvina River. Fedyunkin's 103rd Rifle Corps added from the Stavka Reserve was in reserve to follow through once the German line was pierced.

The 6th Guard Army had a very strong armored component that included two tank brigades, two tank regiments, and two assault gun regiments—a total of over 200 armored vehicles equal to two German panzer divisions. Most of the Soviet armored units had been added after 1 June. During June the 143rd Tank Brigade came from the front reserve, the 47th Tank Regiment from the 10th Guard Army, the 333rd Guard Assault Gun Regiment from the Moscow Military District, and the 335th Guard Assault Gun Regiment from the Stavka Reserve. In addition the 1st Tank Corps with 195 new T34/85 tanks and 42 assault guns was placed immediately behind the 23rd Corps to lead the spearhead after the breakthrough. The 1st Tank Corps had 237 armored vehicles, giving the 6th Guard Army a total of over 450 armored vehicles in comparison with the 100 tanks of a German panzer division.

The Soviet 6th Guard Army artillery was exceptionally strong, including two artillery divisions, a katyusha division, an independent katyusha regiment, a howitzer brigade, and five artillery and mortar regiments. Most of the artillery had been added recently to the army from the Stavka Reserve, the Moscow Military District, and the 11th Guard Army.

The enormous buildup of the Soviet 6th Guard Army in April,

May, and June was indicative of its major role. The powerful artillery support would be used to crush the German defenses, and the enormous number of armored vehicles with ample infantry support would press eastward over 150 kilometers in 15 days.

On 23 June 1944 Beloborodov's 43rd Army, positioned just north of Vitebsk with an assault mission, held a narrow front of only 50 kilometers. The army consisted of the 1st Rifle Corps, the 60th Rifle Corps, and the 92nd Rifle Corps. The 1st Rifle Corps commanded by General N. A. Vasilev held a sector less than 5 kilometers wide with two divisions on the line and one in reserve. The 60th Rifle Corps under General A. S. Lyukhtikov was given an assault assignment and concentrated on a 5-kilometer sector in the center of the 43rd Army. The 92nd Rifle Corps under General N. B. Ibyancksiy screened a very wide sector north of Vitebsk.

The Soviet 43rd Army included the 17th Tank Destroyer Brigade, the 155th Fortified Region (heavily armed with machine guns and artillery), three tank brigades (the equivalent of a tank corps), a tank regiment, and two assault gun regiments. The artillery component of Beloborodov's army was more than doubled in April, May, and June.

By 23 June practically all the Russian units assigned to the 1st Baltic Front reserve had been parceled out to the armies. Even the 1st Tank Corps had been attached to the 6th Guard Army to provide armor to spearhead the drive west to Molodechno. To provide follow-up strength in July, the 14th Rifle Corps was assembled during June from divisions of three different armies in the 3rd Baltic Front. In early July the Soviet command added a tank corps and a rifle corps to the 1st Baltic Front reserve, giving the front a substantial reserve to keep the offensive moving.

At the end of the first blitzkrieg phase of the Russian offensive, the 1st Baltic Front was further reinforced on 8 July by the 2nd Guard Army from the Stavka Reserve. The 51st Army was held in reserve behind the 1st Baltic Front to add fresh power after the first phase. The Soviet 2nd Guard Army and 51st Army had been with the 4th Ukrainian Front in the Crimea in April and was transferred first to the Stavka Reserve in May and then to the 1st Baltic Front on 1 July 1944.

The vast number of reserves available to the Red Army, including two field armies behind the 1st Baltic Front, should lay to rest the theory that had Hitler not intervened, the German generals would have been able to withstand the attack by assuming a mobile defense and adding a few panzer divisions. By June 1944 the Red Army had an overwhelming preponderance of force in White Russia, and the question was not if the Germans could be beaten, but how badly and how soon.

The German Third Panzer Army commanded by General Reinhardt was charged with defending Vitebsk. Facing the Soviet 6th Guards Army was General Wuthmann's IX Corps with the 252nd Infantry Division and Corps Detachment D, created in November 1943 from the remnants of the 56th and 262nd Infantry Divisions, which had suffered heavy casualties in August 1943. The division was supported by the 245th Assault Gun Brigade that had been reformed in April 1943 to replace the battalion lost at Stalingrad.

The German garrison of Vitebsk under General Gollwitzer, the commander of the LIII Corps of the Third Panzer Army, was opposed by the Soviet 43rd and 39th Armies. The German corps included the 206th and 246th Infantry Divisions and the 4th and 6th Luftwaffe Field Divisions. In addition the German Third Panzer Army had the 201st Security Division centered on Lepel, a unit organized to fight Partisans in the rear area. The division had been formed in June 1942 from the 201st Security Brigade and included six infantry battalions, a single artillery battalion, a cavalry squadron of Russian ex-POWs fighting for the Germans, and service elements. Although not intended for or equipped to fight on the front line, the security divisions were pressed into action when Soviet forces broke through the front and scattered the German units.

The seven German divisions had the advantage of well-prepared defenses around Vitebsk; however, the Red Army canceled that advantage by attacking on the less heavily defended northern and southern flanks of the city.

The second day of the offensive, 23 June, brought the Red Army even greater success than the first day. (See Map 6.1.) North of Vitebsk at 0700, the 1st and 60th Corps of the 43rd Army continued their attacks with artillery and air support on Corps Detachment D, trying to hold a strong position at Shumilino. Vasilyev's 1st Soviet Corps of the 43rd Army led by the 306th and 179th Divisions with help from the 71st Guard Division enveloped Shumilino and drove back the scattered elements of Corps Detachment D through the string of lakes in front of the German second defense zone (the Tiger line). Despite German counterattacks, Vasilev's Corps broke through the German second defense zone and crossed the West Dvina River south of Shumilino by evening.[8]

On the German 252nd Division front, Ruchkin's 22nd Guard Corps and Fedyunkin's 103rd Corps of Chistyakov's 6th Guard Army attacked at 0600 on 23 June. The German division was driven out of its defenses and had difficulty in maintaining contact with the ixteenth Army to the north. The 252nd and 56th German Divisions

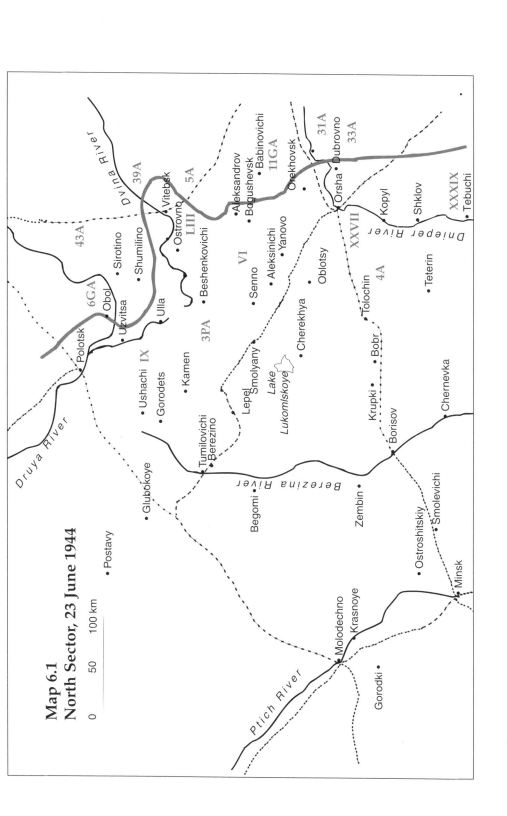

Map 6.1
North Sector, 23 June 1944

0   50   100 km

were beaten and retreated, leaving behind their heavy weapons. To ease the pressure on the two German divisions, at 1700 the 24th German Division and the 909th Assault Gun Brigade attacked the north flank of the 6th Guard Army but by nightfall had made little progress. By the evening of 23 June, Chistyakov's 6th Guard Army and Beloborodov's 43rd Army had advanced 18 kilometers on a sector 20 kilometers wide and were only 2 kilometers from the Dvina River.[9]

On 23 June Butkov's 1st Soviet Tank Corps was ordered to move through the gap in the German line and head for Beshenkovichi, but during the day heavy rain bogged down the tank corps on the poor roads leading to Shumilino, and the tanks did not arrive at the town until late in the evening of 23 June. As a result, General Bagramyan, commander of the 1st Baltic Front, delayed the use of Butkov's tanks until after the infantry had cleared the series of lakes and rivers defended by the Germans. Yermakov's 23rd Guard Corps and Vasilev's 1st Corps advanced 16 kilometers, but on the right Ruchkin's 22nd Guard Corps advanced only 7 kilometers against stubborn German resistance. In the late afternoon of 23 June, Wuthmann, commander of the IX Corps, ordered the German troops to give up the second defense zone and withdraw a further 15 kilometers back to the third defense zone stretching from the Obol area on the West Dvina River to Beshenkovichi. The divisions of Fedyunkin's 103rd and Ksenofontov's 2nd Guard Corps were struggling to catch up with the leading elements of the 6th Guard and 43rd Armies.[10]

As elements of General Lyukhtikov's 60th Corps of Beloborodov's 43rd Army pressed remnants of Corps Detachment D south toward the Dvina River immediately west of Vitebsk on 23 June, the 246th German Division of the city garrison tried to create a defense line on the south bank of the river but was separated by 3 kilometers from Detachment D. By nightfall Soviet antitank guns were firing on the road west from Vitebsk to Beshenkovichi. South of Vitebsk, General Y. M. Prokofiev's 84th Corps of the 39th Army applied pressure on the perimeter while General Bezugliy's 5th Guard Corps cut the Vitebsk-Orsha rail line and drove on toward Ostrovno. Given the advance of Soviet tanks from the south as well, Vitebsk was in serious trouble at the close of the second day.[11]

The rain and low clouds limited the Red Air Force to only 746 sorties. Nevertheless, Soviet aircraft continued to pound German troop movements. Few German fighters were available to protect the ground troops.[12]

On 23 June the Soviet units covering Vitebsk itself were quiet, although the German commander was acutely aware of the Soviet spearheads closing in from the north and southwest of the city. General Reinhardt, the Third Panzer Army commander, wanted to evacuate Vitebsk immediately, but Hitler refused. However, at 1830 Hitler approved the withdrawal of the four German divisions in the city to the second zone of defense, reducing the perimeter by at least half, and at 1930 Hitler approved withdrawal to the third defense zone, crowding the four divisions into a 30-kilometer perimeter. The withdrawal was in anticipation that the garrison would have to fight its way out, since the Russians were rapidly closing the noose. The German garrison received a Hornet 88mm-gun tank destroyer battalion and an assault gun brigade to support the withdrawal.[13]

At the end of 23 June, the Soviet objective of surrounding Vitebsk was nearly achieved. Even more significant, both Butkov's 1st Tank Corps on the north and the Oslikovskiy Horse-Mechanized Group in the south were passing through wide gaps in the German defenses and driving unchecked to the west.[14]

On 24 June Wuthmann's IX Corps planned to hold the line of marshes running southeast from north of Obol through a line of lakes to the Dvina River to Beshenkovichi. However, during the night of 23–24 June, Corps Detachment D collapsed, and the Soviet 60th Corps under General Lyukhtikov penetrated the string of lakes in front of the Tiger line (the second defense zone), breaking through on a wide sector. At 0245 on 24 June Wuthmann ordered the withdrawal to the third defense zone in front of Beshenkovichi on the Dvina River, leaving an 18-kilometer gap between Detachment D and the 246th Division of the LIII Corps defending Vitebsk.[15]

At 0800 on 24 June, Butkov's Tank Corps poured through the gap at Shumilino opened by the 6th Guard Army between the 252nd German Division and the German Sixteenth Army to the north. Tanks moved with difficulty on the poor roads soaked with rain and could not move off the roads into the swamp. The Germans methodically destroyed all bridges as they withdrew, further slowing the tanks. Butkov's tanks reached the Dvina River 6 kilometers south of Ulla at 1100, despite the congested roads, captured a damaged bridge, and crossed the river. By the evening of 24 June, the 67th Guard Division of Yermakov's 23rd Guard Corps of the Soviet 6th Guard Army crossed the Dvina River north of Beshenkovichi and held a 50-kilometer front along the river south of Ulla. The 252nd German Division held the west bank of the Dvina 10 kilometers northwest of Beshenkovichi, but a gap was opening between the division and Detachment D to the south. Better weather on 24 June enabled the 3rd Air Army commanded by General N. F. Papivin to make 1,127 sorties against the Germans.[16]

The counterattacks by the 24th German Division on the northern

ık of the 6th Guard Army had tapered off. During the evening of
24 June, Chistyakov's Guard Army advanced 3 kilometers west
through marshes north of Obol with Ruchkin's 22nd Guard Corps
on the right and Fedyunkin's 103rd and Yermakov's 23rd Guard
Corps on the left. Ksenofontov's 2nd Guard Corps was following up.
The 6th Guard Army reached the West Dvina but did not break
through the German defenses. By the evening of 24 June, the 24th
German Division, reinforced with the 245th and 909th Assault Gun
Brigades, held a line from Obol to the Dvina River. A battalion of the
290th German Division from the 16th Army reinforced the 24th
Division on the west.[17]

On 24 June German Detachment D held the south bank of the
Dvina from Beshenkovichi to 10 kilometers southwest of Ostrovno.
Vasilev's 1st Corps of the 43rd Army had advanced to the West
Dvina northwest of Beshenkovichi and captured several bridgeheads. The tank-supported 60th Corps under Lyukhtikov crossed
the Dvina north and south of Beshenkovichi. By noon Chistyakov's
Guard and Beloborodov's 43rd Armies had crossed the Dvina on
rafts and in boats. Tank destroyer and infantry guns were ferried on
rafts, while the Soviet engineer pontoon units were struggling to
reach the river over muddy roads. By the evening of 24 June, the
pontoons arrived and began ferrying tanks and artillery across the
river. During the afternoon Vasilev's 1st and Lyukhtikov's 60th
Corps continued to advance west of the Dvina toward Lepel.
Bagramyan ordered the 60th Corps to drive forward without
artillery support because there was no time to wait for the ferry to
bring the guns. Instead the front supplied generous air support for
the infantry. Vasilev's 1st Corps continued to attack Ulla and crossed
the Dvina River 6 kilometers south of the town. The 92nd Corps
commanded by N. B. Ibyancksiy continued to exert pressure on
Vitebsk from the north while Prokofiev's 84th Corps of the 39th
Army attacked from the south. Bezugliy's 5th Guard Corps of the
39th Army was moving rapidly to the west toward Ostrovno.[18]

On 24 June the Soviets were torn by the classic problem in
blitzkrieg warfare—how many units to use to close the pocket and
how many to keep pressing forward before the enemy had time to
create defensive positions. General Alexander Vasilevsky, the Stavka
representative coordinating the 1st Baltic and 3rd White Russian
Fronts, urged Bagramyan, the 1st Baltic Front commander, to keep
Beloborodov's 43rd Army moving south because the trap around
Vitebsk had to be closed quickly to prevent the Germans' escape.
Lyudnikov's 39th Army was coming up from the south toward
Ostrovno, and Beloborodov's 43rd Army had to join it on the Dvina,
while Prokofiev's 84th Corps of the 39th Army was attacking Vitebsk

from the south. The German escape route to the west was shrinking with every passing hour. Ibyancksiy's 92nd Corps of the Soviet 43rd Army pressed south to the west bank of the Dvina. By evening the gap between the north and south pincers was narrowed to 10 kilometers west of Ostrovno. During the night of 24–25 June, the east flank of Lyukhtikov's 60th Corps continued to press south against the north perimeter of Vitebsk despite a counterattack by the 246th German Division of Gollwitzer's LIII Corps. The counterattack was repelled with the assistance of a division of Shturmovik ground-attack aircraft from the 3rd Air Army.[19]

On the south side of the Vitebsk road, the 197th German Division of General Pfeiffer's VI Corps folded back from attacks by the 39th Army and retreated to 7 kilometers south of Vitebsk. With a reduced perimeter, Gollwitzer pulled the 4th and 6th Luftwaffe Divisions from the line in the early afternoon of 24 June and sent them west to hold the road from Vitebsk to Ostrovno, but he was not permitted to use his entire corps to break out. Hitler feared that if the divisions tried to break out, all their heavy weapons and equipment would be lost and they would be unable to defend themselves.[20]

At 1900 on 24 June, Hitler granted authority to use three of the four divisions to hold the Ostrovno road, but demanded that the 206th Division continue to hold Vitebsk. The withdrawal of Gollwitzer's LIII Corps to a smaller perimeter allowed Lyudnikov's 39th Army to concentrate Prokofiev's 84th Corps with the 158th and 262nd Rifle Divisions in a narrow sector southwest of Vitebsk and press north against the German 206th Division holding the city. At 2300 on 24 June Bezugliy's 5th Guard Corps of Lyudnikov's 39th Army, led by the 19th and 91st Guard Divisions in the west and the 164th Rifle Division in the east, both with tank support, cut the road on both sides of Ostrovno, trapping the German 4th Luftwaffe Division and the remnant of the 197th Infantry Division in Ostrovno. The remainder of the LIII Corps with 35,000 men was trapped in Vitebsk. A wide gap was torn in the German line from Detachment D west of Ostrovno to remnants of the German VI Corps retreating in the south.[21]

During 24 June the Germans reacted to the crisis. At noon Field Marshal Busch, commander of Army Group Center, requested permission to abandon Vitebsk and requested reinforcement of at least two more divisions to help restore a cohesive front. At 1500 General Zeitler informed the chief of staff of Army Group Center that the 206th Division must remain in Vitebsk and that the road be kept open. To provide reinforcements for General Reinhardt's Third Panzer Army, the 212th and 290th German Divisions would be sent from the north and the 81st Division shifted to Polotsk. The 201st and 221st Security Divisions were sent to the West Dvina River line. The 5th Panzer Division was transferred from Army Group North Ukraine. At 2230 on 24 June, Hitler agreed to the withdrawal of Wuthmann's IX Corps of the Third Panzer Army to the Tiger line but no farther. However, how two battered Germans divisions could stop two Soviet armies was not explained.[22]

On 25 June the Germans tried to hold the Tiger line along the Dvina River, but by noon Beloborodov's 43rd Army continued to cross the river throughout the day on rafts and boats. One of the combat teams of Lyukhtikov's 60th Corps consisted of fourteen tanks, as well as the 417th Regiment of the 156th Division, the 712th Tank Destroyer Regiment of the 17th Brigade, the 28th Guard Gun Artillery brigade, and mortars units.

Yermakov's 23rd Guard Corps of Chistyakov's 6th Guard Army crossed the West Dvina River and held a bridgehead despite ten German counterattacks supported with up to thirty tanks.[23] The Soviet 71st Guard Division was confined to a small bridgehead, but the 67th Division was more successful, and the 51st Guard and 71st Guard Divisions crossed the river in that sector, advanced 10 kilometers west of Beshenkovichi, and crossed the River Svetshanka.

Ksenofontov's 2nd Guard Corps of the 6th Guard Army crossed the Dvina at Beshenkovichi with support from the 3rd Air Army, and Beloborodov's 43rd Army crossed the Dvina at Uzvitsa. Fedyunkin's 103rd Corps of the 6th Guard Army crossed the Dvina at Ulla, 20 kilometers northwest of Beshenkovichi. Vasilev's 1st Corps of the 43rd Army reached Beshenkovichi by the end of 25 June.[24]

The poorly armed German 45th Security Regiment was surrounded at Svetsha. Reinhardt's Third Panzer Army sent the 201st Security Division, the 66th Security Regiment, and the Pershe Cossack Battalion to Wuthmann's IX Corps to help hold back the Soviet 43rd Army. With the IX Corps broken into scattered units, the northern boundary of the Third Panzer Army was changed to return the 24th and 290th Divisions to Sixteenth Army command.[25]

Wuthmann's IX Corps was under constant pressure from the Soviet 43rd and 6th Guard Armies. Beshenkovichi, held by elements of the German Detachment D, was surrounded by Vasilev's 1st and Lyukhtikov's 60th Corps of the 43rd Army advancing toward the Dvina, while the Red Air Force was pounding all the railroads and roads in the area.[26]

At 1330 on 25 June, Reinhardt's Third Panzer Army asked for permission to abandon the Tiger line on the Dvina River and move the remnants of the Wuthmann's IX Corps back to a line running through Uzvitsa, about 35 kilometers southeast of Polotsk, to the Ulla River to give the troops time to establish a defense line before they were overrun by the advancing Russians. The German IX Corps was frantically preparing a defense line on the Ulla River south of Uzvitsa manned by the 201st Security Division.[27]

Permission to withdraw was refused by Hitler, but much of the German Detachment D and an assault gun brigade managed to fight their way out of Beshenkovichi. Multiple columns of Chistyakov's 6th Guard Army and Beloborodov's 43rd Army were fanning out from the gap opened by the collapse of Wuthmann's IX Corps. By the end of 25 June, the pontoon bridges were assembled and tanks and artillery poured across the Dvina River. Butkov's 1st Tank Corps crossed the Dvina south of Ulla in the 6th Guard Army sector and drove west from Beshenkovichi toward Lepel with the intent of taking Kamen and Ushachi the next day, halfway to the Polotsk-Molodechno railway.[28]

West of Vitebsk, the Soviet 43rd Army reached the West Dvina and established bridgeheads on the south bank, crossing the river on boats and rafts. Sixteen- and 30-ton ferries were used to carry tanks and artillery. At 1500 on 25 June, a 30-ton pontoon bridge was erected, and the 10th Guard Tank Brigade crossed and attacked Gneszdilovichi.[29]

Gollwitzer's LIII Corps tried to break out on 25 June. The 4th Luftwaffe Division was surrounded in Ostrovno, and the rest of the corps was either in Vitebsk or scattered along the road leading west under constant heavy air attacks by the Red Air Force. The 206th Division was still under orders to hold the city. By 1400 the 4th Luftwaffe Division had been overrun, while the 246th Division and the 6th Luftwaffe Division were fighting their way west along the Vitebsk-Beshenkovichi road.[30]

Late on 25 June the 179th Rifle Division of Lyukhtikov's 60th Corps met the 19th Guard Division of Bezugliy's 5th Guard Corps of the 39th Army 10 kilometers west of Ostrovno, closing the pocket on Vitebsk.[31] By the end of the day, Busch had committed all of his reserves but had not been able to slow the Soviet advance. Five divisions were encircled in Vitebsk, while the remainder of Reinhardt's Third Panzer Army tried to hold the Dvina and Ulla River lines.

During the morning of 26 June, Wuthmann's IX Corps withdrew to the Ulla River line with the remnants of the 252nd Infantry Division, Corps Detachment D, the 201st Security Division, and a collection of battalions formed into Battle Group de Monteton. While these battered formations were trying to form a defensive line, the Russian attacks continued. Chistyakov's 6th Guard and Beloborodov's 43rd Armies crossed the Dvina at many points. Seven rifle divisions of the 6th Guard Army, two corps of the 43rd Army, and Butkov's 1st Tank Corps all had crossed and were driving westward steadily, overwhelming the poorly armed and dispirited German units. Butkov's tanks continued to cross the Ulla River on 30- and 60-ton ferries 15 kilometers south of Ulla until 1700 on 26 June. At noon units of the 1st Tank Corps moved toward Kamen with the 6th Guard Army. A mobile group of Beloborodov's 43rd Army advanced southwest toward Lepel. Several other tank formations of the 39th Army were moving from south of Vitebsk toward the open southern flank of Wuthmann's IX Corps.[32]

At 1930 on 26 June, the German IX Corps ordered a further withdrawal of 15 kilometers to a line from Uzvitsa to Lake Lukomlskoe. By 2000 the 23rd Guard Corps of the Soviet 6th Guard Army had cleared Beshenkovichi, although some remnants of Detachment D had managed to fight their way out.

The doomed German LIII Corps was still fighting in Vitebsk, with Hitler insisting that they stay there rather than attempting to break out. Lyukhtikov's 60th and Ibyancksiy's 92nd Corps of the 43rd Army from the north and Prokofiev's 84th Corps of the 39th Army from the south were steadily reducing the pocket. At Ostrovno remnants of the 4th Luftwaffe Division were squeezed into a separate pocket under continual air attack.[33]

The next morning, at 0900 on 27 June, Lyukhtikov's 60th Corps and Prokofiev's 84th Corps made the final assault on Vitebsk that was preceded by a massive barrage of artillery and rockets. By noon the defenders had been broken into small pockets. At 0900 Gollwitzer's LIII Corps had sent a radio message that it was under heavy attack and was running out of ammunition.[34]

Small groups of the German LIII Corps had begun to break out of Vitebsk at 0300 on 27 June, but only a few survivors managed to make their way to the ever receding German line during the following weeks. About 8,000 did break out of the first pocket, but were subsequently surrounded again and killed or captured. The Germans lost 20,000 killed at Vitebsk and 10,000 prisoners.[35] The 4th and 6th Luftwaffe Divisions and the 206th, 246th, and 197th German Infantry Divisions actually ceased to exist. After clearing Vitebsk, the two Soviet assault corps rapidly turned and moved west to take part in the ongoing struggle.[36]

By 27 June Wuthmann's IX German Corps had established a defense line from Uzvitsa to Lake Lukomlskoe, but it was a fragile reed of badly mauled formations including the 252nd Infantry Division, Detachment D, the 201st Security Division, and Battle Group de Monteton made up of security and police battalions. All of the units lacked adequate artillery and the heavy weapons that were so essential to block the advance of the Soviet armored columns.[37]

Chistyakov's 6th Guard Army was delayed on 27 June on the northern flank by the 24th German Infantry Division of the Sixteenth Army at Obol (30 kilometers southeast of Polotsk). Ruchkin's 22nd Guard Corps captured Obol by the end of the day. Beloborodov's 43rd Army advanced west from Beshenkovichi toward Lepel on the rail line leading to Orsha. Butkov's 1st Tank Corps, after a brief delay in crossing the Ulla River, attacked Detachment D north of Lepel at Kamen and Ushachi (half way between Lepel and Polotsk). The mobile column formed by Vasilev's 1st Corps of the 43rd Army attacked Lepel, probably at the juncture of Detachment D and the 201st Security Division.[38]

In pursuit, the Russians had formed numerous mobile columns usually composed of a tank regiment and/or an assault gun regiment, a rifle battalion mounted on the tanks, one or more rifle battalions in trucks, engineers with bridging equipment, and a tank destroyer or light artillery regiment. The composition varied with the availability of units; some included a tank brigade and two assault gun regiments for a total of 100 armored vehicles, equal to a panzer division. These columns had the breakthrough power to brush aside the poorly armed German defenders in hastily prepared positions. The columns could maneuver around German positions rather than attack them frontally, which led to the "unhinging" of many German defensive positions and increased the rate of advance. Lyudnikov's 39th Army formed an armored group with the 28th Guard Tank Brigade and the 957th and 735th Assault Gun Regiments. With their mobility and fighting power, the Soviet columns could advance 25 kilometers per day with ease, overcoming the slight delays occasioned by crossing smaller rivers.[39]

The reinforcements for Wuthmann's IX Corps promised by Hitler began to arrive on 27 June. The dangerous gap between Reinhardt's Third Panzer Army and Tippelskirch's Fourth Army was screened by Battle Group Von Gottberg made up of German security and police battalions. Busch, commander of Army Group Center, decided to shore up Wuthmann's IX Corps and placed the newly arrived 212th Division between Detachment D and the 201st Security Division west of Lepel, a crucial junction with roads running in several directions through the marshes.[40]

During 27 June the German IX Corps was forced to withdraw again, this time 10 kilometers west of the Lake Lukomlskoe–Uzvitsa line. The new line ran from Gorodets (about 50 kilometers southwest of Polotsk) to Lepel and the Essa River. Gaps had opened on both sides of that line, and Soviet columns of Chistyakov's 6th Guard Army and Beloborodov's 43rd Army were pressing through, threatening to envelope Wuthmann's IX Corps from both north and south.[41]

The German Sixteenth Army promised an attack from Polotsk to relieve the pressure on the north flank of Wuthmann's Corps, but Malyshev's 4th Shock Army, protecting the flank of Chistyakov's 6th Guard Army, was more than adequate to cope with the feeble attack by three German battalions.[42]

On 28 June there were two gaps, one north of Gorodets, the northern flank of the German IX Corps line, and the other southwest of Lepel. The northern gap between IX Corps and I Corps of the Sixteenth Army was 12 kilometers wide. The Soviet 6th Guard Army continued to exert heavy pressure on the gaps. On the night of 27–28 June, the German 252nd Infantry Division was attacked by Butkov's 1st Tank Corps and Ksenofontov's 2nd Guard Corps while withdrawing during the night from Kamen, and only 300 Germans escaped. Detachment D had only 40 or 50 men in its rifle battalions, many of whom were suffering from foot problems from fighting and retreating in the mud and water of the marshlands for the previous 7 days. As many as 80 men from some battalions of Detachment D were being treated for bad feet. The 201st Security Division was removed from Wuthmann's IX Corps, apparently because it was no longer an effective force after days of front-line combat. The fresh 212th Division with about 500 men in each of its seven battalions was ordered to hold the center of the German IX Corps line on the Lepel-Berezino road.[43]

The attempt to hold Lepel failed when Beloborodov's 43rd Army and a tank brigade of the Horse-Mechanized Group crossed the Essa River at Lepel. At 0745 on 28 June Reinhardt, commander of the Third Panzer Army, ordered the IX Corps to drop back another 10 to 20 kilometers to a line midway to the Berezina River. (See Map 6.2.) The most serious German concern was that Soviet forces would cross the Berezina River, make contact with the numerous Partisans in the huge marsh west of the river, and with their help move quickly 100 kilometers to Molodechno, cutting both the rail and road connection between Minsk, the capital of White Russia, and Vilnius in Lithuania to the northwest.[44] Already the Soviet 277th Rifle Division of General Krylov's 5th Army with tank support was on the Lepel-Begomli road at the Berezina River and crossed the river with forty tanks and a motorized column.[45]

Still under constant pressure, Wuthmann's IX Corps withdrew again during the night of 28–29 June. The overnight retreat went well for the Germans without any attacks by the Russians, who

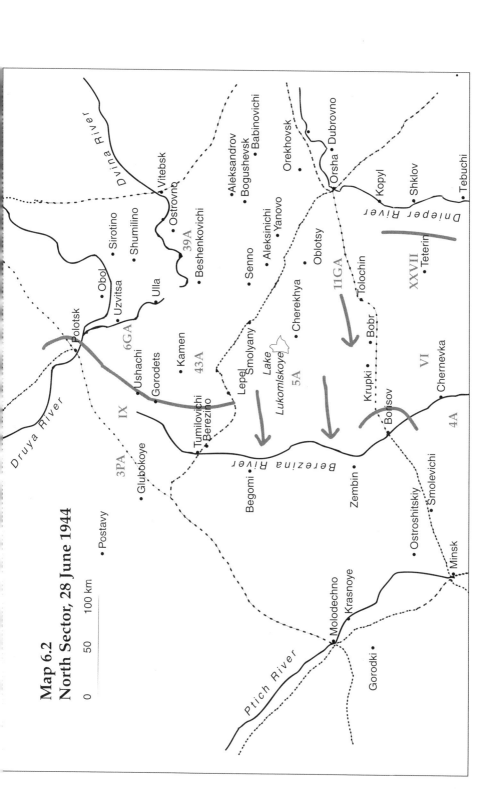

Map 6.2
North Sector, 28 June 1944

0   50   100 km

closed up to the new positions quickly on the morning of 29 June. At noon a tank brigade and a mechanized brigade of Butkov's 1st Tank Corps attacked Ushachi and Gorodets, and Wuthmann's IX Corps was forced to retreat again. The IX Corps was by now reduced to the remnants of the 252nd Infantry Division, Corps Detachment D, and the 212th Division in a small semicircle about 75 kilometers southwest of Polotsk. A gaping hole over 50 kilometers wide stretched north of Wuthmann's IX Corps, giving free rein to Chistyakov's 6th Guard Army. Through the gap Butkov's 1st Tank Corps and Fedyunkin's 103rd Rifle Corps of the 6th Guard Army reached the rail line from Polotsk to Molodechno before noon. The Russians bypassed Polotsk and were on the road to Dvinsk.[46]

To the south, another 70-kilometer gap separated Wuthmann's IX Corps from Tippelskirch's Fourth Army being driven west of the Berezina River, leaving the path open to Molodechno on 29 June. During the night Butkov's 1st Tank Corps swung to the north and took Ushachi and sent tank brigades down the Molodechno-Polotsk rail line, while Wuthmann's IX Corps withdrew again to a line 15 kilometers east of Begomli on the Berezina River. The German troops were worn out, many more were by now suffering from bad feet, and some had not eaten in 3 days because of the continual movement.[47]

During 30 June the Germans again fell back closely pursued by Chistyakov's 6th Guard Army. Early in the morning Butkov's 1st Tank Corps had pushed ahead and crossed the railroad from Polotsk to Molodechno with an open path to Molodechno. On 29 and 30 June the Soviet 159th Tank Brigade of the 1st Tank Corps had advanced 45 kilometers.[48]

In the center of Wuthmann's IX Corps the German 212th Infantry Division had no troops to defend Begomli, and the Russians were building bridges across the Berezina River. By evening the IX Corps held a weak position 15 kilometers east of Glubokoye northwest of the Polotsk-Molodechno railroad. Soviet units were across the Pronia River in the 212th Division sector by nightfall. The 22nd and 23rd Guard Corps of Chistyakov's 6th Guard Army were on the rail line from Daugavpils, Latvia, to Polotsk and were advancing with the help of heavy air support on the afternoon of 30 June.[49]

On 1 July Red Army units were turning the flanks of the 252nd German Division as Wuthmann's IX Corps retreated to Glubokoye. In the afternoon Soviet forces moved through a gap north of Tumilovichi on the Berezina River and penetrated the rear of the 212th German Division. The IX Corps had to retreat again, being pushed to the northwest and leaving the railroad to Molodechno open to the Russians. Chistyakov was heading for Daugavpils.[50]

The 212th German Division could move only to the north because the forest to its rear had few roads and was infested with Partisans, and thus left a huge gap in the German line. As a desperate blocking move, the 391st Security Division, supported by the 519th Heavy Tank Destroyer Battalion with Hornet assault guns, established a position on the road at Postavy about 50 kilometers west of Glubokoye.[51]

Beloborodov's 43rd Army was attempting to round up Reinhardt's Third Panzer Army at Glubokoye while maintaining a link between Chistyakov's 6th Guard Army swinging in a northwest direction and Krylov's 5th Army heading for Molodechno. The Stavka Reserve added the 100th Rifle Corps to the southern flank of the 43rd Army to help maintain a continuous front.[52]

From 29 June to 4 July, the Soviet 6th Guard Army and the 43rd Army advanced 130 kilometers, almost as fast as the infantry could march. By 1 July the German Third Panzer Army had been utterly destroyed and a huge gap was torn in the German line. Gollwitzer's LIII Corps had been eliminated at Vitebsk, and the Soviet 6th Guard Army was chasing remnants of Wuthmann's IX Corps to the northwest. Beloborodov's 43rd Army turned south to close the ring around Tippelskirch's Fourth Army at Minsk.[53]

The performance of the Soviet 1st Tank Corps and General Butkov was criticized because this unit was often bogged down behind the infantry, delayed at each river while waiting for the pontoons to arrive to begin ferrying tanks. The enormous number of vehicles had crammed the poor roads, and there were too few engineers to improve the roads. Lack of adequate transport to move the pontoons up quickly behind the tanks had been a major failing, and as a result the 1st Tank Corps did not play its expected role.[54]

Furthermore, during the following days, a steady stream of German units arrived to slow the Soviet advance and force the Russians to resume the costly battles of attrition. The devastating impact of the surprise attack of 22 June had given the Russians the long-sought prize of Vitebsk and a huge bag of prisoners at comparatively small cost in men and weapons. However, the brief interlude of blitzkrieg war came to an end and the pace slowed to the all too familiar rhythm of the Eastern Front. The effect of the Soviet blitzkrieg had worn thin, and the Russians were once again faced with pushing ahead in slow motion.

Notes

1. G. Niepold, *The Battle for White Russia: The Destruction of Army Group Centre, June 1944* (London: Brassey's, 1987), p. 73; David Glantz, ed.,

1985 Art of War Symposium: From the Dnieper to the Vistula: Soviet Offensive Operations, November 1943–August 1944 (Carlisle Barracks, Penn.: U.S. Army War College, 1985), pp. 272–275, 294–297. The army commanders did expect some form of attack, pp. 258–271; Paul Adair, *Hitler's Greatest Defeat: The Collapse of Army Group Centre, June 1944* (London: Arms and Armour Press, 1994), p. 90; P. Akulov and G. Tolokol'nikov, eds., *V Boiakh za Belorussiu* (Minsk: Belarus, 1970), pp. 241–243.

2. A. M. Samsanov, ed., *Osvobozhdenie Belorussii, 1944* (Moscow: Nauka, 1974), pp. 124, 335; Niepold, p. 78; David M. Glantz and Harold S. Orenstein, eds., *Belorussia 1944: The Soviet General Staff Study* (Carlisle, Penn.: David M. Glantz, 1998), p. 76; F. V. Plotnikov, *v Srazheniia za Belorussi* (Minsk: Belarus, 1982), pp. 50–51; O. Heidkamper, *Vitebsk* (Heidelberg: Vowinckel, 1954), p. 148; Ivan Chistiakov, *Sluzhim Otchizne* (Moscow: Voenizdat, 1975), pp. 220–223; Adair, p. 87; S. P. Kiriukhin, *43-ya Armiia v Vitebskoi Operatsii* (Moscow: Voenizdat, 1961), pp. 76–79.

3. Niepold, p. 73; Earl F. Ziemke, *Stalingrad to Berlin: The German Campaign in Russia, 1942–1945* (New York: Dorset Press, 1968), p. 320; Samsanov, pp. 318–324; Heidkamper, p. 149; Adair, p. 87.

4. Niepold, p. 73; Samsanov, p. 532; Adair, p. 89.

5. Niepold, p. 74; Samsanov, p. 125.

6. Niepold, p. 85.

7. David M. Glantz, *Soviet Military Deception in the Second World War* (London: Frank Cass, 1989), pp. 364, 368; Chistiakov, pp. 216-217; Adair, p. 90.

8. Glantz and Orenstein, p. 76; Kiriukhin, p. 79; Adair, p. 91.

9. Samsanov, p. 125; Niepold, p. 85; Glantz and Orenstein, p. 77; Chistiakov, p. 223.

10. John Erickson, *The Road to Berlin* (Boulder, Colo.: Westview Press, 1983), p. 217; Niepold, p. 79; Albert Seaton, *The Russo-German War, 1941–45* (New York: Praeger, 1970), p. 437; Samsanov, pp. 324–328; Glantz and Orenstein, pp. 77–78.

11. Niepold, p. 81; Glantz and Orenstein, pp. 88–89; Kiriukhin, pp. 81–94.

12. Seaton, p. 438; Glantz and Orenstein, pp. 77–78.

13. Niepold, p. 81; Seaton, pp. 437–438; Heidkamper, pp. 154–155.

14. Niepold, p. 87; Glantz, *1985 Symposium*, pp. 325–327.

15. Niepold, p. 82.

16. Samsanov, p. 127; Glantz and Orenstein, pp. 79–80; Niepold, pp. 88, 97; Plotnikov, p. 52; Akulov and Tolokol'nikov, p. 243; A. M. Vasilevsky, *Delo Vsei Zhizni* (Minsk: Belarus, 1984), p. 458; Adair, p. 94.

17. Glantz and Orenstein, p. 79; I. I. Liudnikov, *Pod Vitebskom* (Moscow: Voenizdat, 1962), p. 67; Chistiakov, pp. 224–227.

18. Niepold, p. 88; Samsanov, pp. 330, 535; Erickson, pp. 217–218; Glantz and Orenstein, pp. 79–80, 89, 92; Glantz, *1985 Symposium*, p. 327; Liudnikov, p. 68; Kiriukhin, pp. 94-102; Adair, p. 94.

19. Erickson, p. 218; Glantz and Orenstein, p. 91; Plotnikov, p. 80; Kiriukhin, p. 102; Glantz, *1985 Symposium*, pp. 327–328; Adair, p. 95.

20. Niepold, p. 82.

21. Seaton, p. 438; Niepold, pp. 88–89; Samsanov, pp. 535–536; Adair, p. 95; Kiriukhin, p. 102; Heidkamper, p. 158.

22. Niepold, p. 100; Glantz and Orenstein, p. 80; Heidkamper, pp. 153–155.

23. Samsanov, p. 338; Glantz and Orenstein, p. 82; Chistiakov, p. 227; Kiriukhin, pp. 103–104; Akulov and Tolokol'nikov, p. 245; Heidkamper, pp. 156–157.

24. Samsanov, pp. 127–128; Glantz and Orenstein, p. 83.

25. Niepold, p. 100; Erickson, p. 220; Glantz and Orenstein, pp. 80–81.

26. Niepold, p. 100; Heidkamper, p. 162.

27. Samsanov, pp. 128–130, 334; Niepold, p. 100; Heidkamper, p. 163.

28. Glantz and Orenstein, pp. 81–82; Niepold, p. 112; Samsanov, p. 130; Kiriukhin, p. 104.

29. Glantz and Orenstein, pp. 82–83.

30. Niepold, p. 101; Seaton, p. 438; Erickson, p. 219; Samsanov, p. 129; Adair, p. 95.

31. Seaton, p. 439; Erickson, p. 219; Glantz and Orenstein, p. 83; Kiriukhin, pp. 106–108.

32. Samsanov, pp. 75, 123; Niepold, p. 114; Glantz and Orenstein, p. 84; Kiriukhin, pp. 114–115; Vasilevsky, p. 460.

33. Samsanov, pp. 338–339; Niepold, p. 115; Adair, p. 97; Heidkamper, pp. 161, 164.

34. Samsanov, pp. 130, 541.

35. Niepold, p. 125; Seaton, p. 439; Erickson, p. 220; Adair, pp. 97–98.

36. Samsanov, p. 541; Seaton, p. 439; Heidkamper, pp. 161–162; Adair, p. 99.

37. Niepold, p. 125.

38. Samsanov, p. 130; Niepold, p. 136; Glantz and Orenstein, p. 85.

39. Samsanov, pp. 542, 546; Heidkamper, p. 165.

40. Niepold, pp. 125–126; Heidkamper, pp. 166–167.

41. Niepold, pp. 125–126.

42. Ibid., p. 126.

43. Ibid., pp 139–140; Heidkamper, p. 168.

44. Niepold, pp. 139–140; Glantz and Orenstein, pp. 85–86.

45. Samsanov, p. 306; Niepold, p. 140; Heidkamper, p. 169.

46. Samsanov, p. 132; Niepold, pp. 140, 153.

47. Niepold, pp. 153–154, 162.

48. Ibid., pp. 164, 173; Samsanov, p. 132.

49. Niepold, pp. 164–165; Samsanov, p. 133; Chistiakov, p. 228.

50. Niepold, p. 174.

51. Ibid., p. 175.

52. Ibid., p. 175; Samsanov, pp. 132–133; Glantz and Orenstein, p. 131.

53. Glantz and Orenstein; p. 131; Chistiakov, p. 229; Plotnikov, p. 127.

54. Glantz and Orenstein, p. 86.

Buildup for the summer offensive was delayed by winter weather. However, masses of troops from the southern fronts were transferred to the center to provide overwhelming numbers for the attack. AUTHOR'S COLLECTION

Soviet light antiaircraft guns along with fighter aircraft provided protection for advancing tanks and permitted the columns to advance in daylight.
AUTHOR'S COLLECTION

By the summer of 1944, Soviet tank factories were turning out thousands of tanks while losses to the Germans had greatly diminished its arsenal. Tank armies, as well as mechanized groups with a tank corps and a cavalry corps, gave the Red Army a superior force. AUTHOR'S COLLECTION

Man-made obstacles and rivers delayed the Soviet advance. This tunnel formed a trap for any tank emerging so Soviet infantry had to advance without support. AUTHOR'S COLLECTION

American lend-lease trucks with four-wheel drive were able to carry infantry right along with the tank columns. AUTHOR'S COLLECTION

Soviet tanks were equipped with handles so that infantry could ride on them and be immediately available to take out German antitank guns. AUTHOR'S COLLECTION

Hastily laid minefields were a constant danger to the advancing Russians. Clearing the minefields was very dangerous and was usually done by Russians who were being punished for some reason. AUTHOR'S COLLECTION

The Soviet navy in the north was bottled up in Leningrad but provided both antiaircraft guns and artillery to defend the city. AUTHOR'S COLLECTION

The Red Army created artillery corps with more than 300 guns. To control the fire required advanced optical equipment. AUTHOR'S COLLECTION

Women were assigned to many Red Army units—usually as medical, communication, and clerical workers. However, sniper battalions were formed with women who had been abused by the Germans. Even experienced soldiers find difficulty in killing individuals over a period of time. The women had no such problem. AUTHOR'S COLLECTION

One of the first tasks after liberating a Russian town was to destroy all vestiges of German rule. AUTHOR'S COLLECTION

The Soviet 76mm gun was the workhorse of the artillery. It was easily placed in position and required only a few men to fire. AUTHOR'S COLLECTION

The rapidly advancing Soviet tank columns surrounded thousands of Germans, many of whom were paraded through the streets of Moscow in a victory parade.

AUTHOR'S COLLECTION

Soviet Sturmovick ground attack planes prevented the Germans from moving on the roads during daylight hours. AUTHOR'S COLLECTION

The huge losses suffered by the Germans were hastily buried in temporary cemeteries. The Germans buried in this cemetery were members of the 3rd Panzer Grenadier Regiment who were killed at Kursk in July 1943. PHILIP FRANCIS

The deadly barrages by Soviet artillery killed many Germans in their elaborate bunkers. The shrapnel from the shells penetrated the helmets, seen here in a makeshift grave. PHILIP FRANCIS

The German Army suffered more killed and missing in June 1944 than in any month of the war. PHILIP FRANCIS

Although the losses suffered by the Germans were heavy in June, in the end the two catastrophic battles in the east and west in June 1944 so weakened the German Army that it brought the war to a speedy end, rather than dragging out for years. PHILIP FRANCIS

CHAPTER 7

Bogushevsk

The objective of the third rupture of the German lines east of Bogushevsk and south of Vitebsk by General I. I. Lyudnikov's 39th Army and General N. I. Krylov's 5th Army of the 3rd White Russian Front was threefold. (See Figure 7.1 for a table of organization of the 3rd White Russian Front northern armies.) The first mission was to facilitate the encirclement of Vitebsk from the south to clear a path for the Oslikovskiy Horse-Mechanized Group, the second to initiate the most spectacular deep penetration in the battle for White Russia, and the third to open the way for the 5th Guard Tank Army commanded by Marshal P. A. Rotmistrov, which would cut off Orsha from the north. The two Soviet armored columns performed a classic exploitation, scattering the German VI Corps and turning the north flank of the German Fourth Army.

The attack south of Vitebsk began in the afternoon of 22 June, when the front-line battalions of the Krylov's 5th Army attacked trench lines of the first German defense zone with artillery support. The 5th Army faced the 299th and 256th Divisions of General G. Pfeiffer's VI Corps, with the 95th and 14th Divisions in reserve. Lyudnikov's 39th Army was primarily concerned with encircling Vitebsk from the south, but General Bezugliy's 5th Guard Corps embarked on a deep penetration action opposed by the 197th German Division of Pfeiffer's VI Corps. Rotmistrov's 5th Guard Tank Army and Oslikovskiy's Horse-Mechanized Group were poised for advance as soon as a clean break had been made.[1]

The main attack was preceded by a 2-hour-and-20-minute bombardment of the German lines by heavy artillery and katyushas and attacks from the air. The air support included the 3rd Fighter Air Corps commanded by General Y. Y. Savitskiy, the 3rd Guard and 213th Bomber Divisions of the 1st Guard Bomber Corps commanded by General V. A. Ushakov, and the 311th Sturmovik Division of the 1st Air Army.[2]

117

Figure 7.1 Northern Armies of the 3rd White Russian Front

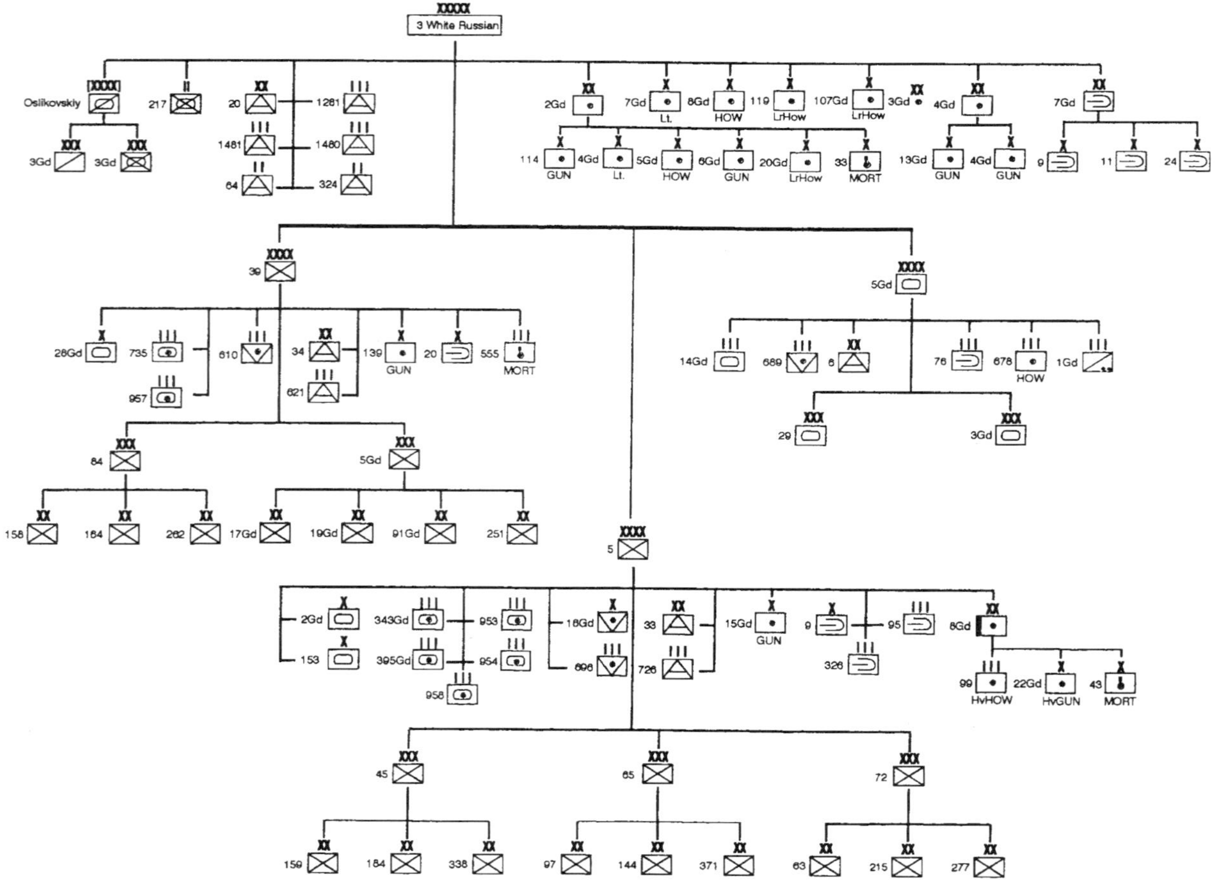

Five Russian divisions, the first echelon of the three corps of Krylov's 5th Army, then assaulted the 299th and 256th German divisions.[3] Krylov's 5th Soviet Army was deployed in two echelons on a 30-kilometer front with the 63rd, 277th, 371st, 97th, and 159th Rifle Divisions in the first echelon. The focal points were the sectors of the Soviet 277th and 371st Divisions. The attacking Soviet divisions had ample armored support. General A. I. Kazariev's 72nd Corps had the 153rd Tank Brigade at Buraki. The 277th Division of Kazariev's corps was supported by the 523rd Tank Regiment, the 513th Tank Regiment with flame throwers, the 954th Assault Gun Regiment, and the 343rd Heavy Assault Gun Regiment.[4] General G. N. Perekrestov's 65th Corps was assisted by the 2nd Guard Tank Brigade, the 395th Heavy Assault Gun Regiment, and the 343rd Assault Gun Regiment, about 100 armored vehicles and equal to a panzer division.

The heaviest blows fell on the German 299th Division as Kazariev's 72nd and Perekrestov's 65th Corps of Krylov's 5th Army hammered 18 kilometers of the German line at the Chernitsa River. The 277th Soviet Division with the support of the 153rd Tank Brigade and the 343rd Heavy Assault Gun Regiment, about eighty armored vehicles and 9,000 men, attacked the thousand Germans of the 530th Regiment of the 299th German Division.[5]

Five battalions of the first-echelon divisions broke through the German lines, and the four second-echelon divisions followed through in the sectors where the greatest success had been achieved. The element of surprise contributed to the success in capturing all three trench lines and breaking through the first German defense zone.

In the afternoon heavy attacks drove the 299th German Division and the left flank of the 256th Division back 2 kilometers and forced them out of the third trench line in the first defense zone. The 277th Division of Kazariev's 72nd Corps with 954th Assault Gun Regiment drove the German 530th Infantry Regiment all the way to the Luchesa River. The Germans responded with an air attack by twenty Ju 87s and a counterattack by elements of the 14th German Division that was beaten off by the Russians with heavy German losses.[6]

Perekrestov's 65th Corps in the center attacked the other regiments of the 299th German Division with the aid of the 2nd Guard Tank Brigade and gained 2.5 kilometers. The 371st and 97th Divisions of the 65th Corps drove through the center of Pfeiffer's VI Corps sector and penetrated to the second zone of defense. The 97th Soviet Division of Perekrestov's corps crossed the Luchesa River.[7]

On the northern flank of Krylov's 5th Army, the 17th Guard Division of Bezugliy's 5th Guard Corps of Lyudnikov's 39th Army hit the northern flank of the 299th German Division on the Vitebsk-Orsha road and Luchesa River. On the southern flank of Krylov's 5th Army, the 45th Corps, commanded by General S. F. Gorokhov, attacked the German 256th Division with help from the 152nd Fortified Region of General K. N. Galitskiy's 11th Guard Army.[8] The German 95th Division in reserve on the Pskov-Kiev road mounted counterattacks with the help of two regiments of the 299th German Division and the 550th Penal Battalion, and that gave the German front-line divisions time to occupy a second defense zone along the Luchesa.[9]

As soon as the first echelon Soviet divisions broke through Pfeiffer's VI Corps sector on 22 June, Krylov's 5th Army quickly advanced its artillery with the help of engineers to greet the German counterattacks with concentrated artillery.[10] Kazariev's 72nd and Perekrestov's 65th Corps advanced up to 4 kilometers, and bridgeheads were established on the Sukhodrovka River. On the night of 22–23 June, three 60-ton bridges were built for tanks and artillery and so were three lighter bridges for trucks.[11] Krylov's 5th Army continued to attack the 299th and 256th German Divisions through the night of 22–23 June.

The first day of the attack south of Vitebsk had been an outstanding success. General I. D. Chernyakovskiy, commander of the 3rd White Russian Front, coordinated the Bogushevsk attack of four armies, a horse-mechanized group, and a tank army compressed into a front just over 100 kilometers wide. The front included, from north to south, Lyudnikov's 39th, Krylov's 5th, Galitskiy's 11th Guard, and General V. V. Glagolev's 31st Armies with the Oslikovskiy Horse-Mechanized Group and Rotmistrov's 5th Guard Tank Army in reserve. The front had a total of 1,169 tanks, 641 assault guns, 1,175 antitank guns (45mm and 57mm), 2,893 guns of 76mm or larger, 3,552 mortars, 689 rocket launchers, 792 antiaircraft guns, 1,864 aircraft, 16,208 machine guns, and 390,000 men.

Glagolev's 31st and Galitskiy's 11th Guard Armies formed the northern pincer of the attack on Orsha, and this operation will be described in the following chapter.[12] Krylov's 5th Army, Oslikovskiy's Group, and Rotmistrov's 5th Guard Tank Army charged westward to Bogushevsk once the German defense line had been pierced. Lyudnikov's 39th Army was the northernmost army holding a comparatively wide, curving sector of over 30 kilometers east of Vitebsk on the face and southern shoulder of the Vitebsk salient. Glagolev had an initial assignment of enveloping Gollwitzer's LIII Corps in Vitebsk from the south and driving off the northern wing of Pfeiffer's VI Corps. Bezugliy's 5th Guard Corps formed the southern pincer of the attack on Vitebsk, while General

Y. M. Prokofiev's 84th Corps held the German divisions in Vitebsk in place.

The two guard divisions of Bezugliy's 5th Guard Rifle Corps had been with the 39th Army since March, but the two rifle divisions had recently arrived to strengthen the assault at the expense of the 33rd Army, which held a passive front. The two rifle divisions of Prokofiev's 84th Corps had held sectors at Vitebsk as part of Lyudnikov's 39th Army since March. The 84th Rifle Corps held more than two-thirds of the army front, providing a thin screen, while most of power of the army was concentrated in Bezugliy's 5th Guard Rifle Corps in a narrow sector about 10 kilometers south of Vitebsk and poised to launch the breakthrough along with Krylov's 5th Army to its left.

The supporting troops of Lyudnikov's 39th Army were strong enough, particularly in armored units, to exploit the breakthrough. Much of the artillery assigned to the 39th Army on 1 June, including four artillery brigades, was transferred to the 3rd White Russian Front reserve before 23 June, and a new artillery brigade, the 139th Gun Artillery Brigade, was formed in May. The 39th Army also had the standard allotment of a tank destroyer regiment, an antiaircraft regiment, a guard mortar regiment, and a mortar regiment. The 34th Antiaircraft Division was added to the army in April.

The armored additions included the 28th Guard Tank Brigade, the 735th Assault Gun Regiment, and the 957th Assault Gun Regiment, all of which would support Bezugliy's 5th Guard Corps. After the fall of Vitebsk, Bezugliy's corps, the 28th Guard Tank Brigade, and two assault gun regiments joined in the exploitation phase.

Krylov's 5th Army received four new divisions and the 152nd Fortified Region during June in preparation for its breakthrough task and subsequent exploitation role. On 23 June Krylov's army had three rifle corps, from north to south, Kazariev's 72nd, Perekrestov's 65th, and Gorokhov's 45th. The 152nd Fortified Region was transferred to Galitskiy's 11th Guard Army in June as the 5th Army concentrated for the offensive.

The 5th Army had a large armored contingent, the 153rd Tank Brigade, the 2nd Guard Tank Brigade, and five assault gun regiments, three formed in May and two from the Moscow Military District in June. This circumstance was unusual because the three new regiments went into action only a month after formation. The usual procedure was to form the regiments in the Moscow Military District and train them for about 2 months before assigning them to an army. The regiments may have been formed from preexisting tank regiments and thus would have had combat-experienced men.

Tank regiments were often reequipped with assault guns and given a new number (at least five tank regiments disappeared from the Soviet order of battle in May 1944). The creation of the assault gun regiments and their immediate assignment to the 5th Army indicated a desire to give the army ample mobile artillery support in view of the important assignment in the offensive.

Krylov's 5th Army artillery was exceptional as well, with the 3rd Guard Artillery Division plus a guard mortar brigade and a regiment. The guard mortar units were especially useful to mobile units in providing close support for advancing armor. The other support troops were standard, an antiaircraft division and a regiment, a tank destroyer regiment, a guard mortar regiment, and a mortar regiment. Krylov's 5th Army with the substantial reinforcements received during June had the offensive power to carry out its major role in the offensive.

Rotmistrov's 5th Guard Tank Army had been with the 2nd Ukrainian Front in April and then moved secretly north to the Stavka Reserve in May. In June the army was placed in reserve behind the 3rd White Russian Front in preparation to exploit the breakthrough south of Vitebsk. This army had ample time to refit, receiving new tanks and crew in May and June, but its move north had been delayed by congested rail lines.

Oslikovskiy's Horse-Mechanized Group was assembled by the 3rd White Russian Front in May and June from Oslikovskiy's 3rd Guard Cavalry Corps and General V. T. Obukov's 3rd Guard Mechanized Corps. Oslikovskiy commanded both the cavalry corps and the group. The Oslikovskiy Horse-Mechanized Group fought as a small tank army, though it lacked the service units of an army and still relied on the 3rd White Russian Front for administrative support.

The 3rd White Russian Front reserve retained a massive artillery component, including four artillery and guard mortar divisions and four independent artillery brigades. Ample antiaircraft protection was provided by a division, three regiments, and two independent battalions. Although the artillery support was considerable, most of the other supporting troops had been distributed to the armies that would play major roles in the offensive.

Facing Krylov's 5th Army, Rotmistrov's 5th Guard Tank Army, and Oslikovskiy's Horse-Mechanized Group was Pfeiffer's VI Corps composed of the 197th, 256th, and 299th Infantry Divisions. The 197th comprised survivors of two battered divisions, neither of which had received sufficient replacements to be reconstituted as a full division, and was almost in the same category as a corps detachment, being filled with experienced but battle-weary men. The division was supported by the 281st Assault Gun Brigade.

The German 256th Infantry Division was a stable division that had spent the entire campaign in the Soviet Union in Army Group Center and, though reduced by attrition, had not suffered the catastrophic losses of many other divisions. The 299nd Infantry Division had been reduced by lack of replacements in the past, but had escaped heavy losses and probably was at full strength in June 1944. The division was supported by the 281st Assault Gun Brigade.

The 95th Infantry Division of Reinhardt's Third Panzer Army was placed in reserve behind the 197th and 299th Infantry Divisions. The 95th Infantry Division had been reduced because of lack of replacements in previous years, but had not suffered heavy losses in defensive fighting since 1943. Through the spring replacement program, the division was at full strength.

In addition, Pfeiffer's VI Corps sector was bolstered by the Army Group Center reserve's 14th Infantry Division, which was placed behind the 256th Infantry Division. The 14th Division had been a motorized division, but, with the shortage of motor vehicles in 1943, was converted to a standard infantry division in July. As a prewar regular division and former motorized division, the unit was of higher quality than most infantry divisions. It was supported by the 667th Assault Gun Brigade, which had been formed by the Ninth Army in August 1942. Pfeiffer's VI Corps also had the 281st Assault Gun Brigade with the 299th Division.[13] The VI Corps was very strong, with three good divisions on the front and two more in reserve and two assault gun brigades holding a 40-kilometer front. The Germans were well prepared, but the Soviet attackers were stronger.

On the second day of the offensive on the morning of 23 June, Lyudnikov's 39th Army launched an attack on the 197th German Division. After a 1-hour artillery barrage starting at 0600, Lyudnikov's infantry stormed the German trenches, broke through, and advanced quickly to the west and southwest. With the 262nd and 164th Rifle Divisions of Prokofiev's 84th Corps on the right and Bezugliy's 5th Guard Corps on the left, all with tank support, the 39th Army crashed through the German 197th Infantry Division. Artillery fire played a major role in destroying the German defenses, while the tanks and assault guns blazed a path for the infantry through the demoralized German defenders.[14]

By 1300 on 23 June, the 262nd and 164th Rifle Divisions of Prokofiev's 84th Corps drove the 197th German Division back to the Vitebsk-Orsha rail line leading south from Vitebsk. The Soviet 164th

Division pushed the 197th German Division in a northwest direction, while the Soviet 262nd Division on the right pivoted, maintaining contact with the 158th Division holding a large sector east of Vitebsk. The 164th Division continued north along the rail line, supported by the 957th Assault Gun Regiment and the 610th Tank Destroyer Regiment. By evening the German 197th Division was driven north to within 15 kilometers of Vitebsk and 8 kilometers west of the railroad.[15]

The Luchesa River was a major obstacle to Bezugliy's 5th Guard Corps as it attacked the German 347th Infantry Regiment of the 197th Division on a 6-kilometer front. The Soviet forces crossed the Luchesa River and cut the Vitebsk-Orsha rail line, advancing 13 kilometers. The German 197th Division was driven back despite help from the 280th Infantry Regiment of the 95th Division.[16]

At 0930 on 23 June, Bezugliy's corps crossed the river, and their engineers quickly installed a 60-ton-capacity bridge for heavy tanks, followed shortly by 24- and 9-ton bridges for light tanks and other traffic. The tanks of the 5th Guard Corps armored column, composed of the 28th Guard Tank Brigade, the 19th Guard Division and the 735th Assault Gun Regiment, moved quickly over the pontoon bridges and raced westward against light opposition.[17]

All four divisions of Bezugliy's 5th Guard Corps were attacking on the front line at 1300 on 23 June. A battalion of the 28th Guard Tank Brigade was attached to the 91st Guard Division on the north; the 19th Guard Division to the left of the 91st Guard Division had another battalion of the 28th Guard Tank Brigade and the 610th Tank Destroyer Regiment; the 17th Guard Division had the 735th Assault Gun Regiment; and the 251st Rifle Division had been added at 1300 to protect the south flank of the advance. By 2300 all of Bezugliy's four divisions had advanced at least an additional 10 kilometers.[18]

To block the advance of the 5th Guard Corps, the Germans planned a counterattack with a regiment of the 95th Division. The 95th Division was placed between the 197th and 299th Divisions on a 14-kilometer front on the Pskov-Kiev road. The German counterattack was supported by tanks, but still failed to slow the Soviet advance.[19]

In the evening of 23 June, having been driven toward Vitebsk, the 197th German Division was transferred to Gollwitzer's LIII Corps. The plan for 24 June was to use the German 4th Luftwaffe Division from the Vitebsk garrison to plug the hole between Vitebsk and Pfeiffer's VI Corps. The gap had opened between Detachment D of Wuthmann's IX Corps and the 197th Division. However, the Germans still held a 20-kilometer-wide corridor open to Vitebsk.[20]

To the south of Lyudnikov's 39th Army, Krylov's 5th Army had its three corps in line on 23 June. It was further reinforced by brigades from Obukov's 3rd Guard Mechanized Corps. Kazariev's 72nd Corps was supported by the 7th and 9th Guard Mechanized Brigades on the right, and Perekrestov's 65th Corps by the 8th Guard Mechanized Brigade and 35th Guard Tank Brigade in the center.[21]

Krylov's 5th Army continued to attack throughout 23 June, driving back Pfeiffer's VI Corps with the support of a heavy artillery barrage and many air attacks. Krylov had penetrated the German second defense zone on 22 June and was heading for the third zone on the 23rd. By noon the German 299th Division had retreated and two tank columns of Krylov's 5th Army had turned south on the Pskov-Kiev road crossing the Luchesa River. By 1300 on 23 June, the German 299th and 256th Divisions plus the 14th Division that had arrived to help were brushed aside and the Red Army units crossed the rail line leading to Orsha. From there, the 9th Guard Mechanized Brigade drove straight west toward Senno with the 45th Tank Regiment, the corps motorcycle battalion, two batteries of the 1823rd Assault Gun Regiment equipped with SU85s, a mortar battery, and the brigade artillery battalion. The 8th Guard Mechanized Brigade came up to hold the gains. The Germans counterattacked, and the Russians claimed four Panthers and three light tanks in exchange for the loss of a single 57mm antitank gun.[22]

To the south, on the right flank of Pfeiffer's VI Corps, the German 256th Division was forced by Gorokhov's 45th Corps to withdraw across the Luchesa River, but Pfeiffer's front was still intact. Krylov's 5th Army had advanced south 13 kilometers on a 26-kilometer-wide sector. By midnight on 23 June, the 5th Army was only 13 kilometers from Bogushevsk. That night Krylov was ordered to turn southeast and advance the 13 kilometers to Bogushevsk. Galitskiy's 11th Guard Army was coming up from the south and would meet the 5th Army at Bogushevsk.[23]

Rotmistrov's 5th Guard Tank Army had still not been fully committed to the battle and was held in reserve for another day. On 23 June the tank army had 524 tanks and assault guns, roughly five times the number in a panzer division.[24]

During the morning of 24 June, Prokofiev's 84th Corps of Lyudnikov's 39th Army mounted a crushing attack on Vitebsk. At 1300 the Soviet 158th Division, holding the east face of the Vitebsk perimeter, launched an attack to hold the German divisions in place. The 262nd Division advanced 6 kilometers from the south, closing in on the corridor leading to Vitebsk. Late in the day the 164th Division attacked at 1900 northward toward the corridor, repulsing a German counterattack of two battalions and ten tanks and assault guns and inflicting heavy losses.[25]

In Bezugliy's 5th Guard Corps sector of Lyudnikov's 39th Army, the 19th and 91st Guard Divisions broke through Pfeiffer's VI Corps at 0600 on 24 June and drove west, while the 17th Guard Division with the 28th Guard Tank Brigade and the 957th Assault Gun Regiment bypassed the German 95th Division on the northern flank of Pfeiffer's corps, crossed the Dvina River about 20 kilometers east of Beshenkovichi in the German corridor to Vitebsk, and established several bridgeheads.[26] The Soviet 91st Guard Division, with the 735th Assault Gun Regiment, advanced unopposed to the Dvina River north of Ostrovno held by remnants of the 4th Luftwaffe Division and the 246th Infantry Division. The Russian 19th Guard Division reached the Dvina at Gnesdilovichi and cut the German 20-kilometer-wide corridor to Vitebsk, joining with Beloborodov's 43rd Army from the north. Late on 24 June Russian tanks entered Pushkari on the Dvina and Bezugliy's 5th Guard Corps advanced to the Dvina north of Ostrovno.[27]

In Krylov's 5th Army sector on the morning of 24 June, the Germans added the 14th Division (less one regiment) between the 299th and 256th Divisions east of Bogushevsk on the southern flank of Pfeiffer's VI Corps opposite Kazariev's 72nd and Perekrestov's 65th Corps of Krylov's army. General M. M. Gromov's 1st Air Army sent 240 aircraft to attack Bogushevsk despite bad weather. Krylov attacked with the 63rd and 277th Rifle Divisions of Kazariev's 72nd Corps, the 371st and 97th Divisions of Perekrestov's 65th Corps, and the 159th Division of Gorokhov's 45th Corps. The 2nd Guard Tank Brigade, reinforced by units of the 144th Rifle Division of the 65th Corps, broke through the defensive zone and advanced 10 kilometers. By noon on 24 June, Krylov's tanks had entered Bogushevsk, and by evening his 215th and 144th Divisions had occupied Bogushevsk.[28]

Oslikovskiy's Horse-Mechanized Group was assembled and passed between Lyudnikov's 39th and Krylov's 5th Armies during the evening of 24 June on its way to Senno, halfway from the railroad to the Ulla River. At 0400 on 24 June, the 3rd Guard Cavalry Corps, with good artillery and air support, plus the help of the 215th Rifle Division, the 153rd Tank Brigade, and army artillery units, attacked the German 95th Division.[29]

Pfeiffer's VI Corps was completely broken on 24 June. During the morning the remnants of the German 197th, 95th, 299th, and 256th Infantry Divisions were still holding a line about 10 kilometers east of Bogushevsk, but by the end of the day the corps had been driven back to Bogushevsk under fierce attacks from Krylov's 5th Army and then was driven from the town by noon on 25 June. The Germans reported that 120 Russian tanks had attacked Bogushevsk.[30]

Pfeiffer reinforced his VI Corps link with Tippelskirch's Fourth Army to the south because the corps was cut off from the rest of Reinhardt's Third Panzer Army. By evening the gap between Wuthmann's IX Corps to the north and the northern flank of Pfeiffer's VI Corps was a gaping 30 kilometers wide, and there were no reserves to close it. This gap would prove the undoing of Army Group Center as the Soviet armored columns poured through it on the following days.[31]

Early on the morning of 25 June, the Germans repulsed heavy attacks on Pfeiffer's VI Corps northwest of Bogushevsk. On the right flank the 256th and 14th German Infantry Divisions were facing northeast, holding on the Pskov-Kiev road.[32]

During the day Lyudnikov's 39th Army solidified its junction with Beloborodov's 43rd Army at Gnesdilovichi, 10 kilometers west of Ostrovno, and tightened the noose around the trapped German garrison in Vitebsk. A series of German counterattacks by two regiments of the 6th Luftwaffe Division and elements of the 206th German Infantry Division supported by tanks and assault guns pounced on the 17th Guard Division, the 164th Rifle Division, the 28th Guard Tank Brigade, a regiment of the 91st Guard Division, and the 2nd Guard Motorcycle Regiment from the 3rd White Russian Front reserve along the corridor at Gnesdilovichi west of Vitebsk. Eighteen attacks were made by the Germans in an attempt to keep the corridor open. Repelling the attacks was aided immensely by Shturmoviks of Gromov's 1st Air Army. Meanwhile, Ibyancksiy's 92nd Corps of Beloborodov's 43rd Army was pushing into Vitebsk from the east.[33]

During the morning of 25 June, Field Marshal Busch, commander of Army Group Center, feared that the Soviet armored columns would pour through the gap at Bogushevsk. A proposed solution was to have the 206th Division evacuate Vitebsk and try to break out with the other three divisions of Gollwitzer's LIII Corps, while Tippelskirch's Fourth Army to the south pulled back 25 kilometers to the Dnieper River. Together the Third Panzer and Fourth Armies could possibly have restored a cohesive front. Hitler had approved the withdrawal of the Fourth Army, but insisted that the 206th Division hold Vitebsk as long as possible to block the main road running through the city.

Fulfilling German fears, during the morning of 25 June Oslikovskiy's 3rd Guard Cavalry Corps overran the German 299th

Division and drove back the 95th Division at Aleksinichi, northwest of Bogushevsk. At 0700 120 tanks of the Horse-Mechanized Group came through Bogushevsk and were 4 kilometers west of the town on their way to Smolyany 30 kilometers west of Senno. The German 2nd Security Regiment was assigned to defend Smolyany, but by 2030 on 25 June, Oslikovskiy's cavalry and tanks with infantry aboard were attacking the town. The cavalry group swept through the gap at Bogushevsk, cut the Lepel-Orsha rail line, and drove on toward Senno. Pfeiffer's VI Corps front collapsed.[34]

Immediately behind the Soviet cavalry corps came two mobile columns, one composed of the 144th Rifle Division of Perekrestov's 65th Corps, the 2nd Guard Tank Brigade, and units of the 5th Army artillery. The other armored group contained the 215th Rifle Division and the 153rd Tank Brigade.[35]

Obukov's 3rd Guard Mechanized Corps supported by the 63rd and 277th Divisions of Krylov's 5th Army attacked Senno directly and occupied it the next day. The next objective was Lepel, 75 kilometers to the west. The cavalry group was then to cross the Berezina River more than 100 kilometers to the west.[36]

At 1130 on 25 June, the shattered remnants of Pfeiffer's VI Corps, completely cut off from Reinhardt's Third Panzer Army by the breakthrough at Bogushevsk, came under the command of Tippelskirch's Fourth Army. The boundary of the Fourth Army was placed at Senno.[37]

On the evening of 25 June, Krylov's 5th Army advanced 20 kilometers. The hastily formed Battle Group von Gottberg formed a thin screen across the 70-kilometer gap between Wuthmann's IX Corps of the Third Panzer Army southeast of Lepel and the 14th German Division holding a position 35 kilometers west of Orsha. The German 14th Infantry Division had retreated south and with the 25th Division was shielding the northern flank of Tippelskirch's Fourth Army.[38]

On the evening of 25 June, Rotmistrov's 5th Guard Tank Army was finally ordered by Marshal Vasilevskiy to advance through the gaping hole on the right of Krylov's 5th Army at Bogushevsk and began driving through the gap in the German lines at 1400 on 25 June, in tandem with Oslikovskiy's Horse-Mechanized Group to the north at Senno.[39] The critical threat to the Germans would erupt the next day.

On 26 June Busch expected the Russians to exploit the gap at Bogushevsk. The remaining units of Reinhardt's Third Panzer Army were being forced back rapidly but were still maintaining a semblance of a front, unlike Tippelskirch's Fourth Army, which was in disarray.[40]

At 0330 on 26 June, elements of the Soviet 158th Rifle Division of Prokofiev's 84th Corps of the 39th Army crossed the Dvina and entered Vitebsk. During the night Lyukhtikov's 60th Corps of the 43rd Soviet Army met the 19th Guard Division of the 39th Army at Gnezdilovichi, closing the ring around Vitebsk. The other two divisions of Bezugliy's 5th Guard Corps (17th and 19th Guard Divisions) also closed up to the West Dvina River further dividing Wuthmann's IX Corps. At 0600 on 26 June, the 262nd Rifle Division, also of Prokofiev's 84th Corps, joined in the attack from the south cutting the main road near the city. West on the road between Ostrovno and Vitebsk, remnants of the German 6th Luftwaffe and 197th and 246th Infantry Divisions counterattacked, hitting the Soviet 17th Guard Division with over 1,000 men and ten to fifteen tanks and assault guns. The German attempt to break out was repelled by the 17th Guard Division, the 164th Rifle Division, the 2nd Guard Motorcycle Regiment, and the 555th Mortar Regiment, which inflicted heavy losses. The escaping Germans were chased down by divisions of the 39th and 43rd Armies.[41]

The Soviet 91st Guard Division still had a regiment north of Ostrovno, but the main body of the division, the 17th Guard Division and the 28th Guard Tank Brigade, was attacking Vitebsk from the western side of the perimeter, trying to eliminate the pocket as quickly as possible. On 26 June units of the 39th and 43rd Armies cleared Vitebsk.[42]

To the west, early in the morning of 26 June, the 159th Soviet Division of Gorokhov's 45th Corps of Krylov's 5th Army had reached Bogushevsk. (See Map 7.1.) The 63rd Rifle Division of Kazariev's 72nd Corps and the 184th Division of Gorokhov's 45th Corps continued to attack southwest from Senno and subsequently held the south and east flank of the advancing 5th Army. The 63rd Division was at Xodtsi, 30 kilometers southwest of Vitebsk, part of a mobile group that included the 153rd Tank Brigade and a heavy assault gun regiment with 152mm assault guns. South of Ostrovno, the 251st Rifle Division of Bezugliy's 5th Guard Rifle Corps of the 39th Army held the northern side of the breakthrough.[43]

On 26 June Obukov's 3rd Guard Mechanized Corps advanced 35 kilometers and took Senno and Cherekhya while Oslikovskiy's 3rd Guard Cavalry Corps moved southwest of Aleksinichi, 10 kilometers south of Senno, to Ianova. Later in the day, the horse-mechanized group reached Lake Lukomlskoe and continued to speed west toward the Berezina River. The German 2nd Security Regiment was overrun at Smolyany by the cavalry corps. Krylov's infantry was following in the footsteps of the cavalry corps and advanced 20 kilometers to the Orsha-Lepel rail line.[44]

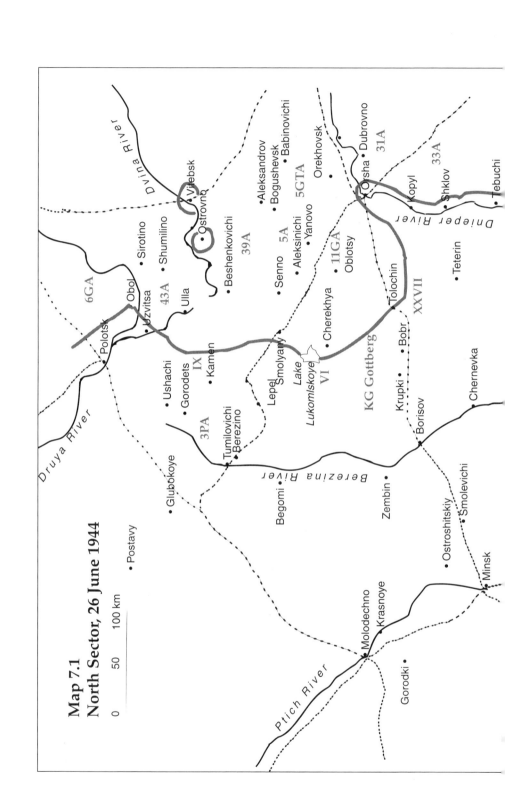

Map 7.1
North Sector, 26 June 1944

0   50   100 km

South of the cavalry corps, Rotmistrov's 5th Guard Tank Army with heavy air support took Tolochin, 50 kilometers west of Orsha, by nightfall on 26 June. The 3rd Guard Tank Corps under the command of General I. A. Bobchenko cut the main road linking Moscow and Minsk west of Orsha. The tank army units continued driving to the west.[45]

The Soviet armored columns were everywhere in the German rear. The horse-mechanized group and Rotmistrov's tank army poured through the gap at Senno and advanced 40 kilometers to Lukomlskoe, Cherekhya, and Tolochin, threatening to cut off Orsha and open a wide corridor to the Berezina River.

On 27 June Beloborodov's 43rd and Lyudnikov's 39th Armies launched the final, decisive assault on Vitebsk. The Soviet 158th and 262nd Divisions of Prokofiev's 84th Corps of the 39th Army attacked from the east after an earthshaking barrage of artillery and katyushas. At 1145 the survivors of the 6th Luftwaffe and 206th, 246th, and 197th Infantry Divisions capitulated. Meanwhile, Bezugliy's 5th Guard Rifle Corps of the 39th Army was rounding up the stragglers from the 4th Luftwaffe and 246th Infantry Divisions in Ostrovno. The 91st Guard Division and the 17th Guard Division of Bezugliy's corps formed a cordon to the west of Vitebsk. By noon on 27 June Red Army troops had taken 7,000 prisoners, and more were coming in. One group of 5,000 Germans broke out of Vitebsk, pushing aside the 2nd Guard Motorcycle Regiment, but were quickly surrounded by the 251st, 63rd, and 184th Rifle Divisions of the Soviet 5th and 39th Armies. Having completed most of its work around Vitebsk, Lyudnikov's 39th Army was marching westward to be placed on the southern flank of Krylov's 5th Army.[46]

While Vitebsk was being crushed, Oslikovskiy's Horse-Mechanized Group moved steadily west from the gap at Senno, encountering few Germans in their way. A leading element of the group was a combat team consisting of a tank battalion from the 35th Guard Tank Brigade and a company of infantry armed with machine pistols. The 3rd Guard Cavalry Corps continued to advance west from Aleksinichi south of Senno. In the afternoon the cavalry corps was west of Lukomli, and Obukov's 3rd Guard Mechanized Corps was 30 kilometers southwest of Senno at Cherekhya.[47]

Following the horse-mechanized group, Krylov's infantry was cleaning up pockets of Germans left behind, advancing 25 kilometers throughout 27 June. The Soviet 277th and 215th Divisions of Kazariev's 72nd Corps destroyed German pockets in the forest and crossed the Usveiku River at Lukomli by evening, and the 144th and 371st Divisions of Gorokhov's 45th Corps reached Cherekhya.[48]

Rotmistrov's 5th Tank Army was attacking German Battle

Groups von Sauken and von Gottberg, which were trying to defend the road to Borisov on the Berezina River. Rotmistrov took Bobr and Krupki, and by 1830 on 27 June, Soviet tankers had penetrated the German screen and were in Krugloe, 50 kilometers southwest of Orsha in the rear of Tippelskirch's Fourth Army.[49] Rotmistrov's armored columns were moving too quickly for the Germans to react: as soon as a German battle group was formed and established a position, the Soviet forces outflanked it and forced the Germans to retreat or be cut off. There were few pitched battles, but the German troops were worn down by constant scrambling, retreating by night, digging in during the early hours of the day, waiting for the Russians, and then retreating again during the next night. Meanwhile, the Soviet armored columns rolled forward led by tanks and motorized infantry in American-built four-wheel-drive trucks that kept moving despite the churned-up dirt roads. The marching Soviet infantrymen were dropping behind, but the armored columns were able to deal with the German battle groups.

On 28 June Krylov's 5th Army and Oslikovskiy's Horse-Mechanized Group reached the Berezina River, pursuing remnants of the German 299th Infantry Division. On the right flank, the 7th Guard Mechanized Brigade of Obukov's 3rd Guard Mechanized Corps chased the 201st German Security Division to the Berezina River. A small Soviet task force of three tanks, some men armed with machine pistols, several antitank guns, and some trucks crossed the Berezina.[50]

Another Obukov task force passed through Cherekhya 30 kilometers southwest of Senno and continued to move west on 28 June. The task force consisted of the 35th Guard Tank Brigade and a battalion of infantry armed with machine pistols in trucks that was supported by elements of the 129th Mortar Regiment, the 334th Guard Mortar Battalion (katyushas), the 743rd Tank Destroyer Battalion, and two batteries of the 1705th Antiaircraft Regiment—an example of the power of the Soviet columns. The task force crossed a canal at 0900 on 28 June and then the Berezina River. The engineers first built a light bridge that enabled the force to take light trucks (probably Jeeps) and then a heavier bridge that supported armored vehicles and two trucks towing 76mm antitank guns.[51]

The 9th Guard Mechanized Brigade of Obukov's 3rd Guard Mechanized Corps, supported by some motorized infantry, the 1823rd Assault Gun Regiment, and a company of the 62nd Engineer Battalion, crossed the Essa River south of Lepel and at noon on 28 June was halfway to the Berezina. With the assistance of engineers, a small wooden bridge was thrown across the Berezina River north of Borisov and provided with air defense to allow the 9th Guard

Mechanized Brigade to cross the river. During the day the engineers assembled a pontoon bridge to carry the tanks of the 35th Guard Tank Brigade.[52]

A few kilometers south on 28 June, the 8th Guard Mechanized Brigade of Obukov's mechanized corps with a company of the 62nd Engineer Battalion started from Bobr, 30 kilometers south of Cherekhya, and crossed the Berezina River near Borisov. The tanks and trucks crossed on a pontoon bridge defended with antiaircraft guns.[53]

Oslikovskiy's 3rd Guard Cavalry Corps reached the Berezina River at Bytcha at 1800 on 28 June and prepared to force a crossing. With the Horse-Mechanized Group plunging ahead west of the Berezina River on 28 June, Rotmistrov's 5th Guard Tank Army turned south into Galitskiy's 11th Guard Army sector and joined the battle around Orsha. Krylov's infantry was moving rapidly behind the armored columns, marching 25 kilometers on 28 June.[54]

By the evening of 28 June, Wuthmann's IX Corps, including the remnants of the 252nd and 212th Divisions and Corps Detachment D, was strung out along the Essa River from Lepel to Gorodets.

On the morning of 29 June, Krylov's 159th and 215th Rifle Divisions were still at Lukomlskoe, 40 kilometers east of the Berezina River, but four mobile columns of Obukov's 3rd Guard Mechanized Corps were forging ahead. The horse-mechanized group simply poured through the gap on its way to Molodechno, the major rail junction 90 kilometers to the west. Obukov reached the Berezina River at Brodi and began a coordinated attack on the west bank of the river. Several bridgeheads were established and the corps advanced 10 kilometers to the south toward Begomli. In 5 days the corps had advanced 180 kilometers and was the first Soviet unit to cross the Berezina River. There were no identifiable German units in the 75 kilometers from the 212th German Division south of Glubokoe to the battle groups defending the flank of Tippelskirch's Fourth Army west of Borisov. Oslikovskiy's 3rd Guard Cavalry Corps ran into stiffer opposition and by evening still had not crossed the Berezina River.[55]

By the morning of 30 June, major units of Krylov's 5th Army and the horse-mechanized group were across the Berezina north of Borisov and streaming west through the gap without opposition. Both corps of the horse-mechanized group were across the Berezina along with three rifle divisions of the 5th Army. This advance posed a severe threat to the rear of the Germans around Borisov, including the 5th Panzer Division and the 14th and 95th Infantry Divisions, which were holding back Rotmistrov's 5th Guard Tank Army and Galitskiy's 11th Guard Army. The objective of Perekrestov's 65th and

Kazariev's 72nd Corps of Krylov's 5th Army and Oslikovskiy's Horse-Mechanized Group was Molodechno, 90 kilometers to the southwest. The units were already 25 kilometers down the road from Begomli on the west bank of the Berezina.[56]

During 1 and 2 July Krylov's 5th Army and the horse-mechanized group advanced 50 to 60 kilometers toward Molodechno, advancing in columns consisting of tanks, motorized infantry, cavalry, and artillery. (See Map 7.2.) On 2 July the 8th Guard Mechanized Brigade reached the Usha River at Molodechno. The brigade sent a task force of five tanks, the 1st Motorized Rifle Battalion, an artillery battery, and a company of 120mm mortars to reach the east bank of the river. The remainder of Obukov's 3rd Mechanized Corps arrived during the next 2 days.[57]

In the early morning of 4 July, the Soviet 35th Guard Tank Brigade launched an attack to cross the Usha River supported by the 7th Guard Mechanized Brigade. The German defenders included elements of the German 5th Panzer Division, two infantry battalions, eighteen Pzkw IIIs and Pzkw IVs, three Tigers, three Ferdinands, eight artillery batteries, and two mortar battalions. Despite the efforts of the 5th Panzer Division, Obukov was soon across the Usha River and took Molodechno.[58]

After the fall of Molodechno, the German 5th Panzer Division and additional reinforcements were able to establish a line along the Vilnya River. The German 170th Infantry Division was on the way, while Oslikovskiy's Horse-Mechanized Group was over 250 kilometers from supply depots behind the startline. The infantry of the Soviet 5th Army was strung out on the roads behind the leading columns.

The first phase of the offensive had come to an end in the northern sector. Then nearly 300 kilometers from supply depots at the railheads east of the start line, supply trucks required 4 days to deliver fuel, rations, and ammunition and return to the depot. With increasing German resistance, greater quantities of munitions were required and stocks held by units at the beginning of the campaign were being exhausted. Until the railroads were repaired, especially the bridges, and the depots moved forward, Soviet forces would be short of supplies. By prodigious efforts on the part of Red Army engineers, the railroads and bridges were quickly repaired and the depots were moving forward by the end of June.

The 2-week blitzkrieg had been a startling success, blasting a hole in the German defenses east of Bogushevsk and driving steadily through Senno to Molodechno. The performance of Oslikovsky's Horse-Mechanized Group had been outstanding in keeping the German defenders continually on the run and unable to form

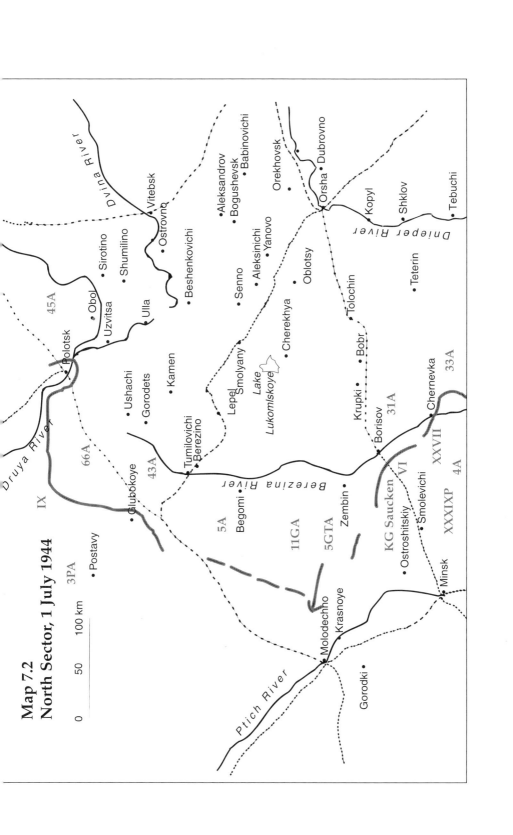

Map 7.2
North Sector, 1 July 1944

0   50   100 km

Dvina River
Druya River
Dnieper River
Berezina River
Ptich River

Lake
Lukomlskoye

Postavy
Glubokoye
Polotsk
Obol
Uzvitsa
Sirotino
Shumilino
Ulla
Ostrovno
Vitebsk
Beshenkovichi
Aleksandrov
Bogushevsk
Babinovichi
Orekhovsk
Orsha
Dubrovno
Kopyl
Shklov
Tebuchi
Senno
Aleksinichi
Yanovo
Oblotsy
Teterin
Ushachi
Gorodets
Kamen
Tumilovichi
Berezino
Smolyany
Cherekhya
Tolochin
Bobr
Krupki
Borisov
Chernevka
Begomi
Zembin
Ostroshitskiy
Smolevichi
Minsk
Krasnoye
Molodechno
Gorodki

3PA
IX
45A
66A
43A
5A
11GA
5GTA
KG Saucken
VI
XXVII
XXXIXP
4A
31A
33A

positions strong enough to delay the Soviet armored columns. Rotmistrov's 5th Guard Tank Army had lagged behind, hindered by its heavy train of supporting units and the need for 60-ton pontoon bridges to cross rivers. Krylov's 5th Army had also played a major role, forming armored columns with tank and assault gun regiments and supporting the columns with truck-borne infantry. However, by the time the Russians reached Molodechno, German reinforcements had arrived and the Soviet infantry and artillery was strung out far behind the armored spearheads. Given a short respite, the Germans were able to begin the process of slowing down the Soviet advance, withdrawing in an orderly fashion, and inflicting heavy losses on the Red Army.

Notes

1. A. M. Samsanov, ed., *Osvobozhdenie Belorussii, 1944* (Moscow: Nauka, 1974), pp. 202, 282; Paul Adair, *Hitler's Greatest Defeat: The Collapse of Army Group Centre, June 1944* (London: Arms and Armour Press, 1994), pp. 90-91; O. Heidkamper, *Vitebsk* (Heidelberg: Vowinckel, 1954), p. 150; A. M. Vasilevsky, *Delo Vsei Zhizni* (Minsk: Belarus, 1984), p. 456.
2. Samsanov, p. 283.
3. Ibid., p. 287; G. Niepold, *The Battle for White Russia: The Destruction of Army Group Centre, June 1944* (London: Brassey's, 1987), p. 74; Heidkamper, p. 150.
4. Samsanov, pp. 282, 288; David M. Glantz and Harold S. Orenstein, eds., *Belorussia 1944: The Soviet General Staff Study* (Carlisle, Penn.: David M. Glantz, 1998), p. 88.
5. Niepold, p. 74; Samsanov, pp. 284–285, 289–291.
6. Samsanov, pp. 289–292; Niepold, p. 74.
7. Samsanov, pp. 288, 292.
8. Ibid., pp. 292–293.
9. Niepold, p. 74.
10. Samsanov, p. 293.
11. Glantz and Orenstein, p. 87; Samsanov, pp. 282, 287; Heidkamper, 151.
12. Samsanov, p. 195.
13. Wolf Keilig, *Das Deutsche Heer, 1939–1945*, 3 vols. (Bad Nauheim: Podzun, 1956–1972), I, Section 82.
14. Ibid., pp. 527–529; Niepold, p. 86; I. I. Liudnikov, *Pod Vitebskom* (Moscow: Voenizdat, 1962), p. 56; Adair, p. 92; F. V. Plotnikov, *v Srazheniia za Belorussi* (Minsk: Belarus, 1982), p. 52.
15. Niepold, p. 81; Samsanov, pp. 530–531; Liudnikov, p. 57; Heidkamper, p. 152.
16. Niepold, p. 82; Glantz and Orenstein, p. 89.
17. Niepold, p. 86; Samsanov, p. 529; Liudnikov, p. 59.
18. Niepold, pp. 81, 86; Samsanov, pp. 531-32, 595; Liudnikov, p. 60.
19. Niepold, pp. 74, 81; Samsanov, pp. 531-32.
20. Niepold, pp. 81–82.

21. Samsanov, pp. 593–594.
22. Niepold, p. 81; Samsanov, pp. 595, 598–599; Adair, pp. 92–93.
23. Niepold, pp. 81, 86; Samsanov, p. 595; Adair, p. 94.
24. David M. Glantz and Jonathan M. House, *When Titans Clashed, How the Red Army Stopped Hitler* (Lawrence: The University Press of Kansas, 1995), p. 360; Niepold, p. 86.
25. Samsanov, p. 534; Liudnikov, pp. 64–65.
26. Samsanov, pp. 74, 532–533; Niepold, pp. 90, 97; Liudnikov, p. 62; Heidkamper, p. 149.
27. Samsanov, pp. 534–535; Niepold, pp. 86, 90, 97; Liudnikov, p. 68.
28. Samsanov, pp. 293, 295, 297; Niepold, pp. 90, 97; Glantz and Orenstein, pp. 90–91.
29. Samsanov, pp. 296, 595; Niepold, pp. 86, 97; Glantz and Orenstein, p. 92; Plotnikov, p. 78.
30. Niepold, pp. 89–90; John Erickson, *The Road to Berlin* (Boulder, Colo.: Westview Press, 1983), p. 218; Heidkamper, p. 157.
31. Niepold, p. 90; Heidkamper, p. 156.
32. Niepold, p. 103.
33. Samsanov, pp. 534–537; Niepold, p. 112; Glantz and Orenstein, p. 92; Liudnikov, pp. 69–71; Heidkamper, p. 157.
34. Samsanov, pp. 74, 298, 473; Glantz and Orenstein, p. 92; Niepold, pp. 103, 106, 112; Heidkamper, p. 157.
35. Samsanov, pp. 298, 473.
36. Niepold, p. 112; Samsanov, pp. 298–299.
37. Niepold, p. 103.
38. Samsanov, p. 74; Niepold, p. 102; Glantz and Orenstein, p. 92.
39. Niepold, p. 112; Glantz and Orenstein, p. 93.
40. Niepold, p. 122.
41. Samsanov, pp. 538–540; Glantz and Orenstein, pp. 94–95; Liudnikov, pp. 72–74.
42. Samsanov, pp. 75, 540; Glantz and Orenstein, p. 94; Liudnikov, p. 75.
43. Samsanov, pp. 302–303, 540.
44. Niepold, pp. 115, 123; Samsanov, pp. 299, 600; Glantz and Orenstein, p. 96.
45. Samsanov, p. 299; Niepold, p. 123; Glantz and Orenstein, p. 96.
46. Niepold, pp. 136–137; Samsanov, p. 303; Liudnikov, pp. 76–77.
47. Niepold, p. 137; Samsanov, pp. 75, 78, 603; Glantz and Orenstein, p. 97.
48. Samsanov, p. 304; Niepold, 137; Glantz and Orenstein, p. 98.
49. Niepold, pp. 127, 130; Samsanov, pp. 75, 78; Glantz and Orenstein, p. 97.
50. Samsanov, pp. 305, 307, 605; Glantz and Orenstein, pp. 99, 132.
51. Samsanov, pp. 602–603.
52. Ibid., pp. 603–604.
53. Ibid., pp. 603–604.
54. Albert Seaton, *The Russo-German War, 1941–45* (New York: Praeger, 1970), p. 439; Glantz and Orenstein, p. 99.
55. Samsanov, pp. 305, 307, 605; Glantz and Orenstein, pp. 99–100, 132–133.
56. Samsanov, pp. 85, 307, 331; Glantz and Orenstein, p. 134.
57. Samsanov, pp. 309–310, 606–608.
58. Ibid., pp. 608–609.

CHAPTER 8

Orsha

The plan for taking Orsha was based on secretly adding 10 days before the attack Galitskiy's 11th Guard Army from the Stavka Reserve to a sector previously held by General V. V. Glagolev's 31st Army. With two corps of the 11th Guard Army and two corps of the 31st Army crowded into a 20-kilometer sector, Stalin expected the attackers to quickly overcome the two defending German divisions and open an avenue for exploitation by Rotmistrov's 5th Guard Tank Army. The southern armies of the 3rd White Russian Front, including the 11th Guard Army and 31st Army, are shown in Figure 8.1.

On 22 June Galitskiy's 11th Guard Army made company-to-regiment-sized attacks on the German 78th and 256th Divisions of General Volkers's XXVII Corps to test the defense. The Germans claimed, despite a heavy artillery barrage supporting the attacks, that all these attacks were repulsed with no loss of ground.[1]

Volkers's XXVII Corps considered the threat of the 11th Guard Army on the flank of the 78th Division more serious and asked to move the 14th Infantry Division from the reserve position and replace it with the army assault battalion. Galitskiy's 11th Guard Army attacks centered on the 78th Assault Division sector of the XXVII Corps, a 15-kilometer front from the main highway to the Dnieper River. On the northern flank of the 78th German Division, two regiments of the Soviet 16th Guard Division of the 16th Guard Corps, supported by the 35th Soviet Guard Tank Regiment and the 345th Guard Assault Gun Regiment, penetrated the first and second line of trenches in the main defense zone only to be stopped by fierce resistance in the final trench line of the zone. The Germans employed 88mm guns and Ferdinand assault guns in the defense against the 63rd Guard Heavy Tank Regiment. The stout defense convinced the 3rd White Russian Front to move the major attack north to the Soviet 5th Army sector.[2]

Figure 8.1 Southern Armies of the 3rd White Russian Front

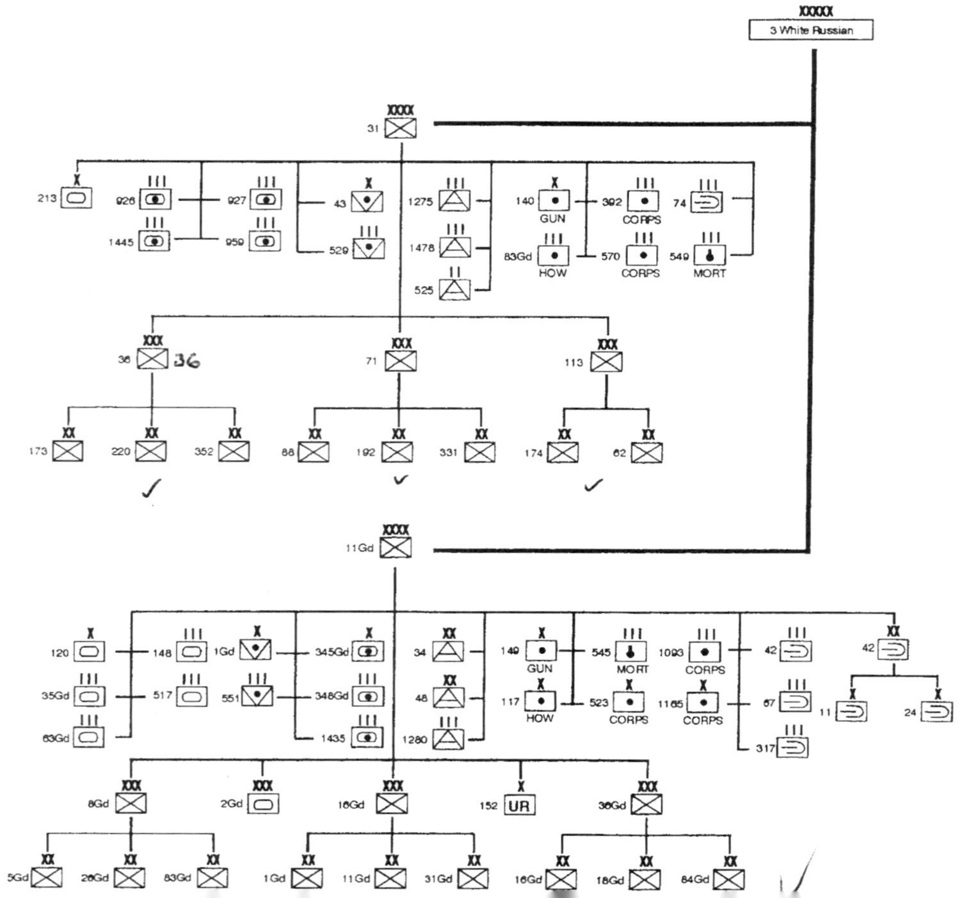

Galitskiy's 11th Guard Army attack gained momentum during the day in General Y. S. Vorobyev's 16th Guard Corps sector. Vorobyev sent in the 31st Guard Division and units of the 152nd Fortified Region to bolster the attack, gaining 3 to 5 kilometers. In Vorobyev's 16th and General M. N. Zavodovskiy's 8th Guard Corps sectors, units of General Burdeyniy's 2nd Guard Tank Corps joined in the battle. On the south flank of the 11th Guard Army, the 36th Guard Corps under the command of General P. G. Shafranov advanced 2 to 3 kilometers. Although the Russians suffered heavy losses, they had penetrated most of the first defense zone by the evening of 22 June. Glagolev's 31st Army attacks, on the other hand, were driven back by heavy artillery and mortar fire.[3] By the end of the first day neither Soviet army had broken through the first defense zone.

The 31st Army had three rifle corps (71st, 36th, and 113th) on a 45-kilometer front. The three divisions of General P. K. Koshevoy's 71st Rifle Corps had been with the army since March. General N. N. Oleshev's 36th Rifle Corps had been transferred from the 33rd Army in June. The 113th Rifle Corps under the command of General K. I. Provalov had come from the 49th Army with two divisions in April.

The supporting troops of Glagolev's 31st Army were exceptionally formidable, including the 213th Tank Brigade, three new assault gun artillery regiments from the Stavka reserve, and a fourth that had been with the army since March. Ample antitank defense was provided by the 43rd Tank Destroyer Brigade and the 529th Tank Destroyer Regiment. Antiaircraft defense was provided by the 1275th and 1478th Antiaircraft Regiments and the 66th Antiaircraft Division. The army artillery included the 140th Brigade, three artillery regiments, a guard mortar regiment, and a mortar regiment.

Galitskiy's 11th Guard Army, between Glagolev's 31st and Krylov's 5th Armies, had been moved from the 1st Baltic Front to the Stavka Reserve on 10 April 1944. From 10 April to 24 May, the 11th Guard Army was camped in the forest in the Nevel area and went through intensive training. This army received 20,000 replacements, bringing the rifle divisions up to an average of over 7,200 men. The army received new Type 1943 76mm guns, additional assault guns, and thousands of machine pistols. The infantry practiced coordinating tactics with tanks, assault guns, and engineers to cross the marshlands and the many rivers to the west.[4]

On 25 May the 11th Guard Army moved up behind the 3rd White Russian Front. On 12 and 13 June the army was moved secretly 300 kilometers to the front in a sector north of the Dnieper River 30 kilometers northeast of Orsha, replacing the 88th and 192nd Rifle Divisions and the 152nd Fortified Region of the 31st Army.[5]

Galitskiy screened most of his sector with Vorobyev's 16th Guard Rifle Corps, while the other two rifle corps (8th Guard and 36th Guard) concentrated in a narrow sector adjacent to Glagolev's 31st Army.

The 11th Guard Army had a generous quota of support units, with two artillery brigades and three corps artillery regiments. The tank destroyer regiment, the antiaircraft regiment, and the mortar regiment were standard allotments. The army also had a guard mortar division plus three regiments, a tank destroyer brigade, and two antiaircraft divisions. The armored component was very strong—a tank corps, a tank brigade, four tank regiments, and three assault gun regiments. Burdeyniy's 2nd Guard Tank Corps with 250 tanks and assault guns was equal to two German panzer divisions.

Most of the support units were added in May and June. Apparently Galitskiy's army had been stripped of most of its supporting units when it was transferred from the 1st Baltic Front in April and then had received new units in May and June. There was a massive influx of support troops from the Moscow Military District, the Stavka Reserve, the 3rd White Russian reserve, and neighboring armies.

On 22 June Galitskiy's Soviet 11th Guard Army was tightly packed on a 25-kilometer front: the 8th and 36th Guard Corps were crammed into less than 10 kilometers, with three divisions on the front and three in reserve. Burdeyniy's 2nd Guard Tank Corps was positioned behind these two corps. Shafranov's 36th Guard Corps had two heavy tank regiments and two assault gun regiments attached, over eighty armored vehicles.[6] Zavodovskiy's 8th Guard Corps was supported by the 120th Tank Brigade and the 1435th Assault Gun Regiment. On the north, Vorobyev's 16th Guard Corps was spread over a 20-kilometer sector, and four battalions of the 152nd Fortified Region overlapped the 256th German Infantry Division sector. The army had from 160 to 250 guns and mortars per kilometer and plentiful air support. All this offensive power was opposed by the German 256th Infantry and 78th Assault Divisions.[7]

Opposing Galitskiy's 11th Guard Army and Glagolev's 31st Army was Volkers's XXVII Corps of Tippelskirch's Fourth Army composed of the 78th Assault Division, the 25th Panzergrenadier Division, and the 260th Infantry Division. The 78th Assault Division was a unique organization in the German army; it had been formed in January 1943 with three regiments, each of which contained a single infantry battalion, two support companies, and an artillery battalion. The divisional artillery regiment had an assault gun battalion, an antiaircraft battalion, and a multiple-barrel mortar (Nebelwerfer) battalion. The theory behind the formation was to provide a limited number of riflemen with a maximum amount of heavy weapons and artillery support. In June 1943 three infantry battalions were added. Although it had then become an ordinary infantry division, its spirit of being an elite unit was alive. On 22 June the 78th Assault Division had an additional infantry regiment attached from the 260th Infantry Division, and to its rear in XXVII Corps reserve was the 501st Heavy Tank Battalion in Orsha.[8]

The German 25th Panzergrenadier Division had been re-formed from the 25th Motorized Division in June 1943, receiving an organic tank battalion and antiaircraft battalion. With motorized infantry, the 25th Panzergrenadier Division had greater flexibility than the marching infantry.

The organization of the German 260th Infantry Division offers an insight into the improvement on the German side of the line during the summer of 1944 in White Russia. This division was re-formed as a three-regiment, seven-battalion formation in April 1944, and during June it was busily improving the defenses of its sector, such work being characterized as an intensive effort. A training school was established for NCOs, an indication that many new recruits had been added during the month. On 20 June March Company 260/20 arrived from Stuttgart with 227 men, mostly returning wounded, but with some new men. Because all of the 260th Division's battalions were up to strength (!), the new arrivals were distributed among all the battalions as personnel above authorized unit strength.

The 260th Division also received new weapons. Along with all of the divisions in the Fourth Army, the antitank battalion received 75mm antitank guns for the 2nd Company. The 3rd Company of the antitank battalion received new 20mm antiaircraft guns. The 1st Company received assault guns and was sent back to Mielau in Germany in mid-June for training. Also in June, the 14th (antitank) Company of all three infantry regiments received a platoon with three 75mm antitank guns and two platoons each with eighteen *ofenröhren*, handheld antitank rocket launchers.

As had most divisions in Army Group Center, the division had suffered from attrition and lack of replacements in the past, but not any unusual loss. The result, in June 1944, was an overstrength division composed mostly of battle-hardened veterans. All three divisions of Volkers's XXVII Corps were better than average and of higher quality than the divisions of Reinhardt's Third Panzer Army.

The 57th Division was sent to Tippelskirch's Fourth Army in June 1944 and was assigned to a sector between the Drut and Dnieper Rivers north of Rogachev on the southern flank of the Fourth Army. The ground was extremely marshy, and the Germans correctly surmised that the possibility of a Soviet attack was very remote.[9] (Soviet attacks developed to the north and south of the sector, and little harm was done to the German 57th Division, which was still intact on 1 July). This sector was ideal for thinning out the defending division by removing a regiment for use in a more endangered area. The 199th Infantry Regiment and a battalion of the 157th Artillery Regiment were added to the German 260th Division, and on 18 June the 480th Infantry Regiment was attached to the 78th Assault Division, increasing to nine the number of infantry battalions in the latter division. The 78th Division would bear the brunt of two corps of Galitskiy's 11th Soviet Army and two corps of Glagolev's 31st Army on 22 June 1944. By the end of that day Volkers, the XXVII Corps commander, was greatly concerned whether the 78th and 256th Divisions could withstand another day of massive attacks.

Volkers's fears for the 78th Division were justified. At 0800 on 23 June, the Soviet forces began a 3-hour artillery bombardment along with air attacks by bombers and Sturmoviks of Gromov's 1st Air Army. These attacks were more devastating than the Germans had ever experienced despite the low clouds and rain that hampered the aircraft. The main blow fell on the German 78th Assault and 25th Panzergrenadier Divisions. The 260th German Division to the south was subjected to very heavy air attacks and then a bombardment of thousands of mortar shells. The division fractured into battle groups after being trampled and losing many men.[10]

By noon on 23 June, Galitskiy's 11th Soviet Guard Army had driven 3 kilometers into the German lines and repelled counterattacks by the 78th Assault Division. Tippelskirch's Fourth Army sent an assault gun brigade, an engineer battalion, and the 61st Security Regiment to reinforce Volkers's XXVII Corps.[11]

At 1425 on 23 June, Tippelskirch requested permission to withdraw 3 kilometers to the second defense zone in the 78th Assault and 25th Panzergrenadier Division sectors because the first zone had been penetrated in many places. Hitler denied this request and instead sent a regiment of the 14th Infantry Division to help shore up the first defense zone. By evening a battalion on the northern flank of Volkers's XXVII Corps had been destroyed, and the survivors fled to the second defense zone, where the Soviet attack was stopped.[12]

In the afternoon of 23 June, Vorobyev's 16th Guard Corps of the 11th Guard Army had penetrated the first zone and advanced 9 kilometers to the second defense zone south of Babinovichi, about 10 kilometers west of Bogushevsk, breaking through the German defenses on the main highway to Minsk and opening a 3-kilometer gap in the 78th Assault Division line. Bagramyan, the 3rd White

Russian Front commander, ordered Galitskiy to reinforce this success with three divisions and, in effect, altered the main direction of the attack from southwest in the direction of Orsha to due west toward Bogushevsk. Galitskiy's 11th Guard Army had closed up to the German second defense zone by the evening of 23 June. South of the 11th Guard Army, Glagolev's 31st Army was still fighting in the first German defense zone east of Orsha.[13]

On the morning of 24 June, the XXVII Corps was ordered to hold Galitskiy's attacks and prevent any further Soviet advance toward Orsha. (See Map 8.1.) The two remaining regiments of the German 14th Division were sent north to help Pfeiffer's VI Corps south of Vitebsk, leaving Volkers with no reserves.[14]

Galitskiy attacked the German 78th Assault Division during the night and morning of 24 June. At 0700 on 24 June, the Germans reinforced the second defense zone 3 kilometers east at Orekhovsk in the path of the 11th Guard Army. In the morning hours of 24 June, Glagolev's 31st Army continued to press the German 25th Panzergrenadier Division still holding the first defense zone on the Dnieper River. The 31st Army advanced 3 kilometers to within 7 kilometers of Dubrovno on both sides of the Dnieper by 1000, but progress was very slow and costly. The heavy Soviet artillery preparation had fallen on empty trenches and artillery positions as the German infantry withdrew during the night, and Tippelskirch reinforced the sector overnight with regiments from the 260th and 286th Divisions.[15]

Despite the desperate German efforts, Vorobyev's 16th Guard Corps on the north flank of Galitskiy's 11th Guard Army overwhelmed the 78th and 14th German Divisions and advanced 10 to 12 kilometers, capturing Babinovichi. To the south, Shafranov's 36th Guard Corps penetrated the second defense zone 4 kilometers north of the main road to Minsk. The original Soviet plan had been to drive along the dry ground north of the main road with Burdeyniy's 2nd Guard Tank Corps, but when Zavodovskiy's 8th Guard Corps broke through the German defenses farther north, Burdeyniy's tank corps was switched to the breakthrough. During the evening of 24 June, the tanks passed northwestward through the swamp, some using the bed of a narrow-gauge railroad, and regrouped north of the Minsk highway on the night of 24–25 June. The next day, the tanks suddenly burst from the swamps at Osinstroy in Zavodovskiy's 8th Guard Corps sector, astonishing the Germans.[16]

At noon on 24 June, Vasilevsky began to move Rotmistrov's 5th Guard Tank Army north to a position behind Krylov's 5th Army, planning to break through at Bogushevsk on the night of 25–26 June and swing around north of Orsha to Tolochin, rather than wait-

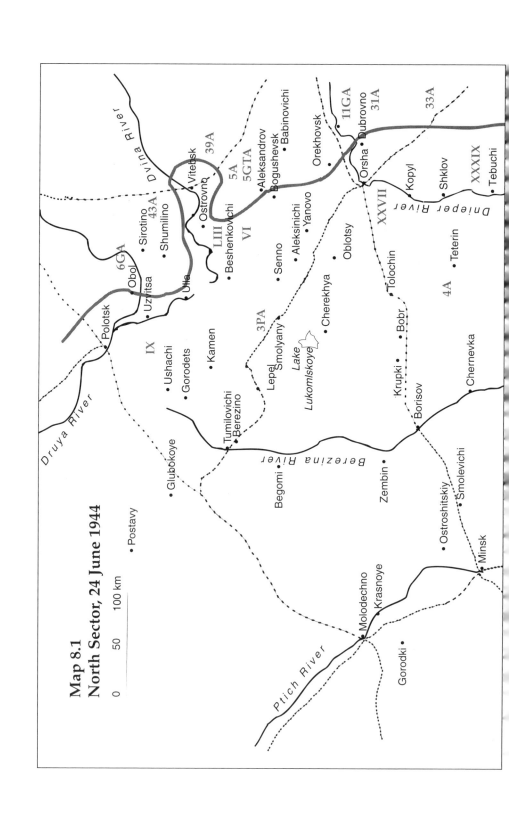

Map 8.1
North Sector, 24 June 1944

0   50   100 km

ing for the 11th Guard Army or the 31st Army to open the more
direct route to Orsha. Here the Soviet commander showed flexibility
in reinforcing success. The move dragged on because of poor lateral
roads. Rotmistrov's tank army had to return to Smolensk by rail and
turn around and move west by rail to Krylov's 5th Army sector, but
the tank army got in place by the evening of 25 June.[17]

Tippelskirch hoped to pull back his Fourth Army 40 kilometers
to the Dnieper River in the afternoon of 24 June. The Fourth Army
was still in good condition despite giving ground and could have
retreated to the Dnieper River with relative ease. Only the 78th
Assault Division had sustained heavy losses. Nevertheless, Hitler
refused to surrender territory willingly and ordered the 260th
Infantry Division on the south flank of Volkers's XXVII Corps
switched to the danger area in the north.[18]

In the early afternoon of 24 June, at 1250, Busch ordered Volkers
to pull back to the Tiger line, the second defense zone, which
stretched from Bogushevsk in the north to Orekhovsk 20 kilometers
northeast of Orsha in the south. The German 14th Infantry Division
and a remnant of the 256th Division of Pfeiffer's VI Corps defended
Bogushevsk. Most of the latter division had lost contact with the VI
Corps and was placed under the XXVII Corps.[19]

At 1425 on 24 June, Tippelskirch requested that the 78th Assault
and 25th Panzergrenadier Divisions withdraw even farther back to
the Hessen defense line, the third defense zone, fearing that
Burdeyniy's 2nd Guard Tank Corps emerging from the forest at
Orekhovsk would turn south and cut off the 78th Assault Division.[20]

Volkers wanted to pull back to a line 3 kilometers east of a line
from Orekhovsk to Dubrovno on 24 June, and on the next day retreat
another 10 kilometers to a line east of Orsha. At 1830 on 24 June,
Army Group Center still insisted that the well-prepared defenses in
front of Orsha be held and that only Volkers's XXVII Corps should
pivot back to the Orekhovsk-Dubrovno line to protect Orsha from
the north. Volkers was also to hold the line of lakes to the north and
try to maintain contact with Reinhardt's Third Panzer Army. The
78th Assault Division withdrew to the third defense zone, the
Hessen line, during the evening of 24 June.[21]

The issue at stake in the dispute was the determination of the
German higher command levels to hold prepared positions, which
had taken so much effort to construct and benefited the defenders,
giving them a decided advantage. Once out of prepared fortifications, the German infantry would face a much more brutal task in
withstanding the Russians, who outnumbered them ten to one in
some sectors. The German corps and division commanders, realiz-
ing that Galitskiy's 11th Soviet Guard Army and Burdeyniy's 2nd

Guard Tank Corps emerging from the swamp were too strong to contain, wanted to trade ground for time, giving the Germans the opportunity to reinforce Tippelskirch's Fourth Army. The local German commanders rightly feared that if they remained in the defenses, the Russians would destroy them.

Although Volkers's XXVII Corps claimed the destruction of 116 Soviet tanks in the 3 days since the attacks had begun, Galitskiy's 11th Guard Army still had hundreds more as it began the attack with nearly 400 armored vehicles.[22]

During the night the 11th Guard Army and the 2nd Guard Tank Corps opened a 7-kilometer gap at Orekhovsk, and at 0030 on 25 June, Volkers's XXVII Corps had exhausted its last reserves in trying to stop the Red Army units roaring down the road leading to Orsha from Orekhovsk. Two bicycle battalions of the German 2nd Security Regiment were placed on the road 20 kilometers north of Orsha, but no German troops were left in Orsha.[23]

During the evening of 24 June, Hitler rejected the idea of pulling the Fourth Army 40 kilometers back to the Dnieper River. Instead, he insisted that the fortifications east of Orsha be held. The badly mauled 78th Assault Division was ordered to maintain contact with the southern flank of Reinhardt's Third Panzer Army, a futile command because the gap was already over 50 kilometers wide. Rather than waiting for Galitskiy's 11th Guard Army to outflank or overrun the German positions, Tippelskirch wanted to retreat swiftly and leave the Russians to bombard empty trenches, while the Germans prepared another line. By shortening its lines, the Fourth Army hoped to accumulate reserves to block the next attack. The German generals blamed Hitler entirely for the impending disasters at Bogushevsk and Vitebsk because he refused to permit the withdrawals, despite the fact that the stubborn German defense was slowing the Soviet advance and exacting large numbers of casualties among the Soviet units.[24]

On 25 June, regardless of Hitler's orders, the 78th Assault Division and other units of the XXVII Corps that were under attack by Galitskiy's 11th Guard Army withdrew, and at 1100 Hitler agreed to the withdrawals. To the south, the 25th Panzergrenadier Division of the XXVII Corps was being driven back to Orsha by Zavodovskiy's 8th and Shafranov's 36th Guard Corps of the 11th Guard Army. Both the German 25th Panzergrenadier and the 260th Infantry Divisions were pressed by Glagolev's 31st Army, which finally ruptured the Dnieper River defense zone and reached Dubrovno, 15 kilometers east of Orsha. The German divisions were reinforced by the German 286th Security Division and the 342nd and 931st Security Regiments, but could not stem the Soviet's tide. The

German 25th Panzergrenadier and 260th Infantry Divisions were ordered to pull back 6 kilometers east of Rudkovscchinato in the Hessen defense zone.[25]

North of Orsha the situation was deteriorating rapidly on 25 June, as the German 78th Assault Division tried to maintain a link to the 25th Panzergrenadier Division to the south. Another security battalion was added to the 78th Division. North of the 78th Division, Rotmistrov's 5th Guard Tank Army launched a furious attack at 1515 on 25 June, sweeping aside Pfeiffer's VI Corps. Soviet bombers and Shturmoviks of Gromov's 1st Air Army repeatedly attacked the German trenches, gun and mortar positions, transport, and reserve units. Rotmistrov's army streamed through a 10-kilometer gap north of Volkers's XXVII Corps, which was ordered to bend its line back to cover Orsha from the north. Pfeiffer's VI Corps was driven south to the west of Orsha as the Soviet tanks poured through the gap to the west.[26]

At 1120 on 25 June, Pfeiffer's VI Corps was transferred to Tippelskirch's Fourth Army with the shattered remains of the 95th, 299th, 14th, and 256th Divisions to hold the gap between Aleksinichi and Volkers's XXVII Corps. The divisions struggled to fight their way to the rear and were constantly harassed by Soviet tank columns. At 1600 on 25 June, the Russians were south of Senno and pursuing the 95th German Division 15 kilometers south of the town. At midnight on 25 June, the German VI Corps had failed to establish any sort of defense line. The 95th, 299th, and 256th Infantry Divisions and the 2nd Security Regiment were under constant attack by Soviet armored columns of Vorobyev's 16th Guard Corps of Galitskiy's 11th Guard Army.

Pfeiffer's VI Corps had been torn to shreds, and a huge 60-kilometer gap was opening between Orsha and the remnants of Wuthmann's IX Corps of Reinhardt's Third Panzer Army at Lake Lukomlskoye. Significantly, the Germans were fleeing in columns that included 600 horsedrawn wagons, while the Russians were following with tanks and truck-borne infantry.[27]

At 1930 on 25 June, Tippelskirch ordered the withdrawal of the XXXIX Panzer Corps under the command of General Martinek to a position south of Orsha halfway back from the original line to the Dnieper River, while Volkers's XXVII Corps was ordered to hold north and east of Orsha. Volkers was in far greater trouble than Martinek: another 15-kilometer gap had opened between the German 78th Assault Division and the 25th Panzergrenadier Division sectors.[28]

By nightfall on 25 June, Galitskiy's 11th Guard Army had advanced 25 kilometers from the startline of 22 June, and the second-echelon divisions were moving forward rapidly to add weight to the attack. After fighting throughout the night, Volkers's XXVII Corps was in the Tiger line from Orekhovsk in the 78th Assault Division sector south to Dubrovno on the Dnieper River on the morning of 26 June.[29]

German reinforcements were on the way at last. The German 5th Panzer Division was moving by train from Army Group North Ukraine, but Battle Group Altrock with three battalions had to be assigned to cover Borisov, where the panzer division would detrain only 60 kilometers from the leading Soviet elements. The Germans feared that the 5th Panzer Division would be met by Red Army units before the tanks could be unloaded.[30]

On 26 June Rotmistrov's 5th Guard Tank Army and Galitskiy's 11th Guard Army advanced 25 kilometers and cut off Orsha on the west, reaching the outskirts of the city. Glagolev's 31st Army crossed the Dnieper River after taking Dubrovno and advanced up to 25 kilometers. Pfeiffer's VI Corps was unable to form a screen between Orsha and Reinhardt's Third Panzer Army to the north as ordered. The survivors of the 14th and 95th German Divisions could not form a defensive line north of Orsha, and Pfeiffer lost contact with his divisions. The rear elements of the corps fled to Borisov, nearly 100 kilometers to the west.[31]

As a result, the Soviet mobile columns were running rampant and threatening the rear of Volkers's corps. At 1100 on 26 June, Burdeyniy's 2nd Guard Tank Corps was at Pogost, 15 kilometers west of Orsha, and the 16th Guard Division of Shafranov's 36th Guard Corps was only 3 kilometers north of Orsha. Galitskiy's 11th Guard Army was 5 kilometers east of Oblotsy and driving south toward Orsha through a gap east of the German 14th Division. By evening on 26 June, Burdeyniy's 2nd Guard Tank Corps had crossed the railroad and main highway 20 kilometers west of Orsha. One brigade of the tank corps turned east to attack Orsha from the west.[32]

Rotmistrov's 5th Guard Tank Army was moving south 50 kilometers west of Orsha, heading for Tolochin. The Germans sent a Tiger tank battalion and a single artillery battalion to defend Tolochin and parry the attack, a very feeble response. By midnight of 26 June, Rotmistrov's tanks and Galitskiy's 11th Guard Army were west of Tolochin and advancing south and west, with advance units heading for the Berezina River. Pfeiffer's VI Corps was no longer an organized formation. Small units were resisting in places, but the Germans had lost control.[33]

On Volkers's XXVII Corps front at 0830 on 26 June, the 78th Assault Division was separated from Pfeiffer's VI Corps by a 12-

kilometer gap. And to the east of this division was a 25-kilometer gap up to the position of the 25th Panzergrenadier Division on the Dnieper River. In an attempt to create a cohesive line, the XXVII Corps retreated hastily to a position southwest of Orsha.[34]

At 1800 on 26 June, Galitskiy attacked Orsha from the north. The attack was preceded by a half-hour artillery barrage, supplemented by a series of heavy air attacks lasting for 2 hours. The 16th Guard Division advanced from the north, and the 84th Guard Division closed in on Orsha.[35]

Glagolev's 31st Army was delayed at Dubrovno, 20 kilometers east of Orsha, but soon captured the town and continued to advance toward Orsha. The German 260th Infantry Division withdrew successfully to the Dnieper by 1800 on 26 June.[36]

The day had been a series of disasters for Tippelskirch's Fourth Army as Rotmistrov's 5th Guard Tank Army and Galitskiy's 11th Guard Army swept around the north flank, while the grinding pressure of Glagolev's 31st Army tied down most of Volkers's XXVII Corps east of Orsha that was desperately trying to block the road to Orsha. Although Pfeiffer's VI Corps was a shambles, Volkers's corps was still a viable formation.

On 27 June Volkers was ordered to hold the Bear line on the west bank of the Dnieper River south of Orsha, as well as fend off attacks from the north and close the gap behind Orsha. All of these tasks were totally beyond the means of the outnumbered XXVII Corps. By midnight of 26–27 June, Galitskiy's 11th Guard Army and Glagolev's 31st Army had already entered Orsha.[37] Early in the morning of 27 June, Volkers's XXVII Corps was split into three groups, with the 78th Assault Division holding the center of Orsha, a battle group standing on the railroad 11 kilometers southwest of Orsha, and another group trying to break out to the south. Ferocious street battles ensued in Orsha, but by 0700 on 27 June, the city was captured. After the battle Glagolev's 31st Army advanced 12 kilometers to the west.[38]

Burdeyniy's 2nd Guard Tank Corps had finally crossed the marsh with the help of its four-wheel-drive trucks and cut the main road from Orsha to Minsk. The corps advanced rapidly in columns of tanks and assault guns, riflemen riding in trucks, and truck-drawn artillery. Glagolev's 31st Army crossed the railroad southwest of Orsha.[39]

During 27 June Martinek's XXXIX Panzer Corps of Tippelskirch's Fourth Army was retreating to the Bear defense zone behind the Dnieper River. At 1040 Tippelskirch reported that Orsha was lost and that the Dnieper River line had been broken. He sought permission to attempt to fight his way west. At 1145 the reply from

Hitler was that the Dnieper line must be held, and, if forced back, the Fourth Army was to establish a new line behind the Drut River, 40 kilometers west of Orsha. However, by noon on 27 June, meeting little resistance, Galitskiy's 11th Guard and Glagolev's 31st Armies covered 20 kilometers and were behind Volkers's XXVII Corps between Orsha and the Drut River.[40]

During 27 June the German Battle Group von Gottberg, a division-sized formation, with Battle Groups von Alrock and Anhalt under its command, was assigned to close the gap between Lake Lukomlskoe on the south flank of Reinhardt's Third Panzer Army and the Minsk highway. The 5th Panzer Division was arriving to hold the Minsk highway, but only advance elements were at Borisov on the southern flank of Battle Group von Gottberg. The remainder of the panzer division was to detrain east of Borisov at noon on 27 June.[41]

Given the hopeless situation, Volkers's XXVII Corps (including remnants of the 25th, 260th, 78th, and 110th Divisions) was permitted to turn and try to escape early on 28 June and, with luck, link up with the 14th Infantry Division, 13 kilometers southeast of Tolochin. Hitler promised that the German 5th Panzer Division would be at Bobr, 30 kilometers west of Tolochin on the main road to Borisov, within the following few days.[42]

During the evening of 27 June, German forces that included some security units, the 505th Tiger Battalion, and the 5th Panzer Division's reconnaissance battalion, engineer battalion, one and a half panzergrenadier battalions, three artillery batteries, and two antiaircraft batteries reached Bobr. However, the armored columns of Galitskiy's 11th Guard Army and Burdeyniy's 2nd Guard Tank Corps were roaming freely and pressing the German rear guards. There was no time to establish a defense at Bobr.[43]

On 28 June Tippelskirch's Fourth Army was fighting its way back, crossing the Drut River and heading for the Berezina River at Borisov 65 kilometers to the west. The gap between the remnants of Reinhardt's Third Panzer Army to the north and Volkers's XXVII Corps of the Fourth Army had grown to 100 kilometers. On the morning of 28 June, the 5th Panzer Division and Battle Group Gottberg were pushed back 5 kilometers from Bobr to Krupki in the middle of the gap by elements of Rotmistrov's 5th Guard Tank Army.[44]

To the west of Bobr, the Berezina line was defended by the 13th Panzergrenadier Regiment of the 5th Panzer Division, the 531st, 350th, and 53rd Security Regiments, other security units, and remnants of the 256th, 14th, and 286th Divisions. The force was equal to about four or five German divisions.[45]

At 0900 on 28 June, Tippelskirch ordered his units to retreat west of the River Drut by that evening. Pfeiffer's VI Corps, with elements of the 14th and 299th Infantry Divisions, was fighting on the west bank of the Drut River and under pressure from Burdeyniy's 2nd Guard Tank Corps and Glagolev's 31st Army. Burdeyniy crossed the Drut by evening.[46]

Volkers's XXVII Corps was ordered to establish a line from the Drut to Chernevka on the Berezina. However, Galitskiy's 11th Guard Army had already penetrated this line and advanced 25 kilometers southward. Galitskiy brushed aside a German battle group and reached the Bobr River by evening. Volkers was trying to avoid being trapped, and by noon broke out to the south with the remnants of the 260th Infantry and 25th Panzergrenadier Divisions.[47]

Tippelskirch was trying to withdraw across the Berezina River, but continual Soviet air attacks delayed all movements. The poor secondary roads were jammed with vehicles of the service units desperately trying to escape the advancing Russians. The small bridges over the many streams that flowed through the marshes collapsed under the heavy traffic, while the major bridges over the Berezina were repeatedly damaged by bombing. Chaos ensued as Tippelskirch lost control of his units, and the retreat turned into a rout.[48]

At noon on 28 June, Busch's Army Group Center formed Combat Group von Saucken composed of the 5th Panzer Division, the 505th Tiger Battalion, and Battle Group von Gottberg. The von Saucken group was also to command any other of Tippelskirch's Fourth Army units north of the Minsk highway. Martinek's XXXIX Panzer Corps headquarters provided the staff for Battle Group von Saucken. The mission of the von Saucken force was to screen the gap between Tippelskirch's Fourth Army and Reinhardt's Third Panzer Army and to destroy elements of the 11th Guard Army advancing on Borisov from the northeast.[49]

Galitskiy's 11th Guard Army was southwest of Krupki in the center of the gap by early evening on 28 June, heading for Borisov on the Berezina River. Burdeyniy's 2nd Guard Tank Corps had crossed the Drut River on the southern flank of the 11th Guard Army and crossed the Berezina at Chernevka 40 kilometers south of the road to Borisov. Zavodovskiy's 8th and Vorobyev's 16th Guard Corps of Galitskiy's army were still 40 kilometers east of the Berezina River at Bobr.[50]

On the morning of 29 June, Tippelskirch was ordered to retreat behind the Berezina River while trying to protect his flanks. Rotmistrov's 5th Guard Tank Army poured through a 50-kilometer breach in the line along with the 11th Guard Army, Burdeyniy's 2nd Guard Tank Corps, Oslikovskiy's Horse-Mechanized Group, and

Krylov's 5th Army. Mobile columns of tanks, assault guns, and infantry riding in trucks fanned out across the rear of the German forces. Still another gap had opened to the south between Borisov and the Drut River, where German divisions protected the north flank of Tippelskirch's army.

The German 5th Panzer Division was sent to close a 50-kilometer gap south of Lepel. Armored columns of Rotmistrov's 5th Guard Tank Army tried to exploit the northern gap but ran into the 5th Panzer Division. Failing to move fast enough, Rotmistrov gave the 5th Panzer Division time to establish a defensive position. Fighting continued throughout 29 June between the 5th Panzer Division and columns of the 5th Guard Tank Army. Rather than bypassing the resistance, Rotmistrov engaged in battles that should have been left to the infantry.[51] The 5th Guard Tank Army moved slowly along the main highway to Minsk and reached the Berezina north of Borisov only a short time before Galitskiy's 11th Guard Army and Krylov's 5th Army. The 5th Army had moved rapidly behind its armored task forces despite the bad roads, swamps, and forest, marching 30 kilometers on 29 June. Advance regiments of Krylov's 5th Army crossed the Berezina at three points on 29 June.

Galitskiy's 11th Soviet Guard Army encountered more resistance at Krupki on the road to Borisov from elements of the German 5th Panzer Division and Combat Group von Saucken. Early in the morning of 29 June, Combat Group von Saucken was on the main highway 6 kilometers west of Krupki east of Borisov and at 1000 was placed under the command of Tippelskirch's Fourth Army, with orders to protect the army's northern flank while the army's divisions fought out of the trap. The combat group was ordered to counterattack Vorobyev's 16th Guard and Zavodovskiy's 8th Guard Corps advancing north of Borisov.[52]

Additional Red Army engineers and river-crossing units were arriving from the Stavka Reserve, enabling more heavy equipment to cross the Berezina. Glagolev's 31st Soviet Army raced forward 40 kilometers on 29 June, chasing remnants of the 78th, 260th, and 25th Panzergrenadier Divisions and reaching the Bobr River south of Krupki at the same time as Galitskiy's 11th Guard Army during the evening of 29 June. The southern flank of Tippelskirch's Fourth Army at Cherven was also under pressure from General V. D. Kryuchenkin's 33rd Army of the 2nd White Russian Front.[53]

Burdeyniy's 2nd Guard Tank Corps was moving quickly westward on the Minsk highway 30 kilometers south of Borisov. By the evening of 29 June, Burdeyniy's 4th and 25th Guard Tank Brigades reached the Berezina River at Chernevka, where they captured a damaged bridge. The Soviet 51st Engineer Battalion repaired the bridge, which was crossed immediately by a column of tanks, motorized infantry, and artillery.[54]

Most of the troops of Tippelskirch's Fourth Army had crossed the Drut River, although a considerable number were still east of the river and under heavy pressure from Glagolev's advancing 31st Army. German communications were crumbling under the strain: Volkers's XXVII Corps lost contact with the Fourth Army from noon on 28 June until 0300 on 30 June as the corps fought its way over the Drut River and back to the Berezina. At midnight on 29 June, Volkers reported that he was trying to cross the Berezina.[55]

Pfeiffer's VI Corps with the 14th and 260th Infantry Divisions was stranded on the east bank of the Drut. Driven south into Martinek's XXXIX Panzer Corps area, by 0400 on 29 June the VI Corps was defending Teterin on the Drut River, over 100 kilometers southeast of Borisov and separated from the rest of Tippelskirch's Fourth Army by another gap opened by Kryuchenkin's 33rd Army.[56]

By nightfall on 29 June, in Minsk, only 60 kilometers west of Borisov, a horde of German service troops and stragglers from various units was out of control. Tippelskirch's Fourth Army had collapsed as remnants of its divisions struggled to cross the Berezina River hotly pursued by Soviet forces. The road to Minsk was open to the Russians except for the pocket of resistance offered by Combat Group von Saucken and the 5th Panzer Division. Adding to German woes, the southern flank of the Fourth Army was under a new attack from Kryuchenkin's 33rd Army.[57]

At 1000 on 30 June, Combat Group von Saucken and the 5th Panzer Division still had a bridgehead east of Borisov and were trying to hold a bridge open to allow the remnants of the Fourth Army to escape. However, Soviet tanks were in sight, coming from the north and south. On 30 June Galitskiy's 11th Guard Army reached the Berezina River. Preceded by a 30-minute artillery barrage and heavy air attacks, the 31st Guard, 1st Guard, 83rd Guard, and 26th Guard Divisions with the help of engineers crossed between 1600 and 1700.[58]

Soviet tanks were attacking Borisov from all points. Rotmistrov's 5th Guard Tank Army had the 29th Tank Corps under the command of General E. I. Fomichev northeast of Borisov and the 3rd Tank Corps under General I. A. Vovchenko southeast of the city. Fomichev's 29th Tank Corps crossed the Berezina at Chernevka, 30 kilometers south of Borisov. Between Borisov and Chernevka was the remnant of the German 14th Infantry Division, as Combat Group Florke screened the west bank along with the rest of Pfeiffer's VI Corps, including elements of the 14th and 299th Infantry Divisions.[59]

On 1 July Galitskiy's 11th Guard Army and Rotmistrov's 5th

Guard Tank Army were still moving rapidly enough to unbalance the Germans. Although river defense lines were quickly penetrated, giving the Germans little opportunity to catch their breath and reorganize, the Red Army advance was often halted too long at the river crossings. The Soviet engineers performed extremely well, building pontoon bridges to carry the tanks across the Berezina River to maintain the drive, but the pontoons were often delayed by colossal traffic jams in the rear of Rotmistrov's army.

While the remnants of Tippelskirch's Fourth Army were fighting for their lives on the Berezina River at Borisov, a far more dangerous development was growing to the north. Krylov's 5th Army and Oslikovskiy's Horse-Mechanized Group were moving toward Molodechno, the rail connection northwest of Minsk, while advance units of the 11th Guard Army were moving from the southwest to cut the rail connection from the southwest. West of the railroad, between Molodechno in the north and Stolbtsy on the southwest, the Nalibotski Forest was infested with Partisans. Therefore, the Germans could retreat only north or south along the rail lines, and if the two rail lines were cut, the Germans around Minsk would be trapped.[60]

Borisov was taken on 1 July by Glagolev's 31st and Galitskiy's 11th Guard Army. The Soviet 5th Guard Division west of Borisov pressed home the attack on the city with tank support and the divisional artillery. The 83rd Guard Division, also on the west bank, attacked Borisov from the north. The 331st Rifle Division of Glagolev's 31st Army attacked from the south. By 0300 on 1 July, the city was in Soviet hands.[61]

During the afternoon of 1 July, Combat Group von Saucken was driven 10 kilometers south of the Borisov, retreating on the Minsk highway. Galitskiy's 11th Guard Army was 15 kilometers west of the Berezina River by the afternoon, and Vorobyev's 16th Guard Corps advanced northwest of Borisov and Zavodovskiy's 8th Guard Corps went due west.[62]

Elements of the 5th Guard Tank Army were still crossing the Berezina at Borisov on 1 July. The tank army had been stalled because of the lack of a bridge capable of supporting the tanks, but the 2nd Guard Engineer Brigade completed a 60- and a 30-ton bridge during 1 July. Marshal Vasilevsky was critical of the tank army for its slow pace and demanded that Minsk be taken by late 2 July.[63]

At midnight the von Saucken group was at Smolevichi, halfway between Borisov and Minsk. Between Minsk and Molodechno the 221st Security Division formed a thin screen on the railroad. Combat Group Florke, south of Borisov, had been driven out of Chernevka by Burdeyniy's 2nd Guard Tank Corps, which had crossed the river and accelerated quickly. (The Germans were trying without success to contain the bridgeheads established by the tank corps.) Burdeyniy, with the help of the 1st Guard Division of the 11th Guard Army, reached the main highway to Minsk and continued to pursue the remnant of Volkers's XXVII Corps.[64]

On 2 July the Soviet mobile columns of the 5th Guard Tank Army continued to press toward the rail lines to the west of Minsk. Tippelskirch's Fourth Army concentrated its forces around Molodechno and tried to close the gap northwest of Minsk. Elements of the 221st Security Division, a police regiment, and an assault gun battalion screened the rail line linking Molodechno and Minsk. During the day reinforcements arrived, including the first units of the 170th Infantry Division.[65]

Battle Group von Saucken reopened the rail line to Minsk from Molodechno with the help of the 5th Panzer Division and the 505th Tiger Battalion. South of von Saucken, Combat Group Gottberg held a position with Combat Group Müller, which consisted of eight battalions and 2,170 men, a panzergrenadier battalion from the 5th Panzer division and the 505th Tiger Battalion. To the south, Combat Group Anhalt with ten police and security battalions held a sector that reached out to Smolevichi and covered Minsk from the north. At Smilovichi, southeast of Minsk, Combat Group Florke with three regiments and stragglers screened Minsk from the south.[66]

Obukov's 3rd Guard Mechanized Corps of the Horse-Mechanized Group cut the railroad 20 kilometers north of Molodechno during the morning of 2 July, and the corps also took Krasnoe south of Molodechno, driving out the German 5th Panzer Division by noon. Other Red Army units were approaching Molodechno from the north, south, and east, including the 3rd Guard Cavalry Corps and Vorobyev's 16th Guard Corps of the 11th Guard Army.[67]

Battle Group von Saucken was still fighting on the Minsk highway. Burdeyniy's 2nd Guard Tank Corps, with elements of Galitskiy's 11th Guard Army and Glagolev's 31st Army, drove the von Saucken group from Smolevichi. The German battle group then withdrew over 50 kilometers northwest to Molodechno, leaving the road open to Minsk. Some reconnaissance units of the Soviet 2nd Guard Tank Corps entered Minsk that afternoon, while the remainder of the force attacked the city from the northeast.[68]

At 0600 on 2 July, Rotmistrov's 5th Guard Tank Army was 18 kilometers northeast of Minsk (the army had lost sixty tanks during the previous few days). By evening the tank army had entered Minsk, with Glagolev's 31st Army following behind.[69]

During the evening of 2 July, General Metz arrived in

Molodechno to take command of all the German units there, including Battle Group Lendle, elements of the 14th and 299th Infantry Divisions, the 31st Police Regiment, and elements of the 18th Luftwaffe Division. To the south, the German defenders had been pushed back toward Minsk. Survivors of Pfeiffer's VI and Volkers's XXVII Corps had filtered back across the Berezina River throughout the day. By midnight 20,000 German survivors were surrounded at Smilovichi and were asking for air supply of rations and ammunition.[70]

On the morning of 3 July, remnants of three corps of Tippelskirch's Fourth Army were trapped on the west bank of the Berezina River, while other detachments of the army had formed a defense around Molodechno.[71] (See Map 8.2.) Battle Group Metz was formed north of Krasnoe on the northern flank of the Molodechno position, with elements of the 221st Security Division and the 170th Grenadier Regiment. The 5th Panzer Division was poised for a counterattack south of Group Metz, but necessary fuel could not be delivered on the limited road network that was crowded with retreating Germans. During the afternoon of 3 July, the 5th Panzer Division finally counterattacked and ran into a Soviet tank column of Galitskiy's 11th Guard Army 10 kilometers west of Ostroshitskiy Gorodok.[72]

Group Florke was holding at Smilovichi at 0800 on 3 July, but was forced back south of Minsk. Group von Saucken was renamed 39th Panzer Corps, and had the task of keeping open the route to Molodechno. Group von Gottberg and the other scratch units of Tippelskirch's Fourth Army in Minsk were instructed to delay the Russians for as long as possible. At 1800 on 3 July, the tanks of Rotmistrov's 5th Guard Tank Army broke into the von Gottberg Group line, thus cutting the road to Minsk.[73]

During the following days the progress of the Red Army lagged considerably. The Soviet armies had been advancing about 20 kilometers per day for 10 days and were nearly 300 kilometers from their depots. Even though they had suffered heavily in the first few days in breaking through the German main line of resistance, in the following days enemy action had cost comparatively little in men and machines. Nevertheless, the wear and tear on the tracked vehicles was considerable, and a growing number were becoming inoperable because of mechanical problems. The initial stocks of fuel and munitions were low, and the pace had to slow to allow the supply trucks to restock the units. A round-trip to deliver supplies required 4 days, and there were not enough trucks or space on the roads to get the supplies forward. At the same time, German resistance was increasing as more fresh divisions arrived from other fronts, stiffen-

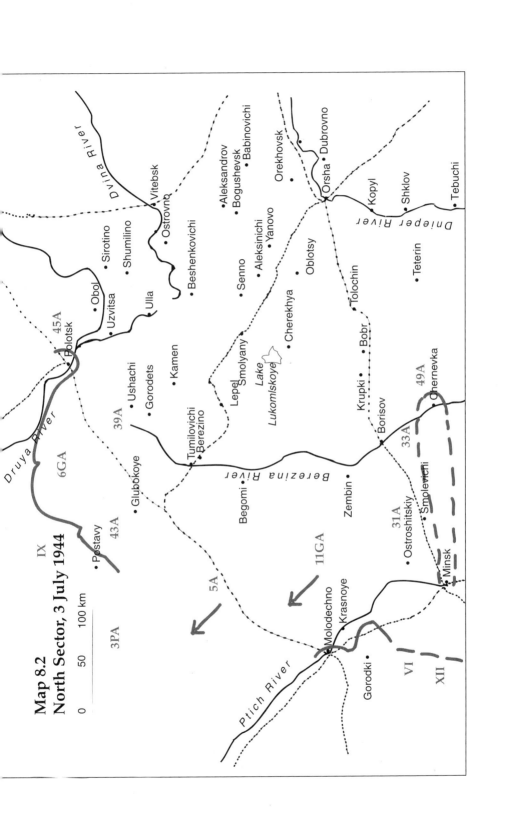

Map 8.2
North Sector, 3 July 1944

0   50   100 km

ing the defensive positions of the survivors of the first 2 weeks. Stouter resistance required greater quantities of munitions and more artillery, which were still stalled by traffic jams in the rear. The element of surprise that was so essential at the beginning of the operation was no longer a factor, and the battle had slowed to a typical Russian campaign of costly grinding out a few kilometers per day against well-prepared German positions.

The logistical problems of even the well-equipped Soviet mobile force in its attempts to maintain a rapid pace over a dismal road network were too great. On the other side, Hitler had banked the existence of Army Group Center on the logistical problems presented by White Russia, and those problems were finally to provide Field Marshal Model with a brief respite that turned a catastrophe into a critical but manageable situation.

Notes

1. G. Niepold, *The Battle for White Russia: The Destruction of Army Group Centre, June 1944* (London: Brassey's, 1987), p. 74; F. V. Plotnikov, *v Srazheniia za Belorussi* (Minsk: Belarus, 1982), pp. 76–77.

2. A. M. Samsanov, ed., *Osvobozhdenie Belorussii, 1944* (Moscow: Nauka, 1974), pp. 466–467, 469; Niepold, pp. 74–75; David M. Glantz and Harold S. Orenstein, eds., *Belorussia 1944: The Soviet General Staff Study* (Carlisle, Penn.: David M. Glantz, 1998), p. 87.

3. Samsanov, p. 467; Niepold, pp. 74–75; Glantz and Orenstein, p. 87; A. M. Vasilevsky, *Delo Vsei Zhizni* (Minsk: Belarus, 1984), p. 457.

4. Samsanov, pp. 446–447.

5. Ibid., pp. 447–454.

6. Ibid., p. 454.

7. Ibid., pp. 454–455.

8. Wolf Keilig, *Das Deutsche Heer, 1939–1945*, 3 vols. (Bad Nauheim: Podzun, 1956–1972), I, Section 81.

9. Georg Tessin, *Verbande und Truppen der Deutschen Wehrmacht und Waffen SS in Zweiten Weltkrieg, 1939–1945* (Osnabruck: Biblio, 1965–1980), V, p. 210; VII, p. 290; Werner von Haupt, *Die 260. Infanterie-Division, 1939–1944* (Bad Nauheim and Dorheim: Verlag Hans-Henning Podzun, 1970), pp. 219–221.

10. Niepold, p. 82; Glantz and Orenstein, p. 89; Paul Adair, *Hitler's Greatest Defeat: The Collapse of Army Group Centre, June 1944* (London: Arms and Armour Press, 1994), p. 101.

11. Niepold, p. 82; Glantz and Orenstein, p. 88; Adair, p. 101.

12. Niepold, pp. 82–83; Adair, p. 102.

13. Niepold, pp. 83, 86; Plotnikov, p. 52.

14. Niepold, p. 83; Glantz and Orenstein, p. 89.

15. Niepold, p. 90; Glantz and Orenstein, p. 90; Vasilevsky, p. 458.

16. Samsanov, p. 469; Glantz and Orenstein, pp. 90–91; Niepold, pp. 90, 98; Adair, pp. 102–103.

17. John Erickson, *The Road to Berlin* (Boulder, Colo.: Westview Press, 1983), p. 219; Niepold, p. 98; Adair, p. 103.

18. Erickson, pp. 91, 96; Adair, pp. 103–104.
19. Erickson, p. 91.
20. Ibid.
21. Ibid., pp. 90–91.
22. Ibid., p. 92.
23. Ibid., pp. 92–93.
24. Ibid., pp. 96–97.
25. Ibid., pp. 104, 106–107; Samsanov, pp. 471, 473; Glantz and Orenstein, pp. 92–93; Adair, p. 104.
26. Niepold, pp. 104, 106; Samsanov, pp. 72, 471.
27. Niepold, p. 104.
28. Ibid., pp. 105–106.
29. Samsanov, p. 472; Niepold, p. 103.
30. Niepold, p. 105.
31. Ibid., pp. 115, 117; Samsanov, p. 474; Glantz and Orenstein, p. 97; Vasilevsky, p. 460.
32. Samsanov, p. 474; Niepold, p. 124; Glantz and Orenstein, pp. 96–97; Adair, p. 105.
33. Niepold, p. 117; Adair, pp. 105–106.
34. Niepold, p. 115.
35. Ibid., p. 117; Samsanov, p. 474.
36. Niepold, pp. 115, 124.
37. Erickson, p. 221; Niepold, p. 126; Samsanov, p. 152.
38. Glantz and Orenstein, p. 97; Niepold, p. 126.
39. Samsanov, p. 475; Niepold, p. 126.
40. Niepold, pp. 126, 128–129; Glantz and Orenstein, p. 98; Plotnikov, pp. 58–59.
41. Niepold, p. 129.
42. Ibid.
43. Ibid.
44. Ibid., pp. 139–140; Glantz and Orenstein, p. 99.
45. Samsanov, p. 476.
46. Glantz and Orenstein, p. 99; Niepold, p. 140.
47. Niepold, p. 141; Glantz and Orenstein, p. 99.
48. Niepold, p. 142.
49. Ibid.; Adair, p. 122.
50. Niepold, p. 140; Samsanov, pp. 476, 616.
51. Glantz and Orenstein, pp. 99–100; Niepold, p. 154; Adair, p. 123.
52. Niepold, p. 156; Samsanov, pp. 477, 618.
53. Niepold, p. 154; Glantz and Orenstein, p. 133.
54. Erickson, p. 226; Niepold, p. 162; Samsanov, pp. 477, 618.
55. Niepold, pp. 154, 156, 159.
56. Ibid., p. 156.
57. Ibid., p. 158; Adair, pp. 124–125.
58. Niepold, p. 165; Samsanov, p. 477.
59. Samsanov, p. 85; Niepold, p. 165.
60. Niepold, pp. 174, 182; Adair, p. 125.
61. Samsanov, p. 478; Glantz and Orenstein, p. 135.
62. Samsanov, p. 480; Niepold, pp. 175, 183.
63. Niepold, p. 183; Samsanov, pp. 479–480; Vasilevsky, pp. 462–463; Adair, pp. 125–127.
64. Niepold, pp. 175, 183; Samsanov, pp. 480, 691.
65. Niepold, p. 186.

66. Ibid., p. 187; Adair, p. 127.
67. Niepold, pp. 186, 193; Samsanov, pp. 309–310.
68. Niepold, pp. 186–187, 193; Samsanov, p. 621.
69. Samsanov, p. 87; Niepold, p. 193; Erickson, p. 227; Adair, pp. 128–129.
70. Niepold, pp. 186–187, 189.
71. Ibid., p. 195.
72. Ibid., pp. 195, 198; Samsanov, p. 480; Adair, p. 130.
73. Niepold, pp. 195, 198, 204; Vasilevsky, p. 464.

CHAPTER 9

Mogilev

The Soviet drive to capture Mogilev in June 1944 was critical to the overall offensive. The German forces holding the sector had a high proportion of very good units, which could not be allowed to reinforce either of the sectors to the north or south. The 2nd White Russian Front, commanded by General G. F. Zakharov, had a primary mission of encircling Mogilev from the north and south and gaining control of the road net through Mogilev to Minsk that was crucial to the total offensive. (Figure 9.1 shows the table of organization of the 2nd White Russian Front.)

The Germans continued to fight tenaciously, inflicting many casualties on Soviet forces. Delayed by the main force of Tippelskirch's Fourth Army and the practically impassable terrain, Zakharov's units made less progress and suffered heavier casualties in the first phase of the White Russian operation than any of their military neighbors. But the 2nd White Russian Front held Tippelskirch's units until retreat was too late, which lead to their encirclement and destruction.

On 22 June 1944 the three armies of the Second White Russian Front, the 33rd, 49th, and the 50th, began the primary task of making a forceful demonstration east of Mogilev to hold in place Martinek's XXXIX Panzer Corps of Tippelskirch's Fourth Army, while major Soviet penetrations were carried out to the north and south. General I. T. Grishin's 49th Army was also charged with moving ahead to break the German line and take Mogilev, opening the one good highway in the sector through the marsh to the west. Faced by five high-quality German divisions in well-prepared positions, the Soviets suffered a high toll in casualties.

At 0600 on 22 June, preceded by a 30-minute barrage, a company from each front-line division of Grishin's 49th Army attacked in the sectors of the German 337th and 12th Divisions to determine the

Figure 9.1   The 2nd White Russian Front

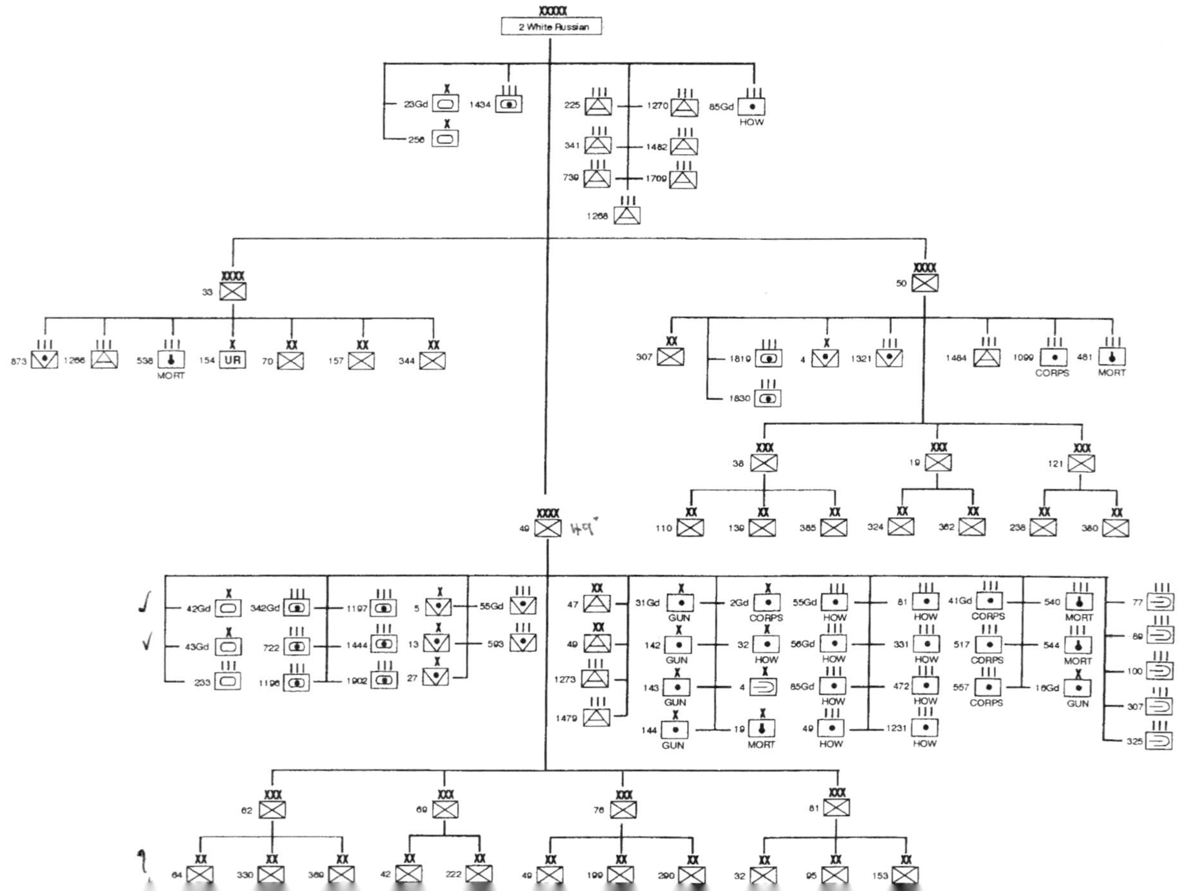

extent of the German defenses. Company-sized attacks on the 110th Infantry Division sector northeast of Kotelovo by General V. D. Kryuchenkin's 33rd Army, and on the 31st Infantry Division by General I. V. Boldin's 50th Army at Golovenchitsy, were launched to deceive the German defenders and keep them guessing about the location of the coming major attacks. The only gain was on a front 300 meters wide.[1]

The German Fourth Army commander saw the attacks on General Martinek's XXXIX Panzer Corps as merely diversions, although he worried that Martinek's artillery was weak in comparison to that of the Russians. On Tippelskirch's south flank, Müller's XII Corps had little contact with the widely spread divisions of the southern flank of Boldin's 50th Army.[2]

During the night of 22–23 June, heavy air attacks by the Soviet 4th Air Army on the German main line of resistance muffled the noise of Soviet tanks and assault guns moving into position. The fog on the morning of 23 June delayed the attack by Grishin's 49th Army until 0700 when a 2-hour artillery barrage successfully silenced the German artillery. Red Army infantry and 200 tanks jumped off at 0900 in the German 337th Infantry Division sector, overrunning all three trench lines of the main defense zone. Grishin reached the Mogilev-Ryasna road to the northeast and crossed the Pronia River. The 337th Division lost six artillery batteries, indicating that the Russians had overwhelmed the infantry in the trenches and captured the artillery before it could retreat. By noon Grishin had advanced 4 to 6 kilometers, but the tanks and assault guns experienced difficulty in crossing the river because the Germans had demolished the two bridges in the area. The poor cooperation between the Soviet armor and the infantry increased the number of casualties for the Red Army riflemen.[3]

The 2nd White Russian Front was relatively small, with only three armies (from north to south, the 33rd, the 49th, and the 50th). North of Mogilev, Kryuchenkin's 33rd Army, equivalent to an army corps, held a wide sector of over 50 kilometers with only three divisions and a fortified region. The Soviet 154th Fortified Region held about 20 kilometers of the army front, and the three divisions held most of the remaining 30 kilometers to the north of the fortified region. Kryuchenkin's army troops were sparse, and included a mortar regiment and an antiaircraft regiment. Obviously, the 33rd Army was performing a screening role between the assault groups designated for Orsha in the north and Mogilev in the south.

Grishin's 49th Army received fresh replacements for its rifle divisions in June to execute its crucial part in the offensive. In early June the army transferred five rifle divisions and received six rested divisions and numerous support troops from the Moscow Military District as well as the Stavka Reserve. On 23 June the army had four rifle corps, two tank brigades, a tank regiment, six assault gun regiments, three tank destroyer brigades, six artillery brigades, a Guard mortar brigade, a mortar brigade, and two antiaircraft divisions, plus many other support regiments.

The Soviet command had concentrated an enormous amount of firepower on a very narrow front to blast through the German defenses and quickly capture Mogilev. The massive influx of supporting units in June added to the potency of the army, which transferred relatively few depleted units to other armies.

In contrast to Grishin's 49th Army, Boldin's 50th Army was widely spread over a 75-kilometer sector, in contrast to a sector of less than 10 kilometers for the 49th Army. Boldin had three rifle corps (19th, 38th, and 121st) with seven divisions plus another independent division.

The 50th Army had a substantial quantity of supporting troops, a tank destroyer regiment, an antiaircraft regiment, a mortar regiment, a corps artillery regiment, and two assault gun regiments. The lack of any guard mortar regiments or any tank units was a clue that Boldin's 50th Army was not to be part of the main breakthrough effort.

The 2nd White Russian Front reserve had very few units to supplant those assigned to the three armies. The reserves included two tank brigades, an assault gun regiment, an antiaircraft division, and three antiaircraft regiments. The limited resources of the 2nd White Russian Front had only one objective, Mogilev, and would have to struggle in the capture of that city because of the strength of the German defenders.

The 2nd White Russian Front was opposed by Martinek's XXXIX Panzer Corps of Tippelskirch's Fourth Army, an unusually strong corps holding the center of the face of the White Russian salient. The stout resistance by this corps would inflict heavier casualties on the Red Army than any of the other German corps during the first 2 weeks of the battle to come. This corps consisted of the 12th, 31st, 110th, and 337th Infantry Divisions. In addition, the Feldherrnhalle Panzergrenadier Division of the Army General Headquarters Reserve was placed in the corps sector. The 12th Infantry Division had retained the nine-battalion structure until October 1943 when, much later than most divisions, it was reduced to seven battalions. The division was well above average in quality.

The 31st Infantry Division had suffered horrible losses in the retreat from Moscow in 1942, but had been lightly engaged for the intervening years and was therefore in good condition in June 1944.

The 110th Division included the 321st Division Group as part of the program to combine understrength divisions while maintaining the division and regiment traditions. The division was supported by the 185th Assault Gun Brigade. The unit had a high percentage of experienced combat soldiers and had probably been moved to Mogilev to reinforce the area most likely to be attacked in June 1944.

The 337th Division was reinforced by the 113th Division Group, which substituted for one regiment in November 1943. The division had a high percentage of veterans and long experience on the Eastern Front, but because of severe losses in the past the division was the weakest in the corps and was the first to break under Soviet attacks.

The Feldherrnhalle Panzergrenadier Division had six motorized infantry battalions in two regiments, a tank battalion, and an anti-tank battalion in June 1944. Earlier in June, the division had provided the cadre for a new 16th Panzer Regiment for the 116th Panzer Division being organized in France, leaving the Feldherrnhalle Division with only one tank battalion instead of a tank regiment with two battalions that was previously part of the division. The division was an elite formation, and its assignment to Mogilev along with the four other high-quality divisions was a testimony to the importance of Mogilev to the German defense. The success of the Germans in withstanding the Soviet attacks in most sectors of Martinek's XXXIX Corps for the first few days was a tribute to the quality of these five divisions.

In the evening of 23 June, German counterattacks halted the Soviet advance. At 2145 the Feldherrnhalle (hereafter FH) Panzergrenadier Division was ordered to defend 20 kilometers of the 337th Division sector and mounted numerous counterattacks. In the 110th Division sector, Kryuchenkin's 33rd Army made little progress because its three divisions and fortified region were widely dispersed over a broad front. However, by the evening of 23 June, Tippelskirch's Fourth Army main defense zone had been penetrated along a 12-kilometer sector to a depth of 8 kilometers in the 337th Division sector.[4]

After a trying day, at 2230 on 23 June, Tippelskirch requested permission to withdraw Martinek's XXXIX Panzer Corps to the second defense zone behind the Dnieper River. The request was denied, and an order was given to hold fast. In the evening, Martinek received three reinforcement battalions (men from the replacement army, including both returning wounded and new recruits) to counter the Soviet advances in the 337th Division sector.[5]

On the morning of 24 June, Grishin's 49th Army, with the help of General D. I. Smirnov's 121st Corps of the 50th Army, renewed its attack against the 337th and FH Divisions 30 kilometers northeast of Mogilev with a murderous 30-minute artillery barrage. Smashing through the main defense zone by noon, the assault opened a gap in Martinek's XXXIX Panzer Corps line east of Chernevka. The 337th Division was disintegrating and had lost most of its artillery. A task force of the Soviet 42nd Division plunged ahead, reaching Chernevka at 1700, and crossed the Basia River.[6]

Grishin's 49th Army turned south into the open northern flank of the 12th Infantry Division. At 1945 on 24 June, Tippelskirch requested but was refused permission to pull back the 12th Infantry Division, then isolated in a salient south of the gap at Chausy. The policy of the German OKH remained firm; prepared defenses were to be held as long as possible. By 2000 the 12th Division was driven back farther west, and only a small battered band of survivors remained of the 337th Division. The 12th Division could not hold its ground well enough for an orderly withdrawal to the next position.[7]

By late evening of 24 June, however, the resistance of the 110th Division to the north of the gap hardened and was slowing the Soviet advance. During the night of 24–25 June, Soviet reinforcements were brought up in the sector between Dribin and Chausy. Kryuchenkin's 33rd Army launched another attack in the evening on the right flank of the 110th Division at Dribin 20 kilometers east of Chernevka.[8]

On Tippelskirch's southern flank during the morning of 24 June, Samarskiy's 19th Corps of Boldin's 50th Army penetrated the 267th Division line at Ludchitsa, but by 1100 on 24 June, the attack was contained. On the 57th Division front to the south, Boldin advanced 10 kilometers west of the Drut River at Podsely in the morning.[9]

The major threat to Mogilev on the evening of 24 June was the deep wedge in the German lines northeast of the city. The FH Division had the task of repelling four Soviet corps moving rapidly toward Mogilev.

At 0600 on the morning of 25 June, the Soviet 49th, 33rd, and 50th Armies launched an attack on the 337th, 12th, and FH Divisions, driving them across the Basia River. At 0840 the 337th Division was pushed back to the River Resta, leaving open the flank of the 110th Division. The 337th Division was preparing to retreat farther to the Dnieper.[10]

Boldin's 50th Army joined in with an attack on the northern flank of the 31st Division and captured Chausy. At 1800 on 25 June, both the 12th and 31st Infantry Divisions were ordered to retreat to the River Resta line. Despite more German reinforcements and fierce resistance, by 2130 that evening, Grishin's 49th Army had broken through the FH Division line, and a column of ninety Russian tanks and infantry in trucks was on the road to Mogilev.[11]

Tippelskirch was in serious trouble by the evening of 25 June. He had planned to withdraw Martinek's Pauzer XXXIX Corps on the following day to a line south of Chernevka, about half the distance from the original front to Mogilev, but this move was unrealistic because the Russians were already west of that line in many places.

At midnight on 25 June, Grishin's 49th Army had advanced a further 4 kilometers south of Chernevka and was approaching the Dnieper River bridges at Mogilev. The 337th Division was scattered, and only Battle Group Schünemann with an infantry battalion, an assault gun brigade, and a tank destroyer battalion was delaying Grishin's advance. North of Chernevka, the 110th Division was holding its own flank but could not stop Kryuchenkin's 33rd Army. The FH Division defense line had been broken, and the 12th Infantry Division south of the FH Division was bending its left flank to prevent Grishin's army from reaching its rear area.[12]

In the south, in Müller's XII Corps sector, the German 57th Infantry Division recaptured Podsely, but Boldin's 50th Army continued to contest the area and recaptured the town by evening. Maintaining the tie between Tippelskirch's Fourth and Jordan's Ninth Armies to the south became a crisis as the 57th Division of XII Corps was pushed northwest away from the Ninth Army boundary.[13] The gap that opened between the 57th Division and the 134th Division of the Ninth Army threatened the rear of the German position at Bobruysk.

After 3 days of battering, Grishin's 49th and Boldin's 50th Armies had finally blasted a hole in Martinek's XXXIX Panzer Corps line, but the Soviet armor available to exploit the break was limited to only two tank brigades, a tank regiment, and six assault gun regiments. Because the Germans had held tenaciously on the main road into Mogilev, Zakharov's 2nd White Russian Front had shifted the weight of its attack to the north through the swamp, thus further limiting exploitation of the breakthrough. However, Müller's XII Corps was on the run on 25 June, and the 49th and 50th Armies had to apply pressure before the Germans could regain their balance and occupy the next defense zone. The 2nd White Russian Front succeeded in breaking the main defense zone with massive infantry attacks with heavy artillery support—the Soviet armored units were repeatedly delayed at the river crossings—leaving the infantry to do the bloody work alone. By evening on 25 June, the German main defense zone was smashed. Grishin's 49th Army had advanced 30 kilometers in the first 3 days of the offensive in the sector north of Mogilev.[14]

On 26 June the three armies (33rd, 49th, and 50th) of the 2nd White Russian Front attacked with orders to reach the Dnieper River north of Mogilev. Kryuchenkin's 33rd Army attack had poor success.

The mobile group with Boldin's 50th Army was achieving nothing at Chausy against the German 12th Division, so the Soviet tanks were shifted to the northern flank of Grishin's 49th Army against Group Schünemann and the 110th Division. The survivors of the 110th Infantry Division fought their way back to the Dnieper River at Shklov by the end of the day. Thereafter the Schünemann group, the remains of the 337th Division, and the FH Division desperately fought to hold open the road to Mogilev on the west bank of the Dnieper to permit others to escape.[15]

V. V. Panyukhov's 81st Corps of Grishin's 49th Army crossed the Dnieper River during the morning of 26 June at Tebuchi, 10 kilometers north of Mogilev. Once across the river, Grishin turned to the northwest to cut off the German forces in Orsha. Before noon other units of the 49th Army had crossed the Dnieper at Polykovichi, north of Mogilev, and cut the Orsha-Mogilev railway northeast of Mogilev.[16]

To the north, Kryuchenkin's 33rd Army captured Gorkiy and advanced 30 kilometers throughout 26 June, forcing the German 260th and 110th Divisions to withdraw to the Dnieper. South of Mogilev in Martinek's XXXIX Pauzer Corps sector on 26 June, the 12th and 31st Divisions held prepared positions east of the Dnieper in the morning, but finally were dislodged during the day by Smirnov's 121st and A. D. Tereshkov's 38th Corps of Boldin's 50th Army, which ground away at Chausy, driving the German divisions back toward Mogilev. By 2200 two corps of Boldin's 50th Army were closing up on the east bank of the Dnieper River.[17]

By the evening of 26 June, Grishin's 49th Army was across the Dnieper in force, and the Germans received the order to evacuate the east bank of the Dnieper. At 2130 Tippelskirch pulled all divisions across the Dnieper to the west bank and concentrated the entire available force to stop the Soviet advance toward Mogilev. On Tippelskirch's southern flank, Müller's XII Corps continued to hold at Ludchitsa, but Jordan's Ninth Army to the south had pulled back to Buda, leaving a 20-kilometer-wide opening in the German line.[18]

The 12th Infantry Division that had defended the main road to Mogilev so tenaciously was sent to garrison that city, which had been designated a fortified area to block the Soviet use of the main road and rail connections. The highway was especially significant because it was the only good road to pass through a 60-kilometer-wide band of swamps and forest that separated the Drut and Berezina to the west.[19]

Tippelskirch had requested that the positions east of Dnieper be abandoned on 23 June, 3 days earlier. Instead, Hitler had ordered the five German divisions to hold the fortifications for 5 days, and so the divisions had been chewed up for no apparent gain. By 26 June the German divisions could no longer escape.[20]

By the next day, 27 June, Zakharov had cleared the east bank of the Dnieper River. Martinek's XXXIX Panzer Corps was retreating under heavy attack from Grishin's 49th Army, which had crossed the Dnieper both north and south of Mogilev. At 0630 Grishin continued to drive back the 337th and FH Divisions north of Mogilev.[21]

In the gap opened between the 110th Division and Mogilev, Grishin's engineers constructed a 16- and a 30-ton bridge across the Dnieper to carry tanks, trucks, and artillery. The Soviet armored columns streamed through the breach and advanced at a blistering pace. The 290th and 369th Divisions of Grishin's 49th Army and Smirnov's 121st Corps of Boldin's 50th Army, following an armored column composed of the 23th Guard Tank Brigade and the 1434th Assault Gun Regiment, struck Mogilev from the northwest and fighting began in the streets during the night. By evening the bridge-head across the Dnieper was 25 kilometers deep, halfway to the Drut River.[22]

As of 1700 on 27 June, Hitler remained insistent that Mogilev and the control of the single road through the marsh to Berezino be held to the last man by the 12th Infantry Division. As Grishin's 49th and Boldin's 50th Armies continued to attack, the Mogilev garrison was left on its own, and the remaining divisions of Martinek's XXXIX Panzer Corps fled west to the Drut.[23]

The 110th Division on the northern shoulder of the Soviet pene-tration was driven north into Volkers's XXVII Corps sector and came under the corps command. The 110th Division was then brushed aside by mobile columns of Kryuchenkin's 33rd Army, which took Kopys after advancing 40 kilometers. Kryuchenkin's infantry divi-sions were struggling to remain abreast as the main Soviet attack flowed along the main road to Berezino on the Berezina River.[24]

South of Mogilev, the 31st Division of Martinek's XXXIX Panzer Corps was pushed into the zone of the 18th Panzergrenadier Division of Müller's XII Corps. This corps retreated to Podsely with its southern flank turned to the west on the northern edge of the gap between the corps and Jordan's Ninth Army to the south. By after-noon on 27 June, Martinek's XXXIX Corps was only 20 kilometers east of the Drut River and under continual attack.[25]

Hitler's stubborn refusal to give ground had weakened during the day and he was considering pulling Tippelskirch's entire Fourth Army, including the XXXIX and XXVII Corps in the north and the XII to the south, across the Drut River to the west bank of the Berezina River. Although Tippelskirch did not take advantage of Hitler's hesitation to withdraw immediately to the Berezina, he did pull Martinek's XXXIX Corps part of the distance back to the Drut River (not the Berezina) at 1540 on 27 June. Tippelskirch worried that retreating all the way to the Drut would turn into a rout; therefore, Martinek was ordered to withdraw the remaining 30 kilometers to the west bank of the Drut on the next day, 28 June.

Throughout 27 June Tippelskirch's army was torn apart by Soviet breakthroughs, both in the north by Grishin's 49th Army and in the south by Boldin's 50th Army. The only hope for the Germans was to retreat faster than the Russians could follow.[26]

On 28 June elements of Grishin's and Boldin's armies closed in on Mogilev and took the city, but only at the price of heavy casualties. The German garrison, primarily elements of the 12th Division, mustered a stout defense: M. I. Glukhov's 76th Corps of the 49th Army cleaned up Mogilev and finally won control of the highway to the west after 7 days of bitter fighting and an enormous butcher's bill. Other elements of the 49th and 50th Armies broke through the German defenses on the west bank of the Dnieper and raced to the Drut River.[27]

At 0900 on 28 June, the remnants of the divisions of Martinek's XXXIX Corps crossed to the west bank of the Drut River pursued by Panyukhov's 81st and H. N. Multan's 69th Corps of Grishin's 49th Army. The Germans held the Drut line throughout 28 June as Grishin's and Boldin's infantry and engineers closed up to the east bank and prepared to cross.

North of Grishin's 49th Army, Kryuchenkin's 33rd Army crossed the Dnieper on 28 June and drove the 25th Panzergrenadier and 110th Divisions back 15 kilometers by 2200. General A. F. Naumov's 62nd Corps of the 49th Army joined Kryuchenkin's 33rd Army to reinforce the drive, pressing back Volkers's XXVII Corps toward the Berezina River.[28]

At 1745 on 28 June, Tippelskirch was ordered to retreat 50 kilometers west to the Berezina River as quickly as possible because of the disasters to the north at Orsha and to the south at Bobruysk. However, the order was too late for the Fourth Army. Its divisions had been ground up trying to hold back Grishin's 49th Army east of the Dnieper, and the survivors were even too weak to delay the pursuing Russians in the flight to the Drut. Martinek's XXXIX Panzer Corps did have enough strength to hold the Drut line for more than a day and then head to the Berezina River, over which the Germans held bridges at Borisov, Chernevka, Berezino, and Brodets.[29]

South of the breakthrough, Müller's XII Corps was desperately trying to escape while under pressure from Boldin's 50th Army. On the southern flank of Müller's XII Corps, Gorbatov's 3rd Army was advancing north of Bobruysk, pushing Jordan's Ninth Army north

toward the bridges over the Berezina River at the rear of
Tippelskirch's Fourth Army. The 31st Division of Müller's XII Corps,
pursued by Smirnov's 121st Corps of Boldin's 50th Army, had
retreated to the Drut River by 2100 on 28 June and planned to cross
the river by morning. Müller wanted to move the division to Pogost
a few kilometers east of Berezino as soon as possible, but the roads
on the west side of the Drut River were too poor for even moderate
speed by trucks. A major catastrophe was brewing because General
K. A. Vershinin's 4th Air Army had bombed most of the bridges,
stranding most of Müller's trucks on the east side of the Drut River.
German engineers feverishly worked on the bridges, but the struc-
tures would not be ready until the morning of 28 June. In the 18th
Panzergrenadier Division sector the bridge over the Drut River was
not open until noon. On 28 June Müller's XII Corps desperately tried
to hold back Boldin's 50th and Gorbatov's 3rd Armies until the next
day to give the 18th Panzergrenadier Division time to escape with its
vehicles and heavy weapons. Time was running out for the Fourth
Army, and saving men would soon take precedence over trucks and
weapons.[30]

Defending the Drut River between Teterin and Belynichi were
Pfeiffer's VI Corps, remnants of the 14th and 299th Divisions, a regiment of the FH Division, the 110th Division, and remnants of the
12th and 337th Divisions under the command of Martinek's XXXIX
Panzer Corps. Having few units to command, the corps headquarters was transferred to head a large battle group to the north, and
the remaining troops were transferred to Pfeiffer's VI Corps command as of 0700 on 29 June.[31] (See Map 9.1.)

On the northern flank of Tippelskirch's Fourth Army, the most
urgent task for Volkers's XXVII Corps was to defend a line south of
the Berezino-Minsk road at Cherven to prevent Red Army forces
from cutting the main escape route from the north once Tippelskirch
crossed the Berezina River. At 1000 on 29 June, Grishin's 49th Army
broke through the FH Division northwest of the Belynichi halfway
between the Drut and Berezina Rivers. The Russians reached the
Berezina River 15 kilometers southeast of Berezino at 1300 on the
afternoon of 29 June.[32]

The retreating divisions of the Fourth Army were under constant
air bombardment on the few roads leading west from the Drut to the
Berezina River. The headquarters of the Fourth Army counted twenty-five air attacks during the day while it moved to the rear. Even
though the German troops reached the Berezina River, the bridge at
Berezino west of Mogilev carried only 8 tons, not enough for even a
light tank. Martinek's XXXIX Panzer Corps was ordered to cross the
Berezina at a 2-ton-capacity bridge being built 15 kilometers north of

Map 9.1
South Sector, 29 June 1944

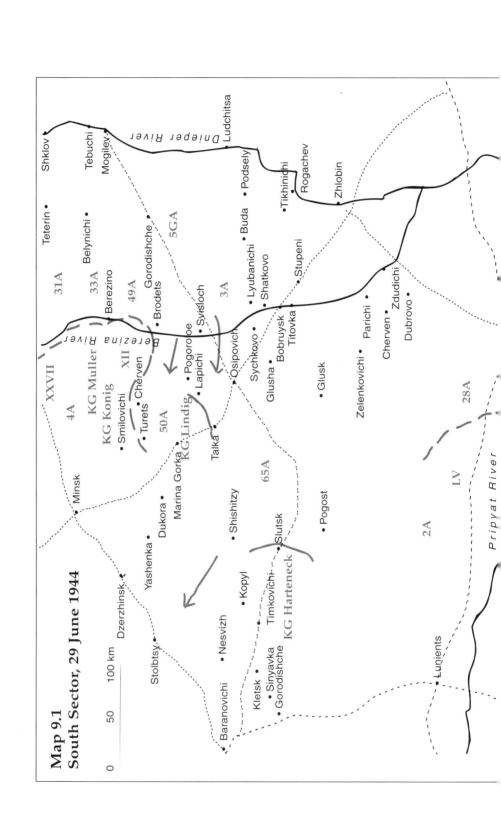

0   50   100 km

Dnieper River

Shklov •
Tebuchi •
Mogilev •
Teterin •
Belynichi •
Berezino •
Gorodishche •
Brodets •
Ludchitsa
Podsely •
Rogachev •
Tikhinichi •
Zhlobin •
Buda •
Lyubanichi •
Shatkovo •
Stupeni •

31A
33A
49A
5GA
3A

Berezina River

XXVII
4A
KG Muller
KG Konig
XII
Smilovichi •
Turets •
Cherven •
Pogoroloe •
Lapichi •
Svisloch •
Osipovich •
Sychkovo •
Glusha •
Bobruysk •
Titovka •
Parichi •
Cherven •
Zdudichi •
Dubrovo •
Zelenkovichi •
Glusk •

50A
KG Lindig
Talka •
65A

Minsk •
Yashenka •
Dukora •
Marina Gorka •
Shishitzy •
Slutsk •
Pogost •

2A
LV
28A

Pripyat River

Dzerzhinsk •
Stolbtsy •
Kopyl •
Timkovichi •
KG Harteneck

Nesvizh •
Kletsk •
Sinyavka •
Gorodishche •
Baranovichi •

Luqients •

Berezino. The road to the main bridge at Berezino was jammed with trucks, most of which would have to be destroyed.[33]

The relentless Soviet air attacks were continual—the bridge at Berezino was hit in the morning and again at noon. The trucks, horses, and troops jammed up waiting to cross were helpless targets for the Soviet aircraft. German engineers repaired the bridge by 1600 on 29 June, and traffic began to flow again.[34]

On the southern flank of the 4th Army, Müller's XII Corps was crossing the Drut River on the morning of 29 June, but the 18th Panzergrenadier Division would not be able to cross until midday. To protect the northern flank, Müller requested that Martinek's XXXIX Panzer Corps slow its withdrawal.[35]

At 0400 on 29 June, advance elements of Grishin's 49th Army reached the Berezina River 10 kilometers south of Brodets and were opposed by elements of the 134th Division of Jordan's Ninth Army. There were also elements of the 707th Division of the Ninth Army defending the bridges over the Berezina River at Brodets, along with 200 stragglers, a battalion of artillery, and three heavy antitank guns. German engineers began building a bridge at Brodets on the morning of 29 June, where two ferries were already in operation. South of Brodets, half of the 12th Panzer Division arrived at 1300 on 29 June to reinforce the Ninth Army near Svisloch, but Gorbatov's 3rd Army was closing in.[36] Many units of Müller's XII Corps were still east of the Drut River: the 18th Panzergrenadier Division crossed around noon, and the 267th, 57th, and 31st Division followed. At 1940 on 29 June, Soviet tanks and motorized infantry reached the Berezina River 8 kilometers south of Brodets and turned north toward Berezino.[37]

All of the units of Tippelskirch's Fourth Army had exhausted their supplies and requested air drops of rations and ammunition. At 2200 on 29 June, Hitler agreed to abandon Mogilev and ordered the garrison to fight its way out, but Soviet forces had already captured the city the previous evening. The attack on Mogilev had succeeded but at great cost to the Red Army: Grishin's 49th Army had taken on five elite German divisions with frontal attacks and meager armored support. Grishin was in disfavor for his handling of this part of the offensive, and the 49th Army had to be withdrawn to refit after the action.

On 30 June Zakharov's 2nd White Russian Front was across the Berezina River at many points and armored columns were moving west toward Minsk 75 kilometers away. Battle Group von Saucken was trying to delay the Soviet forces that were crossing bridges in the Borisov area. Throughout 30 June the FH, 12th, and 337th Divisions were retreating to the Berezina River, and by nightfall the

FH Division was across the river. During the morning of 30 June, all of the troops fighting with Pfeiffer's VI Corps were joined in Battle Group Müller, which held a line facing south at Cherven.[38]

At Berezino, at 1630 on 30 June, Soviet aircraft resumed the persistent attacks on the German columns waiting to cross the bridge over the Berezina River. The main road west of Berezino was held by the 31st and 286th Security Divisions. At 1830 Soviet units attempted to cut the road but were driven off, and the road remained open to the fleeing Germans.[39] To the south, on the east side of the Berezina River, Müller's XII Corps was pushed farther north during the day under relentless pressure from an armored column of Gorbatov's 3rd Army.[40]

On 1 July Battle Group von Saucken, including the 5th Panzer Division, Battle Groups von Gottbert and Florke, and the 14th Division, was holding a line on the Berezina River at Chernevka that was under attack by Kryuchenkin's 33rd Army. The 110th Division of Pfeiffer's VI Corps was crossing the Berezina at Shukovets where two bridges had been built. Also in the area were the 25th Panzergrenadier Division and the 260th Division.[41]

Battle Group Müller with the FH Division was holding Grishin's 49th Army at Duleby northeast of Pogost and trying to escape to Berezino. This group consisted of Müller's XII Corps (the 18th Panzergrenadier, 267th, and 57th Divisions); the 31st, FH, 12th, and 337th Divisions; and the headquarters of the 286th Security Division. On the southern flank of Tippelskirch's Fourth Army, Panyukhov's 81st Corps of Grishin's 49th Army was attacking along the Minsk highway, which was defended by elements of the German 31st, 267th, and 286th Divisions in the Pogost area.[42]

On the Cherven-Berezino road west of the Berezina, Battle Group König (the 12th Grenadier Regiment of the 31st Division, the 27th Fusilier Regiment, and elements of the 286th Security Division) was fighting Tereshkov's 38th and Samarskiy's 19th Corps of Boldin's 50th Army, which had crossed the Berezina north of Brodets. In the late morning of 1 July, Soviet tanks in Cherven drove Battle Group König farther west, and then Boldin cut off Tippelskirch's retreat between Berezino and Cherven and headed for Minsk.[43]

On 2 July Tippelskirch continued to pull his units across the Berezina River under heavy attacks. The 110th Division took command of all German troops crossing at Shukovets. Müller's XII Corps was under pressure at Pogost and repulsed Grishin's attempt to cross the Berezina River north of Berezino. Still on the east side of the river were the FH Division north of the main road and the 18th Panzergrenadier, 337th, and 31st Divisions south of the road.[44]

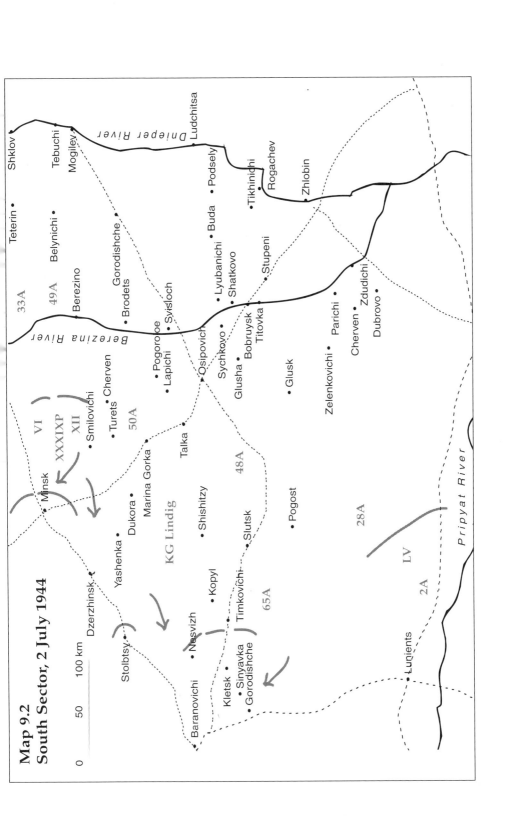

Map 9.2
South Sector, 2 July 1944

0 50 100 km

Dnieper River
Berezina River
Pripyat River

Shklov
Teterin
Tebuchi
Mogilev
Belynichi
Berezino
Ludchitsa
Podsely
Buda
Tikhinidhi
Rogachev
Zhlobin
33A
49A
Gorodishche
Brodets
Svisloch
Lyubanichi
Shatkovo
Stupeni
Pogoroloe
Lapichi
Osipovichi
Sychkovo
Bobruysk
Glusha
Titovka
Glusk
Zelenkovichi
Parichi
Cherven
Zdudichi
Dubrovo
Smilovichi
Turets
Cherven
50A
Talka
48A
Pogost
28A
LV
2A
Minsk
XXXIX P
XII
VI
Marina Gorka
Dukora
Yashenka
Shishitzy
Slutsk
KG Lindig
Dzerzhinsk
Stolbtsy
Kopyl
Timkovichi
65A
Nesvizh
Kletsk
Sinyavka
Gorodishche
Baranovichi
Luqients

Tippelskirch was ordered to pull back to Smolevichi, 35 kilometers west of Borisov and the Berezina River, because Galitskiy's 11th Guard and Rotmistrov's 5th Guard Tank Armies were attacking Minsk from the north behind the Fourth Army. Just before midnight on 2 July, Tippelskirch learned that Burdeyniy's 2nd Guard Tank Corps was speeding south on the open flank, so Tippelskirch sent units of Pfeiffer's VI Corps southwest of Molodechno to set up a defense.[45]

In the south, the 12th Panzer Division was the anchor pin but was needed to protect Stolbtsy. Therefore Battle Group Lindig was ordered to retreat to Dukora late on 2 July and release the 12th Panzer Division for Stolbtsy.[46] (See Map 9.2.)

By the evening of 2 July, the German reinforcements had slowed the Soviet advance, but the troops left behind were lost and would be rounded up by Red Army Forces in the coming days. As the first phase of the struggle ended, the Germans had lost much of the elite force that had defended Mogilev. While the Soviet infantry divisions continued to march forward at a rapid pace and the Soviet engineers repaired the roads and bridges in the newly acquired territory, the Soviet mobile columns were held in check by the German reinforcements. The Red Army, though finally successful in this engagement, was bloodied severely in the final days of the Mogilev campaign by the stubborn German defenders. The next phase of the White Russian offensive would return to the more usual grinding out of minor gains against well-entrenched Germans.

Notes

1. David M. Glantz and Harold S. Orenstein, eds., *Belorussia 1944: The Soviet General Staff Study* (Carlisle, Penn.: David M. Glantz, 1998), p. 100; G. Niepold, *The Battle for White Russia: The Destruction of Army Group Centre, June 1944* (London: Brassey's, 1987), p. 74; A. I. Radzievskii, *Army Operations: USSR Reports, Military Affairs* (Washington, D.C.: Foreign Broadcast Information Service, 1985), pp. 40–45.

2. Niepold, pp. 74–75.

3. Ibid., pp. 82–83; Glantz and Orenstein, pp. 100–101; John Erickson, *The Road to Berlin* (Boulder, Colo.: Westview Press, 1983), p. 220.

4. Niepold, p. 82–84; Glantz and Orenstein, p. 102; Paul Adair, *Hitler's Greatest Defeat: The Collapse of Army Group Centre, June 1944* (London: Arms and Armour Press, 1994), pp. 109–110.

5. Glantz and Orenstein, p. 83.

6. Ibid., pp. 90–91, 103–104.

7. Niepold, pp. 91–92.

8. Ibid., p. 92; Glantz and Orenstein, p. 104.

9. Niepold, p. 92; Glantz and Orenstein, pp. 103–104.

10. Niepold, pp. 103–105; Glantz and Orenstein, pp. 104–105.

11. Niepold, pp. 104–105; Glantz and Orenstein, p. 105.

12. Niepold, p. 107.

13. Ibid., pp. 103, 107.

14. Glantz and Orenstein, p. 105.

15. Niepold, pp. 116–117; Glantz and Orenstein, p. 106; F. V. Plotnikov, *v Srazheniia za Belorussi* (Minsk: Belarus, 1982), p. 112.

16. Niepold, p. 116; Glantz and Orenstein, p. 106; Erickson, p. 220.

17. Glantz and Orenstein, p. 106; Niepold, p. 116.

18. Niepold, pp. 116–118.

19. Ibid.

20. Ibid., p. 122; Adair, p. 146.

21. Niepold, pp. 126, 128.

22. Glantz and Orenstein, p. 107.

23. Niepold, p. 128; Adair, p. 111.

24. Niepold, p. 130; Glantz and Orenstein, p. 108.

25. Niepold, pp. 129–130.

26. Ibid., pp. 131, 136; Adair, pp. 146–147.

27. Erickson, p. 221; Glantz and Orenstein, p. 108; Adair, p. 112; Plotnikov, pp. 76–77.

28. Glantz and Orenstein, pp. 108–109; Niepold, pp. 140–141; Plotnikov, pp. 115–116; Adair, p. 147.

29. Niepold, pp. 142–143; Adair, p. 147.

30. Niepold, p. 141; Adair, p. 148.

31. Niepold, pp. 140–141, 154, 156–157; Adair, p. 148.

32. Niepold, p. 157; Adair, p. 149.

33. Earl F. Ziemke, *Stalingrad to Berlin: The German Campaign in Russia, 1942–1945* (New York: Dorset Press, 1968), p. 323; Niepold, pp. 143, 157.

34. Niepold, pp. 158, 168.

35. Ibid., p. 154.

36. Ibid., pp. 156–157; Adair, p. 150.

37. Niepold, pp. 157–158.

38. Ibid., pp. 165–166.

39. Ibid., pp. 166–167.

40. Ibid., pp. 166, 168.

41. Ibid., pp. 175–176; Adair, p. 150.

42. Niepold, pp. 175–177.

43. Ibid., p. 176.

44. Ibid., p. 188.

45. Ibid.; Adair, pp. 150–151.

46. Niepold, pp. 188–189.

CHAPTER 10

Bobruysk

The monumental task of breaking through the German Ninth Army at two points and enveloping Bobruysk was assigned to three armies of the 1st White Russian Front (3rd, 48th, and 65th Armies) under the command of Army General K. K. Rokossovskiy. After this had been accomplished, the 65th Army commanded by General P. I. Batov would press northwest toward Minsk, the 3rd Army commanded by General A. V. Gorbatov would drive north toward Berezino, and the 48th Army commanded by General P. L. Romanenko would apply pressure in the center. (Figure 10.1 shows the organization table of the northern armies of the 1st White Russian Front.)

Opposing the 1st White Russian Front east of Bobruysk was the German Ninth Army under General Jordan. The sector was quiet on 22 June, the opening day of the offensive, but the German interpretation was that the attacks in the other sectors were a ruse to divert reserves from the south, and that the major objective would be east of Bobruysk at Rogachev. The patrols of the 134th German Division had revealed the Soviet buildup in the sectors of the 35th Guard Corps commanded by General V. G. Zholudev and the 41st Guard Corps under General V. K. Urbanovich opposite the 134th German Division. Each of the three two-battalion regiments of the German divisions was faced with a full-strength Soviet rifle division with 7,200 men. Soviet artillery registration (individual shells fired to determine where shells from each gun would fall) had begun on 17 June. Expecting an attack in the near future, the 134th Division improved its trenches and laid more mines. German air reconnaissance detected 200 Soviet artillery batteries, and the war diary of Jordan's Ninth Army on 22 June forecast a major battle. Jordan realized that the immediate threat at Bobruysk was greater than at Kovel, where the OKH expected the attack to come. The Ninth Army

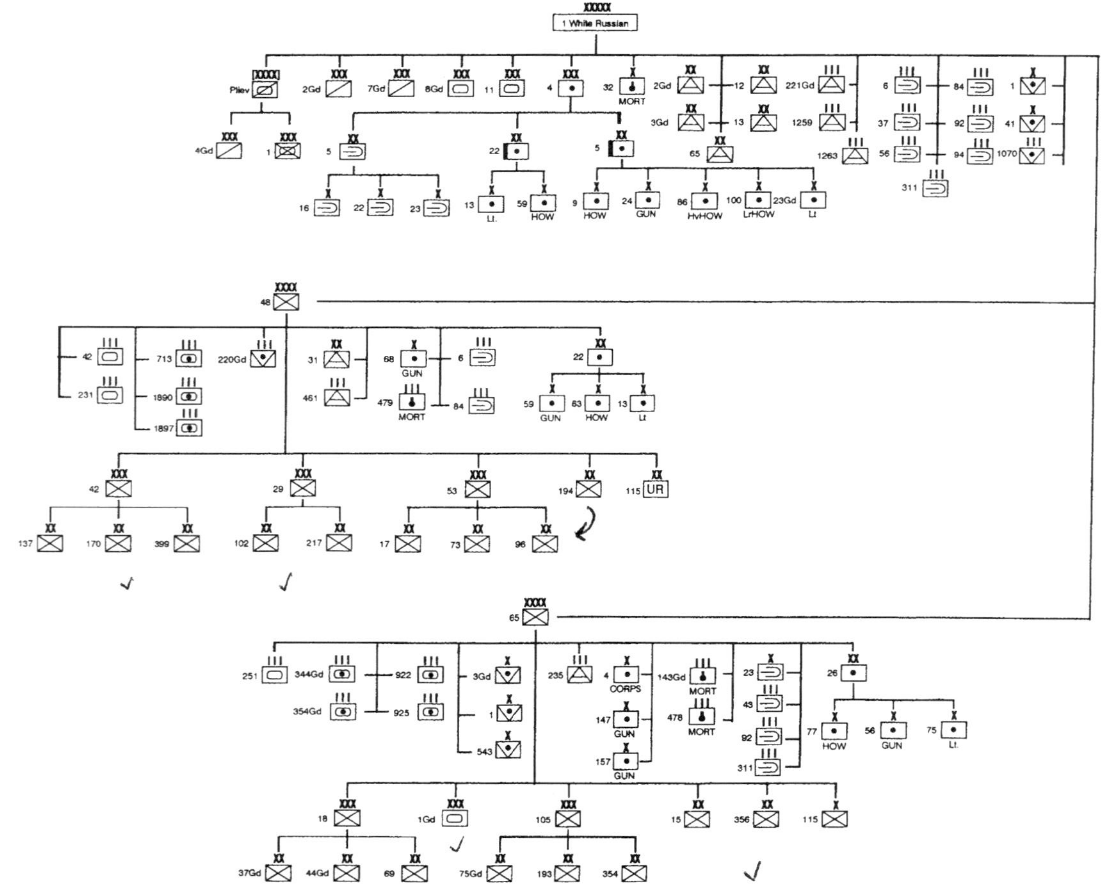

Figure 10.1   Northern Armies of the 1st White Russian Front

war diary expounded at great length that given the odds, the only hope for the army was a mobile defense, trading ground for time to allow reinforcements to arrive from the south. When the Russians had outrun their communications that was the time to counterattack. Jordan was especially opposed to holding fortified cities.[1]

General K. K. Rokossovskiy planned to have the 35th Guard Corps under General V. G. Zholudev and the 41st Guard Corps under General V. K. Urbanovich of Gorbatov's 3rd Army break through the first and second defense lines of General Lützow's XXXV Corps on the west bank of the Dnieper River. After bridgeheads were secured General B. S. Bakharov's 9th Tank Corps and General K. M. Erastov's 46th Rifle Corps would exploit the breakthrough.[2]

In the south, in General Weidling's XXXXI Corps sector, Batov's 65th Army would break through the 35th German Division 10-kilometer front with the 18th Rifle Corps under General I. I. Ivanov and then follow through with the 1st Guard Tank Corps commanded by General M. F. Panov. More than 70 percent of Batov's 65th Army tanks were assigned to the first-echelon divisions. The 17th Guard Tank Brigade supported the 37th Guard and 69th Rifle Divisions on the right of Ivanov's 18th Corps. The 16th Guard Tank Brigade and a 152mm assault gun regiment was attached to the 44th Guard Division in the second echelon behind the 15th Rifle Division on the left. The 15th Guard Tank brigade was attached to the 356th Rifle Division in the second echelon behind the 69th Division. With most of Batov's 350 tanks and assault guns supporting the 18th Rifle Corps, the German 35th and 36th Divisions were faced with the equal of more than three panzer divisions and five infantry divisions.[3]

On 23 June Rokossovskiy opened the offensive against Jordan's Ninth Army with an artillery barrage beginning at 0200. On the northern flank at Rogachev, on the Dnieper River 60 kilometers east of Bobruysk, in Müller's XII Corps sector, the 40th Corps commanded by General V. S. Kuznetsov (129th, 169th, and 283rd Rifle Divisions) of Gorbatov's 3rd Army began with a shattering artillery barrage lasting 45 minutes and then launched regiment-sized attacks on the 267th Infantry and 18th Panzergrenadier Divisions.[4]

In the south, the first echelon of Batov's 65th Army, composed of five rifle divisions (69th, 37th Guard, 15th, 193rd, and 75th Guard Divisions) of General D. F. Alekseev's 105th Corps and Ivanov's 18th Corps, launched twenty-five separate attacks of battalion and regimental size over a 40-kilometer front against the 35th and 36th German Infantry Divisions. The usual attack consisted of three rifle battalions with heavy artillery support. The initial attacks were made without tank support and were contained by German local reserves. However, Jordan pulled a regiment from General Herrlein's LV Corps and moved it behind the 35th German Division, where the main attack was anticipated from Batov's army.[5]

Despite the shattering attacks on 23 June, the German defenders maintained a cohesive front. Rokossovskiy held most of his armored components directly under front control. On the right, reserves were poised in the rear of Batov's 65th Army ready to form mobile columns that would flood into the German rear once the front was broken. The southern breakthrough had much more armored support. Lieutenant General I. A. Pliev's Horse-Mechanized Group, composed of Pliev's 4th Guard Cavalry Corps, the 1st Mechanized Corps commanded by General S. M. Krivoshin, and the 2nd Guard Antiaircraft Division, was in reserve astride the boundary between General Luchinskiy's 28th Army and Batov's 65th Army. The 1st Guard Tank Corps under General Panov was behind Ivanov's 18th Corps of Batov's army.

The 2nd Guard Cavalry Corps commanded by General V. V. Kryukov and the 7th Guard Cavalry Corps under General M. P. Konstantinov were behind the left flank of the 1st White Russian Front along with the 11th Tank Corps and the 8th Guard Tank Corps, units that did not take part in the White Russian operation but were available. These four corps had been transferred to the 1st White Russian Front in April and May. With a total of three tank corps, a mechanized corps, and two cavalry corps, the 1st White Russian Front had the equivalent of two tank armies. With cavalry instead of motorized infantry, Pliev's Horse-Mechanized Group functioned more efficiently than a tank army in the swampy ground south of the Berezina River.

Other 1st White Russian Front reserve troops had included three tank destroyer brigades (1st, 41st, and 3rd Guard), the 1070th Tank Destroyer Regiment, four antiaircraft divisions, three antiaircraft regiments, eight guard mortar regiments, the 35th Mortar Brigade (with guard status), the 5th Guard Mortar Division, and two artillery divisions with a total of nine brigades.

Additional units were added to the 1st White Russian reserve in June. The Stavka Reserve sent the 1st Guard Tank Corps and the 30th Light Artillery Brigade. From the Orel Military District came the 12th Artillery Division, a major increase in the firepower of the 1st White Russian Front. The Moscow Military District added the 4th Corps Artillery Brigade and the 122nd Long-Range Howitzer Brigade, and the Kharkov Military District supplied the 124th Heavy Howitzer Brigade. A total of nine artillery and mortar brigades were added to the eight present. Seventeen artillery brigades was an impressive artillery resource. That some major armored units were not even required to participate indicated the vast resources available to the Red Army.

On the northern flank of the Bobruysk operation, Gorbatov's 3rd Army included six rifle corps, an unusually large number of troops for one army headquarters. The 42nd Rifle Corps commanded by General K. S. Kolganov was transferred to the 48th Army to the south before 23 June. With the transfer of the 42nd Corps and the 115th Fortified Region to the 48th Army, the sector of the 3rd Army was greatly reduced, shedding the responsibility of 50 kilometers of front. The two assault corps (Zholudev's 35th and Urbanovich's 41st) were tightly packed on less than 10 kilometers of front opposite the northern portion of the 134th German Division sector. The two corps along with Andreyev's 29th and Kolganov's 42nd Corps of the 48th Army commanded by General P. L. Romanenko launched a four corps attack on a 20-kilometer front against the 134th and 296th German Infantry Divisions.

The northern sector of Gorbatov's 3rd Army front was held by the 40th Corps commanded by General Kuznetsov and the 80th Corps under General I. L. Ragulya spread out on a wide front to the north facing the 57th German Division. The 46th Corps under General Erastov was in reserve.

Gorbatov's 3rd Army was well supported by a huge armored component on 23 June, including a tank corps, four tank regiments, and ten assault gun regiments. Of the ten assault gun regiments, four came from the 1st Ukrainian Front in June, the 8th Assault Gun Brigade came from the 1st White Russian Front reserve, and the 340th and 341st Guard Assault Gun Regiments came from the Moscow Military District. The 3rd Army included well over 500 tanks and assault guns by 23 June.

Antitank protection was more than adequate: two brigades and four regiments. With 200 heavy antitank guns, the 3rd Army had a powerful breakthrough ability and the support to destroy any German panzer-supported counterattacks.

The artillery included three artillery brigades and two regiments, a mortar brigade and two regiments, and a guard mortar brigade and four regiments, nearly equal to an artillery division. The 28th Antiaircraft Division and the 1284th Antiaircraft Regiment provided solid antiaircraft protection.

At the center of the three armies poised to take Bobruysk was General Romanenko's 48th Army with a dual mission of supporting Gorbatov's 3rd Army in the breakthrough to the north and screening the three German divisions in the triangle formed by the Dnieper and Berezina Rivers.

To relieve Gorbatov of screening duty to concentrate on the assault, Kolganov's 42nd Rifle Corps and the 115th Fortified Region were transferred in June from the 3rd Army to the 48th Army, almost doubling the latter's sector. Occupying nearly 50 kilometers of the front, the 115th Fortified Region held almost half of the army sector. The 53rd Corps under General I. A. Gartsev also had a screening mission and held over 25 kilometers. The remaining two corps, Kolganov's 42nd and Andreev's 29th, were tightly compressed to the north of Rogachev to assist in the breakthrough by Gorbatov's 3rd Army.

Romanenko's 48th Army had few army troops before 1 June: an artillery brigade, two assault gun regiments, an antiaircraft regiment, a tank regiment, a tank destroyer regiment, and a mortar regiment. In June this army received an artillery division, an antiaircraft division, a tank regiment, and an assault gun regiment.

The role of most of the 48th Army was to hold the German units along the Dnieper and the front south of Zhoblin that made a 90-degree turn west to the Berezina River, while Andreev's 29th and Kolganov's 42nd Corps attacked Rogachev to surround Bobruysk from the north.

South of the Berezina River, Batov's 65th Army was tightly compacted on a 20-kilometer front with the task of cracking General Weidling's XXXXI Panzer Corps line and enveloping Bobruysk from the south by pressing up the south bank of the Berezina River. On 23 June the 65th Army had Ivanov's 18th and Alekseyev's 105th Corps in line with the tank brigades of Panov's 1st Guard Tank Corps assigned to support the rifle divisions. The army also had a tank regiment and four assault gun regiments, two coming from the Kharkov Military District in May and two from the Moscow Military District in June. The army had a healthy total of 350 tanks and assault guns, equal to three panzer divisions.

The artillery component was exceptionally strong: a division, three brigades, three tank destroyer brigades and a regiment, a guard mortar brigade and three regiments, two mortar regiments, and two antiaircraft regiments.

The reinforcements added much to the 65th Army's potential of breaking through the German 35th and 36th Infantry Divisions of Jordan's Ninth Army and forming the southern pincers to surround Bobruysk. Most of Batov's units were concentrated in the 18th Corps on the left of the army sector and worked with Luchinskiy's 28th Army in breaking through the Ninth Army. By 23 June Batov's 65th Army had massive support for the breakthrough plus a major mechanized component to exploit the breakthrough with armored columns.

By contrast, the German forces were stretched very thin and had slender reserves. Facing Gorbatov's 3rd Army and the 19th Corps of the 50th Army was Müller's XII Corps, consisting of the 18th Panzergrenadier, the 267th, and the 57th Infantry Divisions. The 18th Panzergrenadier Division had six motorized infantry battalions, an armored reconnaissance battalion, and a tank battalion. This division had long experience and superior mobility.

In the center of Müller's XII Corps, the 267th Infantry Division held a wide sector across marshy ground east of the Dnieper River. The 267th Division had not suffered any unusual losses and had a high proportion of experienced soldiers; it guarded a sensitive area on the southern approach to Mogilev east of the Dnieper River.

The 57th Infantry Division of Müller's XII Corps had suffered heavy losses in the Cherkassy pocket in the Ukraine in February 1944, and had been rebuilt at the Debica Training Camp in Poland in March and April. It had a high proportion of young, inexperienced soldiers along with a cadre of men who had suffered in the disaster at Cherkassy. Not a strong division, it was assigned a wide sector to the east of the Dnieper River that led north to Mogilev in a marshy area where attack was neither expected nor launched.

The three divisions of the XII Corps were more or less a screening force covering the interval between the major communication centers of Mogilev and Bobruysk. In Fourth Army reserve, the 286th Security Division had fought the Partisans and in an emergency could be called on for front-line action.

The XXXV Corps under General Lützow held an extremely wide sector that was south of the XII Corps, stretched to the Berezina River, and covered the rail center of Bobruysk from the east. Lützow's corps included five infantry divisions: the 6th, 45th, 134th, 296th, and 383rd.

The 134th Division had never suffered heavy losses and was filled with experienced soldiers; it held a pivotal sector that was to be hit by the combined weight of most of Gorbatov's 3rd Army and Bakharov's 9th Tank Corps. Anticipating the Soviet concentration, Jordan, the Ninth Army commander, had placed units of the 707th Security Division in reserve behind the 134th Division.

Next in line, the 296th Division had never undergone a catastrophic defeat nor lost a high proportion of its men. It held a vital sector east of the Drut River, and Jordan placed elements of the 45th Infantry Division in reserve behind it.

The 6th Division, although reduced by attrition, had not been rebuilt nor joined with remnants of other divisions. Like all divisions of Army Group Center, the 6th was at full strength in June 1944 and contained a high percentage of experienced soldiers.

The 383rd Division had had no traumatic losses and presumably contained a high percentage of experienced troops.

The 45th Division had recently been reorganized and had a high percentage of young and inexperienced soldiers, but the Austrian cadre was probably of high caliber. The division held a sector east of the Berezina that was not attacked by the Russians.

In addition, the German 20th Panzer Division of the army group reserve was placed in the XXXV Corps area to the rear of the 134th and 296th Division sectors, immediately in the path of the Soviet attack that would cut off Bobruysk from the north. In June 1944 the 20th Panzer Division consisted of a single tank battalion and two panzergrenadier regiments, each with two battalions of motorized infantry. One of the infantry battalions had been replaced by recruits in April 1943, but otherwise the division had suffered from attrition rather than severe fighting. The troops were experienced, but with only a single tank battalion of about fifty tanks, the division was no match for a Soviet tank corps.

The German 707th Security Division was also in reserve in Lützow's XXXV Corps area near Bobruysk. The division was used to control Partisan activity and guard the communications system. It had only one artillery battalion and fewer heavy weapons than an infantry division.

The southern approach to Bobruysk was shielded by Weidling's XXXXI Panzer Corps consisting of the 35th, 36th, and 129th Infantry Divisions south of the Berezina River. The 35th Division had suffered no major defeats, was intact, and had experienced troops.

On the northern flank of Weidling's corps south of the Berezina River was the 36th Infantry Division, which had suffered crippling losses in the Orel offensive in July and August of 1943 and had been reduced to a battle group. The division was rebuilt but had lost many of its experienced men, and the addition of a division group as a third regiment did not help in the morale-building process. Given this situation, the division was below standard and unfortunately was assigned to a sector that would receive the brunt of the attack by Panov's 1st Guard Tank Corps, Batov's 65th Army, and Pliev's Horse-Mechanized Group.

On the southern flank of Weidling's XXXXI Panzer Corps was the 129th Infantry Division. In April 1944 two of its rifle battalions had been replaced by battalions from the 390th Field Training Division that consisted primarily of recruits. In June 1944 the division, with its high percentage of inexperienced troops, would be brushed aside to the south along with the 35th Division as the Soviet juggernaut overwhelmed the 36th Infantry Division to the north.

The quality of Jordan's Ninth Army as a whole was below that of Tippelskirch's Fourth Army. The lower quality of the divisions assigned to Jordan's army may have reflected the OKH belief that the marshy terrain was more favorable to the German defenders and therefore did not require first-class divisions. Three of the German divisions enjoyed strong defensive positions on the west bank of the Dnieper and Drut Rivers, and the other divisions held sectors of marshland adjacent to the Berezina and Dnieper Rivers. The only major east-west road passed through Rogachev in the 296th Division sector securely held by the Germans. Given terrain that was unfavorable to attackers, the Germans did not expect a major attack against that sector and therefore sacrificed quality in the XXXXI Panzer Corps.

On the second day of heavy attacks at 0400 on 24 June, Zholudev's 35th Guard and Urbanovich's 41st Guard Corps of Gorbatov's 3rd Army and Kolganov's 42nd and Andreyev's 29th Corps of Romanenko's 48th Army unleashed another earthshaking 2-hour artillery barrage on Lützow's XXXV Corps at Rogachev in the center of Jordan's Ninth Army. The planned heavy air attacks on the German 134th and 296th Division positions were delayed because of bad weather, but the weight of the attack by eleven rifle divisions of the four Soviet corps fell on two German divisions, the 134th and 296th—eleven rifle divisions against fourteen German battalions. Gorbatov's army made little headway at first because rain hampered the activity of the Red Air Force. Although he took the first line of trenches at 0800, he could move no farther. South of the 3rd Army the terrain was mostly marsh on the east bank of the Dnieper River. Kolganov's 42nd and Andreev's 29th Corps of Romanenko's army were grouped close to the 3rd Army boundary on the east bank of the Dnieper. The rain-swollen Drut River made it hazardous to bridge and made the marshlands even more impassable, especially for tanks, artillery, and heavy weapons. The weather improved in the afternoon, and the Soviet attacks intensified, supported by heavy tanks. Romanenko penetrated the first trench line after 2 hours, and the second trench line was captured at 1130, but the Germans held up any additional advance in the first defense zone until later in the day.[6]

By evening Romanenko had penetrated two more trench lines, advancing 5 kilometers west of Rogachev. The advancing Soviet infantry, with the aid of engineers, built corduroy roads with logs from felled trees to create rough paths through the marshes for the tanks and trucks. Once these roads were available, Soviet armor and truck-borne infantry overwhelmed the German 296th Division and broke into the German rear. Bakharov's 9th Tank Corps was sent in later in the day to exploit the breakthrough. The German 57th

Division on the northern fringe of the attack gave way and the Soviet tanks advanced 10 kilometers.[7]

The German 707th Division was ordered to help at 0745 on 24 June. One regiment was to march on foot from 40 kilometers northeast of Bobruysk and the other was to come by truck from 15 kilometers south of Bobruysk, a testimony to the limited mobility of the Germans in the face of the rapidly moving Soviet tank columns supported by truck-borne infantry and truck-drawn artillery. The 20th Panzer Division also was moved to Lützow's XXXV Corps area as a reserve.[8]

In the south on 24 June, Batov's 65th Army had a successful day, advancing in Weidling's XXXXI Panzer Corps sector and piercing all five German trench lines in the first defense zone. On the right flank of Batov's army near Parichi, 60 kilometers southeast of Bobruysk, a thundering 2-hour barrage in Alekseev's 105th Corps sector began at 0500, followed by repeated air strikes that included heavy bombers. The 75th Guard Division led the attack on the German 36th Division trenches.[9]

The relentless artillery and air attacks began in Ivanov's 18th Corps sector at 0700 on 24 June. At 0900 the 69th and 37th Guard Divisions of Ivanov's corps assaulted the first line of the German 35th Infantry Division trenches and by 1300 had pierced the entire first defense zone with the help of massive air support. By 1400 Ivanov was through the gap in the German line and advanced swiftly to the northwest.[10]

At noon Batov sent the second echelon, composed of more rifle divisions and Panov's 1st Guard Tank Corps, through the gap created by Alekseyev's corps between the German 35th and 36th Divisions. Panov's tank corps attacked at 1800 on 24 June, supported by the 75th, 69th, 15th, and 37th Guard and 354th Rifle Divisions. Panov made steady progress, advancing 20 kilometers, despite some trouble with German Ferdinand assault guns. The Soviet tank destroyer regiments were major players in dispatching the tanks and assault guns supporting the inevitable German counterattacks. The entire 3rd Guard Tank Destroyer Brigade (sixty-three guns) supported Panov's 1st Guard Tank Brigade. At 1600 the tank corps with help from the artillery and aircraft was through the German line and driving northwest toward Bobruysk.[11]

Given the serious nature of the breakthroughs in the south, at 1130 on 24 June, the 20th Panzer Division was ordered to move quickly to 20 kilometers south of Bobruysk at Stasevka behind Weidling's XXXXI Panzer Corps area. The panzers were ordered to move at night beginning at 2100, and were expected to complete the switch by 0900 on 25 June. Several infantry battalions were ordered to move from Herrlein's LV Corps on the southern flank of Jordan's 9th Army.[12]

Before the 20th Panzer Division could close the gap, one of its combat teams was ordered to counterattack in the north. At 1430 on 24 June, most of the 20th Panzer Division was trying to stop the advance of Gorbatov's 3rd Army in the north. By evening Gorbatov had been stopped in the north, but Romanenko's 48th Army in the center continued to advance.[13]

By 1700 on 24 June, Batov's 65th Army had opened a gap 30 kilometers wide and 10 kilometers deep between the German 35th and 36th Divisions. Batov continued to move forward after nightfall, moving a total of 20 kilometers during the day, and reached a point only 8 kilometers from the railroad leading south from Bobruysk. At 2330 the 20th Panzer Division was ordered to assist the 35th Division in closing the gap.[14]

All during the night of 24–25 June, Soviet forces continued to assault Lützow's XXXV Corps west of the Berezina River. In the morning of 25 June, the German 36th Division was driven 5 kilometers back to Zdudichi, half way to Parichi, by Alekseyev's 105th Corps. Batov's 65th Army, led by Panov's 1st Guard Tank Corps and the 3rd Guard Tank Destroyer Brigade, pushed northwest along the Berezina River, advancing 40 kilometers by noon.[15]

Welcome relief for Lützow's XXXV Corps was, however, arriving. At 0600 on 25 June, the motorized elements of the 20th Panzer Division were arriving in the German 35th Division sector. The panzer division was ordered to assist the German 36th Division until the trains carrying the tanks arrived. However, by the time the German tanks were unloaded at 1130, Panov's tanks had moved an additional 6 kilometers to Kovichitsy, more than halfway to Bobruysk. The remnants of the German 35th Division linked up with the 129th Division of Herrlein's LV Corps, leaving a yawning hole of over 40 kilometers in the German line.[16]

The 20th Panzer Division's counterattack was futile. Alekseev's 105th Corps continued to advance and drove the German 36th Division back to Parichi. By 1700 on 25 June, the 35th Division sector was falling apart. The railway leading south from Bobruysk was cut at Zelenkovichi, 40 kilometers south of Bobruysk, and 200 truckloads of Soviet infantry were rolling west. The Russians again built corduroy roads of logs through the marsh to bypass the German roadblocks and move the tanks and trucks around the German positions.[17] (See Map 10.1.)

In the north at Rogachev on 25 June, Lützow's XXXV Corps continued to be pounded by Soviets forces. Kolganov's 42nd and Andreev's 29th Corps of Romanenko's 48th Army crossed the Drut

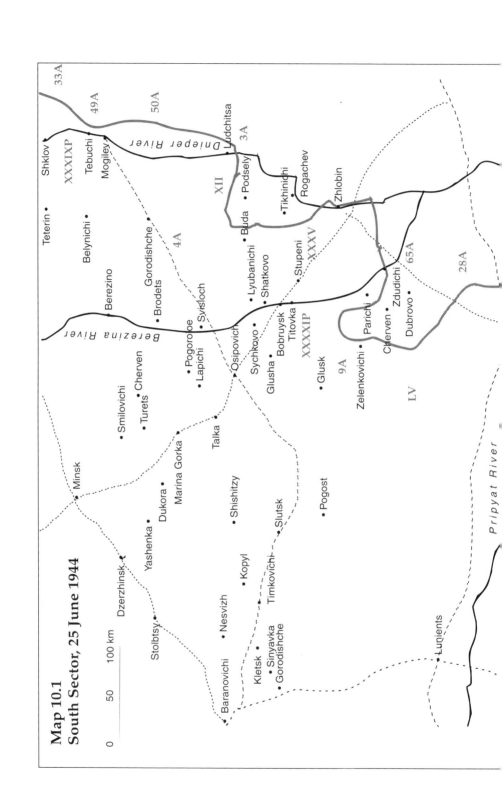

Map 10.1
South Sector, 25 June 1944

River north of Rogachev, but made little progress against the German 296th Division. At 1000 on 25 June, Zholudev's 35th and Urbanovich's 41st Corps of Gorbatov's 3rd Army attacked the 134th German Division. At noon Bakharov's 9th Tank Corps joined in the assault after changing sectors to advance through a marsh where German defenses were weak. The tank corps crossed the Mogilev-Bobruysk road and quickly advanced 10 kilometers toward Bobruysk during the day, reaching the Dobritsa River by evening. Kuznetsov's 40th, Urbanovich's 41st, and Ragulya's 80th Rifle Corps of Gorbatov's 3rd Army followed Bakharov's 9th Tank Corps, which had ample air support. The gap between the Lützow's XXXV Corps and the German 57th Division to the north opened to 15 kilometers, but Gorbatov's 3rd and Romanenko's 48th Armies made far less headway than Batov's 65th Army.[18]

In the center, Jordan wanted to pull back the three German divisions (6th, 383rd, and 45th) between the Berezina and Dnieper Rivers at Zhlobin to provide reserves to stop the Soviet advances to the north and south. Jordan proposed that the entire army be pulled back to Bobruysk to save it from being encircled by Soviet pincers from the north and south. Busch, Army Group Center commander, refused to allow the withdrawal on the mistaken grounds that the Russians could not move supplies through the marshlands in the gaps in Jordan's front and would soon be forced to halt. Busch was unaware of the capabilities of the American-built 2.5-ton trucks and the impact that large numbers of these trucks had on bolstering the Red Army's logistics system.[19]

At 2230 on 25 June, Jordan told Busch that the Soviet units were attacking with more than 300 tanks in two tank corps and a cavalry corps, while the 20th Panzer Division had only 40 tanks. Again Jordan wanted to withdraw, but Busch repeated the foolhardy instructions from Hitler that Zhlobin must be held. Regardless of the order, the Ninth Army pulled out regiments and battalions from the divisions in the Zhlobin salient on 25 June to form combat groups in an attempt to shore the defenses to the north and south.[20]

By midnight of 25 June, Lützow's XXXV Corps in the north was being forced west of the Dnieper and Drut by Gorbatov's 3rd Army supported by Bakharov's tank corps and two corps of Romanenko's 48th Army. The Russians were driving due west toward Bobruysk and threatening to cut off six German divisions (134th, 296th, 6th, 383rd, 45th, and 36th) in a pocket southwest of Bobruysk. By 25 June the refusal to permit the retreat of the divisions at Zhlobin was these divisions' doom. The XXXV Corps was falling apart, and finally the German 383rd Division was ordered to move by truck out of the Zhoblin salient to Bobruysk at 0900 on 26 June.[21]

By midnight of 25 June, Weidling's XXXXI Corps was split apart. On the north side of the gap, the 36th Division was at Parichi, while on the south side, the remnant of the 35th Division was at Kovichitsy and Zelenkovichi with the 20th Panzer Division. Jordan's entire 9th Army front was collapsing under massive attacks.[22]

By the morning of 26 June, Panov's 1st Guard Tank Corps, with 252 tanks and assault guns, and the Pliev Horse-Mechanized Group, with 321 tanks and assault guns, had passed through the gap in Weidling's XXXXI Corps sector. The 1st Guard Tank Corps was 20 kilometers southwest of Bobruysk with few Germans available to stop it. The German 35th Division was on the Ptich River west of the railroad south of Bobruysk with a 40-kilometer gap between the two divisions (35th and 36th) and Bobruysk to the northwest. The 35th Division was ordered to hold wherever possible, and although this division did launch some counterattacks, Weidling's XXXXI Corps was disintegrating.[23]

At 0900 on 26 June, the 20th Panzer Division was ordered to abandon the 35th Infantry Division and move north to block Panov's advancing 1st Guard Tank Corps southwest of Bobruysk to close the gap. General Kurt Zeitler, Chief of the German General Staff, was furious that the 20th Panzer Division had been used first to help the 35th Division, and then was being moved in a roundabout route to try to protect Bobruysk, thus wasting valuable time.[24]

During 26 June Panov's tank corps and Alekseev's 105th Rifle Corps bypassed Parichi and pressed northward toward Bobruysk. At 1015 Panov was 15 kilometers south of Bobruysk on the Parichi road west of the Berezina River. By evening the tank corps had reached Titovka, a few kilometers south of Bobruysk, and had taken an essential bridge over the Berezina.[25]

During the evening of 26 June, the German 36th Division was able to hold Parichi on the west bank of the Berezina with elements of the 20th Panzer Division. The 16th Air Army commanded by General S. I. Rudenko flew 526 sorties to assist Panov's 1st Guard Tank Corps at Titovka north of Parichi. By nightfall the 36th Division had retreated across the river to join with remnants of Lützow's XXXV Corps, also retreating from the Zhoblin salient. With the support of Alekseev's 105th Rifle Corps, Panov continued north on the Parichi road and was within 6 kilometers of Bobruysk by evening.[26]

Fighting continued during the night as Batov's 65th Army followed elements of Panov's 1st Guard Tank Corps around Bobruysk and cut all the roads to the west and northwest. Batov reached Osipovichi, more than 50 kilometers northwest of Bobruysk, by evening.[27]

Northwest of Bobruysk on 26 June, Bakharov's 9th Tank Corps crossed Lützow's XXXV Corps rear to the north with a lightning stroke that reached Startsy by evening, cutting the main road to Mogilev. Bakharov caught up with the columns of retreating Germans, and his tanks shot up the trucks, while the German troops fled into the forest. The trapped Germans blew up their trucks, blocking the road and delaying the 9th Tank Corps. Zholudev's 35th and Urbanovich's 41st Corps followed closely behind the tanks.

Gorbatov's 3rd Army crossed the Berezina at Titovka, drove through the German 134th and 707th Divisions, and headed direct for Bobruysk. By noon of 26 June, the 707th German Division was isolated at Buda, and the 134th Division at Tikhinichi was under heavy attack from the 3rd Army. The XXXV Corps turned and tried to break out to the north, but was stopped by Gorbatov. The 296th, 6th, and 45th Divisions were all being pushed west toward the Berezina River south of Bobruysk by Romanenko's 48th Army. By 1900 on 26 June, the 134th German Division was shattered and in flight and Bakharov's 9th Tank Corps was 15 kilometers from Bobruysk, about to cut the road to Mogilev.[28]

Soviet aircraft continually attacked the Germans on the roads. Throughout 26 June the 20th Panzer Division, in its moving from the Weidling's XXXXI Corps sector in the south to Parichi, was held south of Bobruysk by air attacks. During the first 3 days of the offensive, Rudenko's 16th Air Army flew 8,000 sorties against Army Group Center.[29]

By the evening of 26 June, Romanenko's 48th Army had captured Zhoblin and pursued the three divisions of Lützow's XXXV Corps to the west. Romanenko crossed the Berezina River at Stupeni, 10 kilometers south of Bobruysk.[30] Panov's 1st Guard Tank Corps and elements of Romanenko's army were northwest of Bobruysk by the end of the day. Throughout 26 June the Soviet armored columns had bypassed German road blocks and were roaming freely in the German rear through gaps north and south of Bobruysk. The German divisions that had tarried in the Zhoblin salient were desperately trying to escape under continuous attacks.[31]

During the night of 26–27 June, Soviet heavy bombers struck Bobruysk with a pattern bombing raid. At midnight Panov's 1st Guard Tank Corps with over 200 tanks cut the road into Bobruysk at Titovka, a few kilometers southeast of the city, isolating the German 36th Division at Parichi to the south.[32]

At 0815 on the morning of 27 June, Romanenko's 48th Army attacked and drove remnants of German divisions into Bobruysk. A German counterattack at Titovka against Bakharov's 9th Tank Corps by the 383rd Infantry Division and a tank battalion and panzergrenadier battalion of the 20th Panzer Division cost the Germans many casualties but did not reopen the road. The last effort to take a bridge across the Berezina failed, and most of the 20th Panzer Division and remnants of several other divisions were trapped on the east side of the Berezina. At 1130 another German attack at Titovka opened a railway bridge, the only avenue of escape for a mob of Germans fleeing to Bobruysk.[33] Some German troops were able to cross the Berezina into Bobruysk despite continuous Soviet air attacks. At 1900 526 aircraft attacked the Germans around Titovka.[34]

On the east bank of the Berezina River, the German 296th, 6th, and 45th Divisions from the Zhoblin salient retreated to within 4 kilometers of Bobruysk under pressure from Romanenko's 48th Army. During the morning, German air reconnaissance detected from 3,000 to 4,000 trucks and wagons on the road from Zhlobin to Bobruysk, only 10 kilometers southeast of Bobruysk. North of Bobruysk, the German 707th and 134th Divisions were retreating to the River Ola under constant attack by the 3rd Army. An armored column of Gorbatov's 3rd Army was closing the noose from the east, reaching Shatkovo on the Berezina River a few kilometers north of Bobruysk. Bakharov's 9th Tank Corps cut all the roads and bridges over the Berezina northeast and east of Bobruysk.[35]

At 1700 on 27 June, Lützow's XXXV Corps stopped trying to break through at Titovka and turned north to link up with the 707th and 134th Divisions retreating north between the Drut and Berezina Rivers. Gorbatov drove west during the evening through the gap between the German 707th and 57th Divisions to the north and reached the Berezina at Lyubanichi, 40 kilometers north of Bobruysk. By 2230 the 3rd and 48th Armies had hunted down and killed or captured the survivors of Lützow's XXXV Corps trying to escape to the north.[36]

To the west, at 0430 on 27 June, twenty-five tanks of Bakharov's 9th Tank Corps had reached Osipovichi, 40 kilometers northwest of Bobruysk, and cut the rail line to Minsk. At 0700 Jordan ordered the 383th Division to hold Bobruysk, while the rest of the Germans trapped in Bobruysk tried to break out of the pocket in a northwest direction along the railroad to Osipovichi. Busch countermanded the order at 0915, demanding that all efforts be made to reopen the roads, but to hold fast. At 1600 on 27 June, Hitler changed his mind and ordered Jordan to fight his way out northwest along the railroad to Osipovichi, leaving the 383th Division behind to hold Bobruysk, the same order that had been reversed that morning.[37]

At 1600 on the same day, Alekseev's 105th Corps, Bakharov's 9th Tank Corps, and Panov's 1st Guard Tank Corps attacked Bobruysk from the northwest and south. The German battle groups, hastily assembled in the city, were pushed into a smaller and smaller circle but fought tenaciously and refused to surrender.[38]

During the evening of 27 June to the northwest, at Osipovichi on the escape route from Bobruysk, a battle group under General Lindig, consisting of stragglers and an engineer battalion, was forced to give ground as Panov's tank corps drove toward Minsk.[39] Battle Group von Bergen was formed in Minsk with a training division headquarters and security battalions to protect Minsk until the 12th Panzer Division could be unloaded from incoming trains. By the evening of 27 June, a tank company and two motorized infantry companies of the 12th Panzer Division had arrived.[40]

By nightfall on 27 June, Lützow's XXXV and Weidling's XXXXI Panzer Corps were fleeing north on both sides of the Berezina River pursued by armored columns of Panov's 1st Guard Tank Corps and Bakharov's 9th Tank Corps. Bobruysk was surrounded, and the Russians were reducing the pocket. For the Germans one thread of hope was the arrival of the 12th Panzer Division and a battle group built around the 390th Field Training Division, but this was a feeble response to the advancing juggernaut.

During 28 June Hitler was reluctant to move the German panzer divisions at Kovel to help the beleaguered Army Group Center because he anticipated an attack by the 1st White Russian and 1st Ukrainian Fronts. To facilitate the allocation of reserves, Hitler made Field Marshal Model commander of both Army Group North Ukraine and Center, allowing Model to decide how much he should weaken the Kovel area in favor of Army Group Center.[41]

Jordan's Ninth Army was in desperate straits, with isolated units scattered over 150 kilometers on the morning of 28 June. Most of the army, from 40,000 to 70,000 men, were trapped around Bobruysk. A wide gap yawned between the fragments of Jordan's army and the German Second Army to the south, and another gap had opened between the fleeing XXXV Corps and the remnants of Tippelskirch's Fourth Army still holding south of Borisov.[42]

A flood of German stragglers poured into Bobruysk during the night of 27–28 June, including units of the 20th Panzer Division and the 36th, 45th, 707th, and 134th Infantry Divisons. At 0400 on 28 June, Romanenko's 48th Army, Alekseev's 105th Corps, and Panov's 1st Guard Tank Corps attacked the city from the south, east, and west, while Gorbatov's 3rd Army pressed in from the north. The 16th Air Army launched heavy raids on the city, trying to break the morale of the defenders.

The German commander in Bobruysk continually requested permission from Army Group Center to break out during the day; the response was to leave one division in Bobruysk and allow the others to try to escape. The closest established German line was over 50 kilometers to the northeast at Osipovichi.[43]

At noon on 28 June, the pressure west of Osipovichi on the German 12th Panzer Division and the 390th Training Division decreased, and a line was formed by Battle Group von Bergen at Talka, about 30 kilometers northwest of Osipovichi. The respite probably was the result of Gorbatov's 3rd and Romanenko's 48th Armies turning south to clean up Bobruysk and blocking the German breakout at Svisloch, rather than pressing on to Minsk. At any rate, Panov's 1st Guard Tank Corps and Batov's 65th Army were stalled at Osipovichi.[44]

On 28 June most of the fresh 12th Panzer Division had arrived at Marina Gorka on the Ptich River, 50 kilometers northwest of Osipovichi and 55 kilometers south of Minsk. The panzer division had three possible courses: first, to help delay Panov's 1st Guard Tank Corps in moving up the main road to Minsk from Bobruysk; second, to delay Bakharov's 9th Tank Corps from threatening the southern flank of Tippelskirch's 4th Army; and, third, to move down to Slutsk to help the 4th Panzer Division stop the Pliev Horse-Mechanized Group that had broken through north of Herrlein's LV Corps. The decision was made to use the 12th Panzer Division along with Battle Groups von Bergen and Lindig to stop Panov's 1st Guard Tank Corps and Batov's 65th Army at Talka on the main road to Minsk.[45]

Finally, shortly after noon on 28 June, Hitler gave permission for all units to abandon Bobruysk. Romanenko's 48th Army relieved the 3rd and 65th Armies during the day and took on the task of cleaning out the city. The German defenders counterattacked with tanks and assault guns, destroying many Soviet tanks, but by evening the 48th Army had taken 6,000 prisoners.[46] At 2300 that night the German breakout began. It was led by the 20th Panzer Division, with the 383rd Division being the last to leave at 0200 on 29 June. From 10,000 to 15,000 Germans with a dozen assault guns and tanks led the breakout, attacking the 356th Rifle Division and the 1st Guard Motorized Brigade of Batov's 65th Army. Despite Soviet efforts to reinforce the northwest sector of the ring, the Germans broke through the 356th Rifle Division in a series of attacks launched at 2330 on 29 June. Even though the Germans suffered severe losses, they managed to escape. At 0230 on 30 June, the Germans were through the Soviet line and had reached Sychkovo, halfway to Osipovichi, while the rear guard troops were still fighting in Bobruysk. At Sychkovo the Germans met the 15th Guard Tank Brigade of Panov's tank corps that was rolling up the main road to Minsk, but the Germans managed to keep moving.[47]

At 0300 on the morning of 29 June, the first elements of the main group of Germans fighting their way out of Bobruysk were at Svisloch, while the rear guard, the German 383rd Division, was pulling out of the Bobruysk. The soldiers of this division suffered heavy losses but managed to escape.[48]

At 1000 on 29 June, the final attack on the city was launched by Gorbatov's 3rd Army from the north, Batov's 65th from the south, and Romanenko's 48th Army from the east. The 1st Guard Motorized Brigade, the 1001st Assault Gun Regiment, and the 455th Mortar Regiment advanced into Bobruysk from the north, while the 15th and 16th Guard Tank Brigades joined with Alekseev's 105th Rifle Corps in the final attack from the southwest. The 354th and 356th Rifle Divisions led the way in crossing the Berezina River from east of Bobruysk. However, the German 383rd Division was still fighting on the northern fringe of the city at 1300.[49]

By 1700 on 29 June, the German breakout group led by the 20th Panzer Division was near Svisloch, only 20 kilometers from the German battle groups blocking the road to Minsk south of Marina Gorka. Battle Group Lindig had assumed command of the 12th Panzer Division and Group von Bergen at noon, and was holding a line south of Marina Gorka astride the main road at Talka, 80 kilometers southwest of Minsk.[50]

However, both flanks of the blocking force were open, and the Russians were advancing though both gaps. Ivanov's 18th Corps of Batov's 65th Army, led by the 17th Guard Tank Brigade of Panov's 1st Guard Tank Corps, was advancing from Osipovichi. Ivanov bypassed Group Lindig to the south and headed west on 29 June toward Baranovichi.[51]

The 17th Guard Tank Brigade was the core of a combat team driving toward Marina Gorka with a tank destroyer regiment, an assault gun regiment, and an engineer battalion. The team advanced from Svisloch, driving back the 12th Panzer Division, and crossed the Svisloch River at Lapichi, halfway between Svisloch and Talka, threatening the southern flank of Tippelskirch's Fourth Army.[52]

The Germans did not use the 12th Panzer Division to protect the flank of the Fourth Army at Cherven because German panzer units were unable to leave the roads in the forests, as could the Russians, and could bring only the leading tanks of the attacking unit to bear. Therefore the 12th Panzer Division was committed to defending the road to Minsk, but only half of that division had arrived by the evening of 29 June to face Panov's 1st Guard Tank Corps and Batov's 65th Army moving northwest from Osipovichi.[53]

At midnight on 29–30 June, Hitler designated Minsk a fortified city, and Jordan's Ninth Army was ordered to improve its defenses. At that time, there were only 1,800 stragglers and limited-service men in the city. On the road to Minsk at Talka, halfhearted attacks by Panov's 1st Guard Tank Corps were repelled by a battalion of the 12th Panzer Division. By late afternoon more elements of Batov's 65th Army were arriving at Talka.[54]

A new Soviet adversary, Burdeyniy's 2nd Guard Tank Corps of Galitskiy's 11th Guard Army, had raced through the gap between Orsha and Mogilev and reached the Berezina River at Svisloch. The 12th Panzer Division counterattacked with three panzergrenadier battalions, a tank battalion, and three artillery battalions from Lapichi. The panzer division managed to keep the door ajar for the fleeing survivors of Lützow's XXXV Corps. The attack saved 10,000 German troops, but the remaining 60,000 Germans who had escaped from Bobruysk were killed or captured.[55]

Battle Group Hoffmeister, about 30,000 men of Lützow's XXXV Corps that had broken out of Bobruysk, reached the bridge at Svisloch before noon and reported that the group had lost 12,500 men and was short of rations, medical supplies, and ammunition. By late afternoon of 29 June, the Germans had been driven out of Svisloch by Burdeyniy's 2nd Guard Tank Corps and were fighting their way north under heavy pressure from Gorbatov's 3rd Army. At 1500 the 12th Panzer Division was ordered to try to aid the fleeing survivors on the morning of 30 June.[56] (See Map 10.2.)

Panov's 1st Guard Tank Corps and other units of Batov's 65th Army were moving west from Osipovichi to Shishitsy, bypassing the Germans at Talka and threatening Minsk from the south. Battle Group Meinecke, less than a battalion, was sent south to block the advance. At 2000 on 29 June, 700 Soviet tanks and trucks and 5,000 men were reported advancing toward Shishitsy.[57]

Batov's 65th and Gorbatov's 3rd Armies were driving the survivors of Lützow's XXXV and Weidling's XXXXI Corps northwest, toward Minsk between the Ptich River on the west and the Berezina on the east. Moving so fast, the Russians were threatening to cut into the rear of Tippelskirch's Fourth Army. The 12th Panzer Division was shuttled about in an attempt to halt the progress of the Soviet armored columns across a 70-kilometer-wide gap, but the panzers could do little more than delay the Soviet columns for a few hours.

At 0200 on 1 July, a battalion of the 12th Panzer Division attacked Svisloch in an attempt to rescue Group Hoffmeister, which had about 35,000 men moving north out of Bobruysk and was cut off from the 12th Panzer Division by Burdeyniy's 2nd Guard Tank Corps in Svisloch. The 12th Panzer Division attack was beaten off, but about 15,000 unarmed Germans were able to cross the river south of Svisloch during the day and walk to Marina Gorka, 50 kilometers to the west, within the next few days. At Marina Gorka the

Map 10.2
South Sector, 30 June 1944

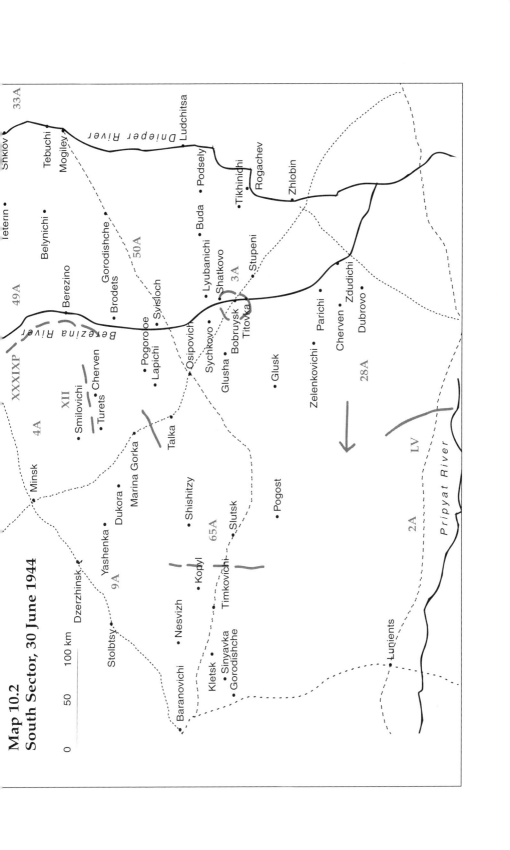

0   50   100 km

Minsk

Dzerzhinsk

Stolbtsy

Yashenka

Dukora

Marina Gorka

9A

Baranovichi

Nesvizh

Kopyl

Kletsk

Sinyavka

Gorodishche

Timkovichi

Slutsk

65A

Shishitzy

Talka

Pogost

Lunjents

2A

Pripyat River

LV

28A

Zelenkovichi

Parichi

Cherven

Zdudichi

Dubrovo

Glusk

Glusha

Bobruysk

Titovka

Sychkovo

Osipovich

Pogoroboe

Lapichi

Sysloch

Turets

Cherven

Smilovichi

XII

XXXIXP

4A

49A

Berezina River

Berezino

Brodets

Gorodishche

50A

Lyubanichi

Shatkovo

3A

Stupeni

Buda

Podsely

Tikhinichi

Rogachev

Zhlobin

Ludchitsa

Dnieper River

Mogilev

Tebuchi

Belynichi

Teterin

Shklov

33A

survivors from Bobruysk boarded trains for Minsk and beyond. At 1830 on 1 July, the stream of survivors had ceased, and the panzer-grenadier battalion retreated westward 20 kilometers to Pogoroloe northeast of Lapichi after midnight.[58]

Battle Group Lindig, including the major part of the German 12th Panzer Division and the 390th Security Division, was still hold-ing Panov's 1st Guard Tank Corps and Batov's 65th Army on a nar-row front at Lapichi and Talka, but the Russians were outflanking them on the north and south. From the north, Gorbatov's 3rd Army was pouring through a gap south of Cherven, threatening to out-flank Group Lindig from the south. South of Marina Gorka, Batov was overwhelming Group Meinecke, north of Shishitsy, which was trying to screen the gap between Jordan's Ninth Army and Herrlein's LV Corps far to the south.[59]

Gorbatov and Batov sent armored columns around the flanks of Group Lindig to head for Minsk, while Romanenko's 48th Army continued to push remnants of Tippelskirch's army west. To avoid encirclement, at noon on 1 July, Battle Group Lindig was ordered to withdraw during the evening to a line just east of Marina Gorka, and it did so by 0200 on 2 July.[60] Marshal Model abandoned any hope of holding Minsk on 1 July, and ordered Jordan to withdraw to the edge of the Nalibotski Forest between Stolbtsy and Molodechno.[61]

During the morning of 2 July, Battle Group Lindig held Marina Gorka for a few hours, but by noon was driven north by Panov's 1st Guard Tank Corps. During the afternoon, the battle group, including the 390th Training Division with six security battalions, tried to hold a line 10 kilometers east of Dukora and was ordered to move back to Dukora by evening. However, by the afternoon of 2 July, Panov had pursued Battle Group Lindig to Dukora, only 20 kilometers from Minsk. Later in the day, Panov forced the battle group west along a road from Dukora to Stolbtsy, leaving the southern flank of the Fourth Army and the road to Minsk open. To the south of Dukora, Battle Group Meinecke was screening the gap between Slutsk and Dukora.[62]

In Minsk fifty-three trains loaded with 15,000 unarmed German survivors were stranded as the rail lines were cut, and stragglers interested only in escape refused to help defend the city. By 2 July Model had abandoned Minsk and concentrated Battle Group Lindig with the German 12th Panzer Division south of Stolbtsy.[63]

On the night of 2–3 July, the 12th Panzer Division set off for Stolbtsy, passing between Dukora and Minsk at 0600 on 3 July. The bad roads were clogged with hundreds of Germans fleeing on foot, but many of the refugees were picked up as replacements for the division. The 5th Panzergrenadier Regiment joined Battle Group Meinecke to protect the movement from the south by forming a screen around Yashenka, 25 kilometers west of Dukora. Despite repeated Soviet attacks, the screen held until the 12th Panzer Division had reached Stolbtsy during the evening of 3 July. Only a few stragglers survived from Battle Group Lindig, which had included the 390th Training Division.[64]

By 3 July Jordan's Ninth Army, which held the sector east of Bobruysk, had been reduced to prisoners in Soviet camps and unarmed stragglers desperate to escape. Model abandoned Minsk and concentrated his forces to delay the Soviet drive southwest toward the rail center at Baranovichi. The Red Army's destruction of the German Ninth Army was a devastating loss that left a gaping hole in German defenses.

However, logistics did finally catch up with the Russians. Faced by a German panzer division, the 1st Guard Tank Corps needed ammunition and fuel. Separated from supply depots by nearly 300 kilometers, trucks needed 4 days to make a round-trip. The need to repair the railroads destroyed by the retreating Germans and to move supply depots closer to the front was as much a factor in the pause in the offensive as the arrival of German reinforcements.

As supplies arrived, the attack resumed but at a slower pace. In the days following the battle for Bobruysk, the Russians would clean up numerous pockets of Germans east of Minsk and regroup to begin the second phase of the operation. The blitzkrieg was over, and advances through alerted German defenses would exact a high price.

Notes

1. G. Niepold, *The Battle for White Russia: The Destruction of Army Group Centre, June 1944* (London: Brassey's, 1987), pp. 75–77; Werner von Haupt, *Geschichte der 134. Infanterie Division* (Weinsberg: Herausgegeben vom Kamardenkreis der Ehemaligen, 134. Inf.-Division, 1971), p. 220.

2. A. M. Samsanov, ed., *Osvobozhdenie Belorussii, 1944* (Moscow: Nauka, 1974), p. 359.

3. Ibid., pp. 626, 630; A. I. Radzievskii, *Army Operations: USSR Reports, Military Affairs* (Washington, D.C.: Foreign Broadcast Information Service, 1985), pp. 16–17, 27–28; P. Akulov and G. Tolokol'nikov, eds., *V Boiakh za Belorussiu* (Minsk: Belarus, 1970), pp. 284–285.

4. Niepold, p. 82; Samsanov, p. 623; Paul Adair, *Hitler's Greatest Defeat: The Collapse of Army Group Centre, June 1944* (London: Arms and Armour Press, 1994), p. 114.

5. Niepold, p. 84; Akulov and Tolokol'nikov, p. 232

6. David M. Glantz and Harold S. Orenstein, eds., *Belorussia 1944: The Soviet General Staff Study* (Carlisle, Penn.: David M. Glantz, 1998), p. 110;

Albert Seaton, *The Russo-German War, 1941–45* (New York: Praeger, 1970), p. 439; Niepold, p. 99; Haupt, p. 221; Adair, pp. 114–115.

7. Niepold, pp. 93, 98–99; John Erickson, *The Road to Berlin* (Boulder, Colo.: Westview Press, 1983), pp. 221–222.

8. Niepold, p. 93.

9. Samsanov, p. 579; Niepold, pp. 98–99; Akulov and Tolokol'nikov, pp. 232–233; S. P. Kiriukhin, *43-ya Armiia v Vitebskoi Operatsii* (Moscow: Voenizdat, 1961), p. 112.

10. Samsanov, p. 579; Glantz and Orenstein, pp. 110–111; P. I. Batov, *V Pokhodakh i Boiakh* (Moscow: Voenizdat, 1966), pp. 416–419.

11. Niepold, p. 84; Samsanov, pp. 265, 508, 572, 578–579; Erickson, p. 222; Glantz and Orenstein, p. 111; Batov, pp. 419–420.

12. Niepold, pp. 93–94; Erickson, p. 223; Adair, p. 115.

13. Niepold, p. 94.

14. Ibid., p. 95.

15. Ibid., p. 107; Samsanov, pp. 508–509; Adair, pp. 116–117.

16. Niepold, p. 107.

17. Ibid., p. 108; Erickson, p. 223; Samsanov, p. 580.

18. Niepold, pp. 108, 112; Samsanov, pp. 359–60, 508; Glantz and Orenstein, pp. 113–114; F. V. Plotnikov, *v Srazheniia za Belorussi* (Minsk: Belarus, 1982), pp. 100–101; Akulov and Tolokol'nikov, p. 233; Adair, p. 117.

19. Niepold, pp. 108–109.

20. Ibid., p. 109.

21. Ibid., pp. 109, 111, 118.

22. Ibid., p. 110.

23. Ibid., pp. 120, 122; Samsanov, p. 430; Adair, p. 117.

24. Niepold, pp. 118–119; Adair, p. 118.

25. Glantz and Orenstein, p. 112; Niepold, pp. 118–119, 122, 124; Batov, pp. 421–422.

26. Niepold, pp. 124, 137; Samsanov, pp. 580, 632.

27. Glantz and Orenstein, p. 112; Niepold, p. 137; Samsanov, pp. 580, 633–635; Adair, p. 117.

28. Niepold, pp. 119, 120, 124; Samsanov, pp. 147, 580; Erickson, pp. 223–224; Glantz and Orenstein, pp. 114–115; Plotnikov, pp. 101–102.

29. Niepold, pp. 120–121, 138; Samsanov, p. 264.

30. Glantz and Orenstein, p. 115.

31. Samsanov, p. 147; Adair, p. 118; Niepold, p. 137.

32. Niepold, p. 131.

33. Ibid., p. 133; Plotnikov, pp. 68–69; Glantz and Orenstein, p. 116.

34. Niepold, pp. 131, 133; Glantz and Orenstein, pp. 117–118; Akulov and Tolokol'nikov, p. 233.

35. Niepold, pp. 131–132, 137; Samsanov, p. 147.

36. Niepold, pp. 133–134, 137.

37. Ibid., pp. 131–133; Batov, pp. 422–423; Adair, pp. 135–136.

38. Glantz and Orenstein, pp. 119–120; Plotnikov, p. 103; Akulov and Tolokol'nikov, p. 235; Niepold, p. 134.

39. Niepold, p. 134.

40. Ibid., pp. 134–135; Adair, p. 135; Rolf Hinze, *East Front Drama— 1944: The Withdrawal Battle of Army Group Center* (Winnipeg, Manitoba: J. J. Fedorowicz Publishing Inc., 1996), pp. 38–39.

41. Earl F. Ziemke, *Stalingrad to Berlin: The German Campaign in Russia, 1942–1945* (New York: Dorset Press, 1968), p. 324; Adair, pp. 136–137; Hinze, pp. 42–43.

42. Niepold, pp. 139, 143.
43. Ibid., p. 144; Adair, p. 137; Hinze, p. 42.
44. Niepold, p. 145; Glantz and Orenstein, pp. 120–121; Hinze, p. 39.
45. Niepold, p. 145; Adair, p. 139; Hinze, p. 39.
46. Samsanov, pp. 581, 635; Erickson, p. 224; Niepold, pp. 143–144; Hinze, p. 39; Glantz and Orenstein, pp. 119–120.
47. Niepold, p. 145; Samsanov, p. 635; Glantz and Orenstein, pp. 120–121; Adair, p. 138.
48. Niepold, p. 159; Samsanov, pp. 265, 581, 636; Adair, pp. 138–139.
49. Niepold, p. 163; Samsanov, pp. 149, 510; Glantz and Orenstein, p. 122; Akulov and Tolokol'nikov, p. 235; Batov, p. 425.
50. Hinze, p. 46; Niepold, p. 159.
51. Niepold, pp. 160, 163; Erickson, p. 224; Adair, p. 140; Hinze, p. 41.
52. Samsanov, pp. 636–638.
53. Hinze, p. 40; Niepold, p. 160.
54. Niepold, pp. 168, 170.
55. David M. Glantz and Jonathan M. House, *When Titans Clashed, How the Red Army Stopped Hitler* (Lawrence: The University Press of Kansas, 1995), p. 208; Niepold, pp. 168, 170, 173; Adair, pp. 140–141.
56. Adair, p. 140; Niepold, p. 169.
57. Niepold, p. 170; Adair, pp. 141–142.
58. Niepold, pp. 178–179; Adair, pp. 140–141; Hinze, pp. 47–48.
59. Niepold, pp. 178–179; Hinze, p. 49.
60. Niepold, pp. 179, 181.
61. Ibid., p. 182; Hinze, p. 50.
62. Niepold, pp. 189–190; Samsanov, pp. 150, 623; Hinze, pp. 50–51.
63. Adair, p. 128; Seaton, p. 441; Niepold, p. 190.
64. Niepold, p. 199; Adair, p. 142; Hinze, pp. 51–53.

CHAPTER 11

The Southern Shoulder

The objective of General K. K. Rokossovskiy's 1st White Russian Front armies on the southeast corner of the White Russian salient was to break through the LV and XXXXI Corps of the German Ninth Army, race west to Slutsk and Baranovichi, and block the route of German reinforcements from Kovel. The western armies of the 1st White Russian Front protected the left flank of the Soviet mobile columns that exploited the breakthrough and prevented the German Second Army from helping out to the north. (Figures 11.1 and 11.2 show the organization tables of the central and western armies of the 1st White Russian Front.)

On the first 2 days of the battle, 22 and 23 June, the three corps of General A. A. Luchinskiy's 28th Army pressured the flank of the German 35th and 129th Divisions, driving them toward the railroad south of Bobruysk. On 23 June Luchinskiy's 28th Army attacked and met with stubborn resistance. General F. I. Perkhorovich's 3rd Guard and General P. K. Batitskiy's 128th Corps drove back the southern flank of the 35th Infantry Division and, together with General Batov's 65th Army, advanced up to 10 kilometers on 24 June. On the same day, the Pliev Horse-Mechanized Group, consisting of his 4th Guard Cavalry Corps and General S. M. Krivoshein's 1st Mechanized Corps, was committed at 1630 to assist Luchinskiy against the 129th Division of Weidling's XXXXI Panzer Corps. By evening the tanks of the Pliev group had advanced 20 kilometers.[1]

The southern shoulder of the White Russian salient was held by General Herrlein's LV Corps of Jordan's Ninth Army and Weiss's Second. Only Herrlein's corps was attacked by Rokossovskiy in the opening days of the offensive; Weiss's Second Army front was quiet. Opposed to Herrlein's LV Corps was Luchinskiy's 28th Army and Pliev's Horse-Mechanized Group. Opposing Weiss along the Pripyat River were the 61st, 70th, 47th, 8th Guard, and 69th Armies, none of

Figure 11.1 Central Armies of the 1st White Russian Front

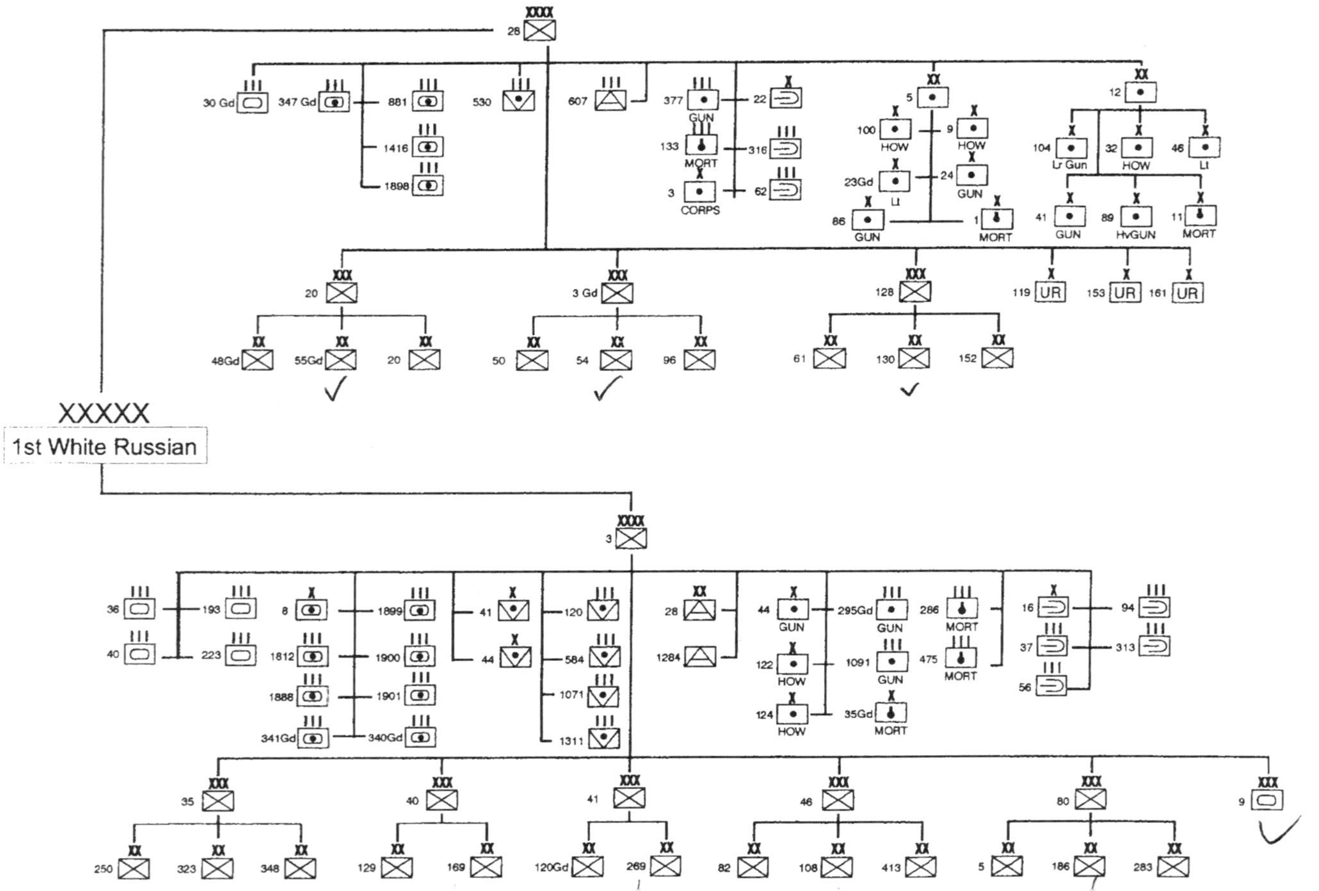

Figure 11.2 Western Armies of the 1st White Russian Front

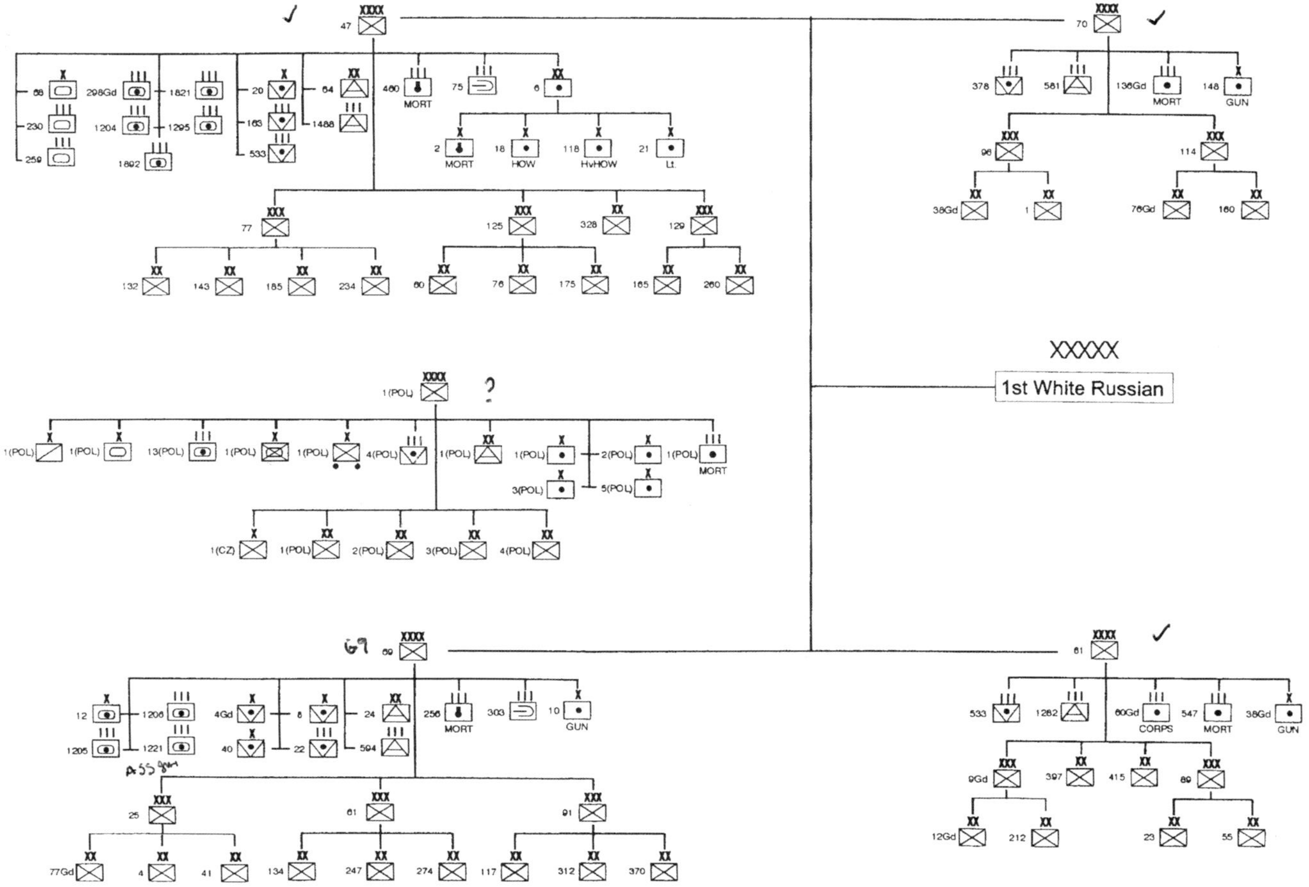

which was actively engaged during the first 2 weeks of the offensive. However, these armies provided ample reserves when needed and prevented Weiss from sending divisions to Army Group Center.

Luchinskiy performed the major role in the breakout in the south with three rifle corps compressed on a 25-kilometer front versus the 35th and 129th Rifle Divisions. The remainder of the front was screened by three Soviet fortified regions. The army's three rifle corps (20th, 3rd Guard, and 128th) had three divisions in each. General Perkhorovich's 3rd Guard Corps held a narrow 5-kilometer sector on the right. General N. A. Shvarev's 20th Rifle Corps held a 5-kilometer sector to the left of the 3rd Guards Corps, and General Batitskiy's 128th Corps held a wider sector to the left of Shvarev. Most of the divisions had served in the south with either the 28th Army or the Coastal Army in April.

On 1 June Luchinskiy's 28th Army had the bare minimum of support units allocated to a field army: an artillery regiment, a tank destroyer regiment, an antiaircraft regiment, and a mortar regiment. However, during June, massive reinforcements arrived. From the Moscow District came a guard breakthrough tank regiment, an assault gun regiment, and a corps artillery brigade. The Kharkov Military District provided three assault gun regiments. An artillery division and a guard mortar brigade came from the 1st White Russian Front reserve, and two guard mortar regiments came from the 69th Army. An artillery division came from the Orel Military District. In the last week of June, the Stavka Reserve provided a tank regiment and an artillery brigade, and the Moscow District sent two tank regiments. Over 200 armored vehicles were added to the army in the same month.

Facing the German Second Army were a half-dozen Soviet armies on the left flank of the 1st White Russian Front. The 61st Army held a large sector to the left of the 28th Army with two guard rifle corps, the 89th and the 9th. The 61st Army had a small allotment of supporting units: an artillery brigade, a corps artillery regiment, a tank destroyer regiment, an antiaircraft regiment, and a mortar regiment. The army had no assigned guard mortar regiments.

The 1st Polish Army had been formed with Soviet officers as the cadre along with Soviet citizens born in Polish provinces and refugees from Poland. This army had four infantry divisions and mechanized units, equal to those of a Soviet tank corps; these, combined with the strong artillery forces, made the army far more effective. The Poles were held in reserve on the left flank of the 1st White Russian Front.

The remainder of the armies were grouped around Kovel. The 70th Army was a small one with two rifle corps (96th and 114th), an artillery brigade, a tank destroyer regiment, an antiaircraft regiment, and a mortar regiment. A noteworthy addition was the 3rd Sniper Battalion of sharpshooters to pick off unwary German soldiers, an indication of the army's defensive role.

The 47th Army was the next in line, with three rifle corps and ten divisions. The army troops were substantial, a tank brigade and two regiments, five assault gun regiments, a tank destroyer brigade and two regiments, an artillery division, and an antiaircraft division.

The 69th Army consisted of three rifle corps (25th, 61st, and 91st) that had been transferred from the Stavka Reserve in April. The army had an unusually large tank destroyer component, three brigades and a regiment, a heavy concentration of over 220 antitank guns. The 69th Army had also received three guard mortar regiments and three assault gun regiments (more than 120 armored vehicles) from the Stavka Reserve in April. The 69th Army had the standard allotment of other units, two artillery brigades and a regiment, an antiaircraft division and regiment, a tank destroyer regiment, and a mortar brigade and regiment, all of which had come from the Stavka Reserve in April.

The southern breakthrough had seen very substantial armored support, the Pliev Horse-Mechanized Group, consisting of the 4th Guard Cavalry Corps and the 1st Mechanized Corps, placed behind Luchinskiy's 28th Army. With cavalry instead of motorized infantry, the Horse-Mechanized Group functioned more efficiently than a tank army in the swampy ground north of the Pripyat Marshes. The horses were able to keep pace with the tanks more easily than truck-borne infantry.

Holding the corner of the German position was General Herrlein's LV Corps (the third corps of Jordan's Ninth Army), covering a wide sector with only two divisions. The 292nd Infantry Division was on the eastern flank bordering the XXXXI Panzer Corps. The troops were probably well seasoned, with a minimum number of young soldiers because the division had not suffered catastrophic losses.

The 102nd Infantry Division, which held the west half of the LV Corps sector, was reinforced by the 216th Division Group, which had replaced the 233rd Infantry Regiment in November 1943.

Over 300 kilometers of the southern shoulder that ran through the Pripyat Marshes was held by the Second Army with a thin screening force. Nearly half of the sector was held by the XXIII Corps, with the 203rd Security Division on the east and the 7th Infantry Division on the west. The 7th Infantry Division had suffered devastating losses in the Orel operation.

The 203rd Security Division included two three-battalion security regiments, a single artillery battalion, and some Russian POW units. All German security units were composed of older men with a minimum of heavy weapons required to fight Partisans. Both divisions merely provided a screen to prevent intrusion by small Soviet units because the ground was too wet for major operations. The corps reserve consisted of the 17th Special Brigade with three security battalions and the 1st Hungarian Cavalry Division at the railroad junction at Luninets.

The German XX Corps held another wide sector west of the XXIII Corps with the 3rd Cavalry Brigade and Corps Detachment E. The 3rd Cavalry Brigade included a cavalry regiment with three battalions, an artillery battalion, an assault gun battalion, a heavy-weapons battalion, and a Cossack battalion. The brigade was stretched over a 60-kilometer sector and constituted a thin screen.

The Corps Detachment E was a division-sized unit consisting of remnants of the 86th, 137th, and 251st Infantry Divisions, and was assigned the low risk duty of screening a 60-kilometer sector in the Pripyat Marshes during that same June. Given the composition of survivors of battered divisions, the unit did not possess cohesion and was of little combat value. The corps reserve included the 4th Cavalry Brigade.

The VIII Corps held the narrowest sector on the eastern end of the Second Army with its southern flank only 40 kilometers from Kovel. The corps included the 12th Hungarian Reserve Division, the 211th Infantry Division, and the 5th Jäger Division. The 12th Hungarian Reserve Division had been added recently to the corps to screen the less sensitive eastern part of the corps sector. The Hungarian units did not fight well in Russia and were usually confined to security duty fighting the Partisans. However, the perceived need to bolster the defense near Kovel probably led to the addition of the Hungarians to enable the remaining divisions to concentrate in the west sector.

The 211th Infantry Division, holding a 20-kilometer sector, had received remnants of the 321st Infantry Division in the fall of 1943 to rebuild with after having been mauled in battles around Bryansk in July 1943. Made up of survivors of two battered divisions, the 211th Division probably had less cohesion, although 9 intervening months had allowed time for wounds to heal. Given its assignment to a significant sector, the German high command had confidence in the units.

The 5th Jäger Division, with specialized training, was probably better than average and had not suffered severe losses since 1941. The 904th Assault Gun Brigade with sixty assault guns was attached, and the corps reserve 237th Assault Gun Brigade was stationed immediately behind the division, giving it a powerful armored component equal to a panzer division.

Deep in Second Army reserve, under the II Hungarian Reserve Corps, were the 23rd and 5th Hungarian Reserve Divisions engaged in fighting Partisans. The Hungarians lacked front-line combat experience.

In all, the Second Army was a weak force whose task was to screen the Pripyat Marshes to prevent the incursion of small Soviet units and to fight the Partisans in the area. As the battle unfolded to the north, the Second Army had few available resources to help its neighbors.

Those neighbors would soon need a great deal of help, and the Second Army would be forced to part with its slender reserves. On 25 June Luchinskiy's 28th Army broke into the lines of the German 35th and 129th Divisions in five places. Having sent most of its battalions north to help the other divisions of Weidling's XXXXI Panzer Corps, the 129th Division was reduced to regimental level. During the day, the 129th Division was forced to rotate to the west by Luchinskiy's 28th Army, leaving a gap on the northern flank of Herrlein's LV Corps. Battle Group Schirmer, with three training battalions, was formed to hold the gap between the 129th and remnants of the 35th Division.[2]

Batitskiy's 128th Corps and the 153rd Fortified Region pressed the next German division to the south, the 292nd, to withdraw so as to keep contact with the north. At 1600 on 25 June, Busch, Army Group Center's commander, ordered the division to hold and bend back only on the northern flank. General Ivanov's 18th Corps of the 65th Army scattered the German 35th Division, and the remnants were forced to retreat to the west, further widening the gap south of the 36th Division.[3]

On the morning of 25 June, the Pliev Horse-Mechanized Group moved through the gap opened by Luchinskiy and Batov. The group advanced quickly in the afternoon, pursuing the 35th Division. At 1630 the group passed through Luchinskiy's army and raced forward with little opposition toward Glusk, driving before it the German 35th Division. Pliev advanced 30 kilometers the first day and 40 kilometers the second, cutting all roads south and southwest of Bobruysk, and crossed the railroad south of Bobruysk by the evening of 26 June.[4] The German 129th Division, south of the 35th Division, was also forced to wheel to the west to protect the northern flank of Herrlein's LV Corps.[5]

On 26 June Pekhorovich's 3rd Guard Corps and Pliev's Horse-Mechanized Group forced the 35th Division back more than 40 kilometers to the Ptich River, west of the railroad, leaving a 40-kilometer gap between this division and the 36th Division to the north. The Germans were still ordered to hold wherever possible, and the 35th Division did launch some counterattacks. However, there were no reserves to fill the breach north of the 35th Division, and Weidling's XXXXI Panzer Corps front was falling apart.[6]

On 26 June Herrlein's LV Corps was holding a line on the Ptich River, but Pliev's group with 321 tanks had crossed the river north of Glusk at 1500, threatening to outflank the German 35th and 129th Divisions. The horse-mechanized group, led by the 40th Guard Cavalry Regiment of the 10th Guard Cavalry Division, took Glusk, 50 kilometers southwest of Bobruysk, on the southern shoulder of the gap between the 35th and 36th Divisions, and was moving unopposed and quickly to the west. The 10th Guard Cavalry Division was on the main road to Slutsk, a major rail and road center 80 kilometers to the west, with a road connection to Bobruysk and a rail connection to Mogilev. Luchinskiy moved steadily forward, following the retreating 129th Division, which was closing up to the Ptich River at Kazarichi.[7]

On 27 June Pliev's 4th Guard Cavalry Corps and the 54th Guard Division of the 3rd Guard Corps headed due west for Slutsk and took Star-Dorogi on the Mogilev-Slutsk Railroad, only 60 kilometers from Slutsk. Krivoshein's 1st Mechanized Corps was at Glusk, 30 kilometers to the southeast, driving back the badly battered elements of the 35th Division. At 1700 on 27 June, Soviet units were flowing freely through the gap to the north of Luchinskiy's 28th Army.[8] (See Map 11.1.)

The 129th and 292nd Divisions of Herrlein's LV Corps continued to hold the Ptich River line under moderate pressure from the three fortified regions and Batitskiy's 128th Corps of Luchinskiy's 28th Army. Herrlein's LV Corps was driven steadily west and south by Luchinskiy, creating an ever widening gap between the corps and the rest of Jordan's Ninth Army. At 1630 on 27 June, the other three divisions of Herrlein's LV Corps were ordered to pull back from the Ptich River to avoid being cut off from the north.[9]

Pliev's 4th Guard Cavalry Corps advanced from Star-Dorogi on the way to Slutsk. By the evening of 28 June, the 30th Cavalry Division brushed aside two German battle groups defending Slutsk and reached the outskirts of the town. Slutsk was on the main road from Bobruysk to Baranovichi and was the rail center for the German divisions coming from the south. Battle Group Schirmer was attempting to delay the advance of Krivoshein's 1st Mechanized Corps and Luchinskiy's 28th Army, but at 2200 the 9th Guard Cavalry Division of the Pliev group crossed the river at Slutsk and Krivoshein joined in the attack from Glusk.[10]

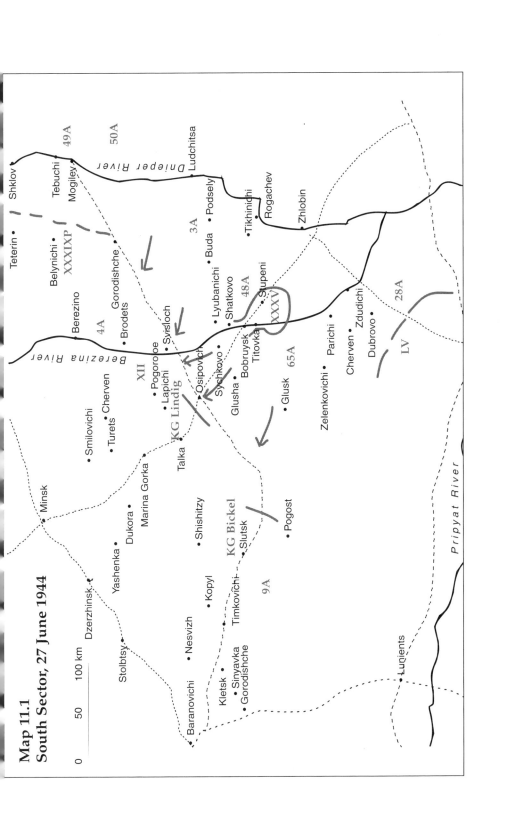

Map 11.1
South Sector, 27 June 1944

Weiss's Second Army on the Pripyat River was not under pressure from Soviet units. However, as the Russians advanced across the Second Army's rear to the north, Weiss had to make adjustments to protect his flank. Battle Group Bickel, with Jordan's Ninth Army weapons training school troops, was 20 kilometers east of Slutsk along with Battle Group Rojahn with a German cavalry regiment. Weiss was ordered to pull back General Tiemann's XXIII Corps to maintain a link with Herrlein's corps. Weiss then began to thin out his line to send units north to help the Ninth Army. The 1st Hungarian Cavalry Division, in the army reserve, was the first to be dispatched to the north from Luninets.[11]

Although most of the Army Group Center was in some difficulty, Herrlein's LV Corps was stable with only minimal pressure from the three fortified regions of Luchinskiy's 28th Army. However, Pliev's group was racing westward on the northern flank, forcing Herrlein to retreat. On 29 June only a string of isolated German units remained at Slutsk under the command of General Harteneck, commander of the I Cavalry Corps. During the day, Luchinskiy's 28th Army and Krivoshein's 1st Mechanized Corps poured through the gap at Slutsk in the rear of Weiss's Second Army. The 4th Guard Cavalry Corps attacked Slutsk from the north, east, and south on 29 June; the 32nd Guard Cavalry Regiment and the 151st Tank Regiment were the first in the city at 1000.[12]

The remainder of Herrlein's corps (the 129th, 292nd, and 102nd Infantry Divisions) retreated 30 kilometers on 29 June in an attempt to protect its northern flank. The gap between Herrlein and the battle group at Slutsk had widened to 60 kilometers. However, help was on the way. Throughout 29 June the first three trains of the 4th Panzer Division had arrived in Baranovichi, 90 kilometers west of Slutsk, and the 28th Light and the 7th Panzer Divisions were ordered to follow.[13]

On 30 June Pliev's group drove Battle Group Harteneck from Slutsk. The Germans fought hard, but the combined efforts of Red Army cavalry, motorized infantry, and tanks prevailed. The 9th Guard Cavalry Division reached the center of the city, while the 10th Guard Cavalry Division cleared the northern part of the city. Resistance ended at 1130. The German 5th Cavalry Regiment did counterattack and manage to retake the western part of the town, but the Russians held the remainder.[14]

After the capture of Slutsk, Pliev's 4th Guard Cavalry Corps was ordered to advance west to Stolbtsy and Gorodeya to cut the Minsk-Baranovichi railroad and prevent German reinforcements from reaching Minsk. Krivoshein's 1st Mechanized Corps was sent southwest directly toward Baranovichi.[15]

But German reinforcements were arriving. The first units of the 4th Panzer Division to arrive in Baranovichi on 30 June were sent east to block the main road 20 kilometers west of Slutsk and stop Krivoshein. The 1st Hungarian Cavalry Division from the Second Army was on its way to cover Baranovichi along with the 4th Panzer Division. The 28th Division was in transit and would arrive on 1 July at Dzerzhinsk, halfway between Minsk and Stolbtsy, 40 kilometers southwest of Minsk. The 28th Division was ordered to halt the advance of Pliev's 4th Guard Cavalry Corps.[16]

To the south, the 129th Division of Herrlein's LV Corps and the remnant of the 35th Division pulled back nearly 50 kilometers westward from their position on the previous day. The other two divisions of the corps, the 292nd and 102nd, slowly retreated, keeping contact with the 129th Division.[17] On the south side of the gap between the Slutsk and Herrlein's corps, the 129th and 35th Divisions and the rest of the LV Corps were placed under the command of the Second Army's XXIII Corps as Battle Group Tiemann.[18]

In the gap on 1 July, the 6th German Cavalry Brigade of Battle Group Harteneck delayed the advancing Pliev group 6 kilometers west of Slutsk. The 4th Guard Cavalry Corps bypassed the German cavalry to the north by going through Kopys; south of Slutsk, the 1st Mechanized Corps passed through Pogost on its way to Baranovichi. Elements of the 4th Panzer Division counterattacked at Kopys, while the German 6th Cavalry Brigade withdrew.[19]

Throughout 1 July six battalions of the German 28th Light Division were expected. The first three were to unload at Stolbtsy on the Baranovichi-Minsk rail line and defend that town as the southern flank of a line along the railroad to Minsk. However, the arrival of the 28th Division was delayed nearly a day by Partisans' sabotage of the railroad. At 1700 on 1 July, the Soviet 30th Cavalry Division was racing to reach the railroad at Stolbtsy before the 28th Division arrived, so the Germans sent a company of tanks from the 4th Panzer Division to Stolbtsy from Baranovichi to delay the Soviet cavalry.[20] Further, a panzergrenadier battalion from Battle Group Lindig was ordered to block the road from Bobruysk to Minsk to Stolbtsy. However, the battalion could not move until evening, probably because of incessant Soviet air attacks on the roads.

To assist the 4th Panzer Division holding south of Stolbtsy, the 1st Hungarian Cavalry Division reached Sinyavka, 45 kilometers to the south, during the day.[21] The Soviet armored columns were moving rapidly to cut the only rail line open south of Minsk, but the Germans were bringing in three divisions that could hold Pliev's group if they arrived in time. And time was crucial.

At 0515 on 2 July, Pliev's 4th Guard Cavalry Corps reached the

Niemen River at Stolbtsy and at 0600 entered the town. At 1000 units of the cavalry corps, the 30th Cavalry Division and the 151st Tank Regiment, attacked the town from the south. A panzergrenadier battalion from the 12th Panzer Division retook the western side of the town, but the vehicle bridge had been destroyed and the Russians had taken the railroad bridge, thereby cutting the rail line to Minsk.[22]

The 10th Guard Cavalry Division and the 128th Tank Regiment took both Gorodeya, 20 kilometers southwest of Stolbtsy, and Nesvizh, 10 kilometers south of Gorodeya, early in the morning of 2 July. Pliev was driving quickly over a 40-kilometer front. Battle Group Harteneck, with the 4th Panzer Division and the 1st Hungarian Cavalry Division, was ordered to retake Nesvizh, but lacked fuel and could not begin, an indication of Partisan success in disrupting rail traffic.[23]

The German 4th Cavalry Brigade retreated toward Battle Group Harteneck at Kletsk, 20 kilometers south of Nesvizh, under pressure from Krivoshein's 1st Mechanized Corps driving west from Slutsk toward Baranovichi, and the infantry of Batov's 65th and Romanenko's 48th Armies was coming up behind the Pliev's group.[24]

In the evening of 2 July, the 12th Panzer Division was ordered to move to Stolbtsy to defend the Neman River. The rest of Battle Groups Lindig and Meinecke were sent to Stolbtsy, in effect abandoning the Minsk-Bobruysk road and leaving it open to Red Army units.[25]

On 3 July, in Stolbtsy, with the rail and road connection with Baranovichi cut by Pliev's group, elements of the 20th Panzer Division and remnants of many other units fought northwest along the Neman River into the Nalibotski Forest. By 1800 German engineers had built a bridge across the Neman near Turets, about 30 kilometers northwest of Stolbtsy. The bridge was to serve as an escape route for thousands of Germans fleeing Minsk, and throughout the night German stragglers crossed the bridge and fought their way southwest to Baranovichi.[26]

During the morning of 3 July, Jordan's Ninth Army (4th Panzer Division, 4th Cavalry Brigade, 1st Hungarian Cavalry, 28th Light Division, 12th Panzer Division, and other units) was given the name Battle Group von Vormann and attached to the Second Army holding the southern shoulder of the salient.[27]

A counterattack by two battalions and forty tanks of the 4th Panzer Division from Baranovichi went well on the morning of 3 July, retaking Nesvizh, 50 kilometers east of Baranovichi, before 0900 and driving the 24th Cavalry Regiment of the 10th Guard Cavalry

Division from Gorodeya 20 kilometers northward by 1100. At Stolbtsy the 30th Cavalry Regiment of the 9th Guard Cavalry Division, supported by the 1815th Assault Gun Regiment, captured the town and held it despite German armored attacks. At 1800 twenty German tanks and an infantry regiment were repulsed. The 9th Guard Cavalry sent in the 34th Cavalry Regiment, a tank regiment, two guard mortar battalions, and a tank destroyer regiment from the 4th Guard Cavalry Corps reserve to reinforce the 30th Cavalry Division. However, Pliev's 4th Guard Cavalry Corps had been halted south of Stolbtsy.[28]

More German reinforcements were arriving. Thirteen trains carrying the German 28th Light Division arrived at Baranovichi and Gorodeya during 3 July, where the Russians counterattacked at 2200. Battle Group Harteneck, including the 1st Hungarian Cavalry Division, stopped Krivoshein's 1st Mechanized Corps at Kletsk, 20 kilometers south of Nesvizh. To the southwest, the German 4th Cavalry Brigade was pushed northwest toward Kletsk by Krivoshein as he drove toward Baranovichi, threatening the rear of the Germans around Stolbtsy. Soviet forces reached the rail line from Luninets south of Baranovichi and began to advance toward Baranovichi, reaching Sinyavka in the rear of Battle Group Harteneck. However, German reinforcements stabilized the front around Baranovichi, and efforts by Battle Group Harteneck and the other units around Baranovichi successfully rescued 25,000 men from the Bobruysk area by 3 July.[29]

From 22 June to 3 July, Luchinskiy's 28th Army and Pliev's Horse-Mechanized Group had forced the Germans to withdraw 250 kilometers to Stolbtsy. After the initial breakthrough, Krivoshein's 1st Mechanized Corps and Pliev's 4th Guard Cavalry Corps had taken the lead, advancing an average of 20 kilometers per day. The rifle divisions of Luchinskiy's 28th Army marched doggedly on behind the spearheads and kept the southern flank of the penetration secure. Weiss's Second Army and Herrlein's LV Corps were forced to withdraw to protect their flank, but on 3 July German and Hungarian reinforcements finally halted the Soviet cavalry group at Stolbtsy and forced Pliev to wait until Luchinskiy's 28th Army caught up before resuming the attack.

In early July the Soviet advance along the southern shoulder of the White Russian salient was halted because the armored columns lacked sufficient power and supplies to overcome the increasing German resistance. The Red Army had to pause until the infantry, artillery, and supplies caught up to the armored spearheads. The progress of the Russian blitzkrieg finally ground to a halt on the southern shoulder as the first phase of the offensive ended, and after a short pause the grueling second phase would begin, again with mounting Soviet casualties.

Notes

1. David M. Glantz and Harold S. Orenstein, eds., *Belorussia 1944: The Soviet General Staff Study* (Carlisle, Penn.: David M. Glantz, 1998), p. 111; A. M. Samsanov, ed., *Osvobozhdenie Belorussii, 1944* (Moscow: Nauka, 1974), pp. 153, 430; G. Niepold, *The Battle for White Russia: The Destruction of Army Group Centre, June 1944* (London: Brassey's, 1987), p. 99.
2. Niepold, p. 108.
3. Ibid., pp. 107–108; F. V. Plotnikov, *v Srazheniia za Belorussi* (Minsk: Belarus, 1982), pp. 64–65.
4. Niepold, p. 120; Glantz and Orenstein, p. 112.
5. Niepold, pp. 107, 112, 120; Samsanov, p. 430.
6. Niepold, p. 120; Samsanov, p. 430.
7. Niepold, pp. 122, 124, 137; Samsanov, p. 430, 509; Glantz and Orenstein, p. 113.
8. Niepold, pp. 134–135.
9. Ibid., pp. 135, 146.
10. Samsanov, pp. 431–432; Niepold, p. 146.
11. Niepold, p. 146.
12. Ibid., p. 161; Samsanov, p. 432.
13. Niepold, pp. 161–162; Rolf Hinze, *East Front Drama—1944: The Withdrawal Battle of Army Group Center* (Winnipeg, Manitoba: J. J. Fedorowicz Publishing Inc., 1996), p. 78.
14. Samsanov, p. 433; Niepold, p. 171.
15. Samsanov, p. 433; Paul Adair, *Hitler's Greatest Defeat: The Collapse of Army Group Centre, June 1944* (London: Arms and Armour Press, 1994), p. 142.
16. Niepold, pp. 170–171; Adair, p. 142; Hinze, p. 48.
17. Niepold, p. 171; Hinze, pp. 75–78.
18. Niepold, p. 181.
19. Ibid.
20. Ibid., pp. 179–181; Samsanov, p. 434; Hinze, p. 48.
21. Niepold, p. 181; Adair, pp. 142–143.
22. Samsanov, pp. 150, 433–434; Hinze, p. 49; Niepold, p. 189.
23. Niepold, p. 191; Samsanov, pp. 433–434.
24. Niepold, pp. 191, 193; Samsanov, p. 433; Hinze, p. 54.
25. Niepold, p. 191; Adair, pp. 142–143; Hinze, p. 55.
26. Niepold, p. 199; Adair, p. 143; Hinze, pp. 57, 59–60.
27. Neopold, p. 200; Hinze, p. 58.
28. Samsanov, pp. 437–438; Niepold, p. 200; Adair, p. 144.
29. Niepold, pp. 200–201; Hinze, p. 62.

CHAPTER 12

Conclusion

A diversion on a second front in Europe requested of the Soviet Union by the Western Allies produced the worst defeat suffered by the German army in World War II. In the battle to drive the Germans out of White Russia, the Red Army ruptured the German defenses within a few days, and Soviet task forces of tanks, cavalry, and mechanized infantry plunged through the gaps to roam freely behind the German lines, cutting off numerous pockets of demoralized units, and completely disrupting Army Group Center. Soviet supplies, artillery, and fresh units bypassed the fortified areas on the rough tracks and pontoon bridges close behind the spearheads. As the Soviet mobile troops moved west, the Germans were unable to close enormous gaps in their line for days at a time. When the Germans attempted to establish a defensive position during the course of the battle, the Russians quickly concentrated men, weapons, and tanks to overwhelm the German defenders before they could dig in properly.

The situation changed after the first 2 weeks of the White Russian operation ended on 3 July, when the arrival of German reserves and Soviet logistics problems slowed the Red Army's advance. The first phase of the plan for the operation had been achieved 12 days before the planned date. The unexpected rapid pace had created an enormous supply problem. The Soviet divisions and mobile corps had begun the attack with enough fuel, rations, and munitions to last about 3 days. When the initial load of supplies was exhausted, trucks were sent forward from depots east of the startline to deliver fresh supplies and were probably able to return within 2 days. However, by 3 July, the Soviet supply problem intensified when the nearly 300-kilometer round-trip required up to 4 days.

The average daily requirement for 168 rifle divisions, 10 tank

221

corps, 3 cavalry corps, 2 mechanized corps, and 15 tank brigades was 69,513 tons, excluding the needs of the artillery divisions, assault gun and tank regiments, and other units. With a 2-day turnaround, the supply situation was manageable, but a 4-day turnaround meant there would be a severe shortfall even if demand was less than the 69,000 tons per day. With a 4-day turnaround, only 31,000 tons could be delivered to the front daily. The four fronts had only 60,649 trucks with an average capacity of 2 tons for a total of 121,298 tons or enough to provide supplies for 1.75 days if all the trucks were used for supply. Of course there were many variables: not all units were 300 kilometers from the depots, some depots may have been moved forward by 3 July, the turnaround may have been shorter on the four improved roads, and the infantry would have used less ammunition because it was not heavily engaged. On the other hand, the armored units used far more fuel in their rapid advance, and most of them were a distant 300 kilometers from their depots. The armored units required at least 9,000 tons per day, about one-third of the amount that could be delivered, leaving 22,000 tons for the infantry and the other units, slightly more than one-third of their needs. In the early days of July, Red Army engineers worked frantically to repair the rail lines to enable moving the depots forward. As a result, the Soviet mobile columns did continue to move forward though at a slower pace.

Operations continued at the end of the first phase. Minsk was viciously attacked from all sides, as the Soviet armored spearheads converged on the city, capturing it on 3 July. The fall of Minsk cut off large numbers of Germans in many pockets east of Minsk.[1] Soviet rockets, artillery, and air attacks pounded the pockets one by one, beginning on 5 July, until they lost contact with Army Group Center.[2]

North of Minsk the second phase of the operation was under way. Ruchkin's 22nd and Yermakov's 23rd Guard Corps of Chistyakov's 6th Guard Army were driving the German Sixteenth Army westward from Polotsk.[3] On 5 July Chistyakov and Malyshev's 4th Shock Army were racing unheeded through a gap south of the German Sixteenth Army heading for Vilnius. Remnants of Wuthmann's IX Corps of Reinhardt's 3rd Panzer Army at Postavy were being driven steadily westward. Closer to Minsk, Weidling's XXXXI Panzer Corps was retreating west of Molodechno despite arriving German reinforcements, and Pfeiffer's VI Corps was retreating through the forest west of Minsk.[4]

South of Minsk, on 3 July, Weiss's Second Army was pulling back as Soviet armored columns raced westward in the army's rear. Weiss launched a counterattack on the 30th Cavalry Division at

Stolbtsy but could not prevent the Soviet cavalrymen from taking the town.[5] Pliev's 4th Guard Cavalry Corps and units of Bakharov's 9th Tank Corps on its right were ordered to drive for Baranovichi and then on to Slonim while Krivoshein's 1st Mechanized Corps was to pass south of Baranovichi.[6] On 5 July Pliev encountered Battle Group von Vormann, which included the 4th Panzer Division, the 1st Hungarian Cavalry Division, the 28th Light Division, and the 3rd German Cavalry Brigade at Baranovichi. By 6 July von Vormann had been driven back, and Pliev's cavalry and motorized infantry were well on the road to Slonim.[7]

On 5 July the second phase was in progress, with the Red Army on the move against disjointed German resistance. However, German panzer and infantry divisions were arriving daily, along with a miscellany of other units, which gradually slowed the Soviet rate of advance as the Germans traded ground for time to regroup. No more pockets developed because the wary Germans retreated as soon as their flanks were threatened.

Still, the Red Army was able to inflict the catastrophic defeat of Army Group Center by the application of eight factors: concentration of force, deception, surprise, leadership, timing, use of terrain, training, and better technology.

Overall Soviet numerical superiority in men was not as great as the Germans claimed, but the Russians did concentrate force in the crucial areas. The Red Army had about twice as many men as the Germans on the Eastern Front, but the Russians usually were able to muster a much greater ratio in assault areas. The Soviet superiority factor was far more than two to one in weapons. The noteworthy change in 1944 was that the Red Army was more skilled. Victories were won with improved combat techniques on the part of the Red Army as well as with greater numbers of men and weapons.[8]

An example of concentration was the formation of horse-mechanized groups, a combination of a corps of cavalry and a corps of mechanized infantry, which provided two of the spearheads that swept forward after the German line was breached. In the first 2 weeks of the offensive, the two cavalry groups operated more effectively than Rotmistrov's 5th Guard Tank Army. The Soviet armies without armored corps had sufficient independent tank brigades and regiments and assault gun regiments, truck-borne infantry, and motorized artillery to create mobile armored columns. These ad hoc mobile columns were often as strong as German panzer divisions.

Once the six penetrations by the Red Army had been achieved, its rifle divisions surrounded the German fortified cities of Vitebsk, Orsha, Mogilev, and Bobruysk, as well as pockets of Germans east of the Berezina River and around Minsk. The capture of the surrounded fortified cities was supported by the artillery that bombarded the garrisons at leisure, while the Red Air Force subjected the cities to heavy air attacks.

In view of their hopeless situation some of the German garrisons surrendered; many of the prisoners taken in the early weeks of the offensive came from the surrounded cities. Despite their defeats in France and on the Eastern Front, most of the Germans continued to fight tenaciously for many reasons: patriotism, pride in their units, fear of reprisal if they surrendered, knowledge of the horrible conditions in the Soviet prisoner of war camps, belief in Hitler's promises of secret weapons that would change the course of the war, and the presence of military police who arrested those who deserted their units. This tenacity was a major factor in slowing down the Soviet juggernaut in the early days of July.

Deception was a major component of the Soviet success in the first phase from 23 June to 3 July. The ruse was so clever that even after the beginning of the fighting, Hitler and the General Staff were still convinced that the attack was only a diversion. The deception was so convincing that they viewed the offensive as a trap to draw German panzer divisions into the salient, subsequently to be surrounded when the real offensive was launched in the south at Kovel. Had the Germans reacted in time, their reserves at Kovel could have been moved to improve the odds before the Russians destroyed so many divisions in the first phase of the offensive.

The argument can also be made that the Germans could have done little to alter the outcome. At Vitebsk delaying the retreat by 2 or more days with the help of several panzer divisions could not have altered the overwhelming Soviet superiority in men and material. Pulling the four low-quality German divisions out of Vitebsk on the limited road network would have exposed them to devastating air attacks and the vengeance of well-trained Soviet mobile units. The German panzers could have done little to slow the overwhelming power of the Red Army. Although more Germans would have been able to escape capture, many more would have been killed in fierce inequitable battles. At Stalingrad the German Sixth Army had held fast and tied up Soviet armies, giving Manstein an opportunity to patch together a front. The fortified city strategy may have given the Germans precious time to rescue the few remnants that escaped the opening onslaught in White Russia.

Surprise provided two major benefits. The Russians suffered few casualties after breaking through the German front line in the first phase and made sizeable gains. However, after 3 July, the Russians paid a heavy price in casualties and equipment when the element of surprise vanished. For example, Rotmistrov's 5th Guard Tank Army began the offensive on 23 June with 524 tanks and assault guns and still had 307 in operation on 5 July after 12 days and 260 kilometers of fighting. By 16 July, only 12 days later, the tank army had only 50 serviceable tanks after moving 190 kilometers in the face of increasing German resistance.[9]

When the element of surprise wore thin during the remainder of the White Russian operation, Soviet losses were heavy. Attacking German defenses in the second half of 1944 was more formidable than in previous years, and most Soviet victories were bought at a high price. The length of the Eastern Front was shortened considerably as the Germans were driven back, enabling the Germans to increase the number of men per kilometer of front. In addition, German defenses were more sophisticated and tougher to crack. Breaking through the German first defense zone later in 1944 without the element of surprise required far more effort than in previous years.[10]

One of the reasons the Russians were able to impose such a devastating defeat on the Germans in June 1944 was bold leadership. Stalin was putting more confidence in his generals, even though he made clear that when he acceded to suggestions that were counter to his ideas, generals making such recommendations would bear full responsibility for their outcome and could face demotion, or worse, if the actions failed.[11]

By contrast, the German generals had less freedom to command because Hitler lacked confidence in his generals' ability to make major decisions, and he exerted more and more control over the detail of operations. On the other hand, the generals placed much of the blame for the defeat on Hitler, on his inability to make timely as well as quality decisions and on his obsession with holding ground.

The failure of Hitler's personal military leadership led to the bomb plot of 20 July 1944, 2 weeks after the first phase of the White Russian operation. The attempted assassination showed the decline of the German generals' confidence in their leader. The disaster in White Russia, attributed by the German generals directly to Hitler's fortified city concept, goaded them into action after years of plotting his demise. The planning of the assassination jeopardized the German situation in White Russia because the *Valkerie* units, formed in the Replacement Army for use in an emergency, were held back by the plotters to implement the coup once Hitler was dead instead of being dispatched quickly to White Russia.

Timing was a crucial ingredient in the summer of 1944. Soviet intentions could not be concealed for an indefinite period. Given the need for concealment, the Russians used the railroads and highways only at night, which slowed the buildup. The original plan called for the attack to begin in mid-June, when the roads were dry. However, the delay in moving Rotmistrov's 5th Guard Tank Army caused by the clogged railroads forced Stalin to postpone the attack until 22 June.

Stalin was probably unaware of the possible weather problems in late June, having spent his youth in a seminary rather than working in the fields. The summer solstice (22 June) was often marked by heavy rain in Eastern Europe, and in fact heavy rains did fall in White Russia on 22 and 23 June, severely hampering air support for the Soviet offensive and turning the dirt roads into streams of mud. The rivers, swollen by the heavy rains, raised the water level and the speed of the current, a combination that made the construction of pontoon bridges more difficult, especially on the Drut and Berezina Rivers, delaying the advance of Rotmistrov's 5th Guard Tank Army after the battle began.

The Soviet general staff's study of the White Russian operation was critical of Rotmistrov because his army was delayed at the rivers while the rifle divisions moved ahead and pursued the Germans. Rotmistrov was continually delayed by his inability to cross rivers: the increased need for pontoon battalions and other bridging units had not been anticipated. As a result, the tank army's huge service and support elements created a massive traffic jam at each river crossing. The bridging units that were available were often delayed by road conditions because their trucks were heavily loaded and more easily bogged down. Until a 60-ton pontoon bridge was constructed, the heavy tanks could not cross, and apparently the tank army was reluctant to proceed without its support.

The difficulties of Rotmistrov's 5th Guard Tank Army were therefore directly related to the weather. Pontoon bridges were difficult to assemble at any time, and all the more so when the river banks overflowed and the current was swift. Even though the Soviets bypassed the German strongpoints, as the Germans retreated they destroyed the bridges, and under the excruciating conditions created by the rain the rivers were very difficult to cross. Launching the offensive 2 weeks earlier could have met with good weather and speeded up the operation. The decision to delay because of the plodding movement of the 5th Guard Tank Army postponed its role until the end of the first phase of the offensive.

Despite the problems of Rotmistrov, the timing combined with the other factors resulted in a successful campaign. One reason the Russians could not continually replicate the stunning victory was the time factor. Although deception was critical to a blitzkrieg against a strong opponent, time was needed to set the trap to draw German reserves away from the crucial sector, and to create the illusion that the assault area presented no threat. In future operations, the Russians believed that time was not on their side if they were to acquire Eastern Europe before the war ended.

With the expectation of an early end of the war after the invasion of France, the Soviet Union was faced with the prospect of the restoration of the Polish government in exile and the rapid reconstitution of Germany with Western Allied assistance. With a renewed Germany and an unfriendly Poland in the future, the Soviet Union would have been in the same strategic position as in 1939, and the death of over 28 million Soviet citizens would have been for naught. The Soviet concern for its position after the war was verified in October 1998, when the British government declassified a tentative Western Allied plan made in 1945 to attack the Soviet Union with the assistance of the German army after the German surrender. Very likely Stalin was aware of this negative attitude toward the Soviet Union, and trusted the United States and Britain no more than they trusted him. Given the situation, Stalin forced the Red Army to drive ahead with frontal attacks against well-prepared German defenses at a cost of thousands of lives to gain as much ground as possible, including Berlin. Had there been more trust among the Allies, the time pressure would have been eased and the Red Army would have been able to prepare its attacks as leisurely as had Montgomery in the spring of 1945.

The Soviet use of the terrain was especially brilliant because the German generals had assumed that the Russians would have the same lack of mobility in the marshes as the German army. The German infantry divisions could withdraw successfully only at the plodding speed of a horsedrawn wagon, which was not much more than 30 kilometers per day on good roads. On muddy roads, the horses pulled the wagons at an even slower speed and could not move at all in the marshes during wet weather because the wagon wheels sank to the hubs in mud. The German generals mistakenly assumed that with capable rearguard actions on the good roads, the Germans could delay the Red Army's rate of advance.

The Germans' assumption that the terrain favored them was the justification for their holding the fortified cities. Giving up the elaborate defenses at Vitebsk would have unleashed the mass of Soviet armor and artillery on the hard-surfaced road that passed through the city to Lepel. Until Vitebsk was taken, no good road was available to supply the 1st Baltic Front and the northern flank of the 3rd White Russian Front, forcing the Russians to use the poor roads and tracks bypassing the city. Once the city had surrendered, the road was cleared for Soviet use.

At Mogilev the Russians made a frontal attack to gain control of the road and suffered massive losses. At Bobruysk the Soviets avoided the fortified area of Rogachev and struck south of the city through the wetlands and, with the help of Lend Lease trucks, cut the roads leading west. The Soviets then gobbled up the Germans fleeing from the Dnieper River and trapped them in a colossal traffic jam at the bridges crossing the Berezina. The Red Army used the terrain to destroy the roadbound Germans.

With excellent training, most Soviets units were able to overcome the terrain problem. The luxury of being able to withdraw entire armies from the front for weeks allowed the Red Army to give several weeks of intensive training to the units scheduled for assault roles. The troops practiced attacking with artillery and tank support. They practiced with new weapons, including the latest models of machine pistols and antitank guns. Most beneficial of all, they trained with engineers to overcome the natural obstacles encountered in the swamps. Even though the weather made the swamps more formidable than expected, the Soviet units were able to overcome the obstacles and press on with the attack.

Technology played a major role in the success of the campaign. The Soviet mechanized infantry brigades traveling in American-built trucks were at the heart of the White Russian offensive. The Russians were able to move these four-wheel-drive vehicles, along with tanks, through the swamps, carrying motorized infantry and supplies and towing guns. Well-balanced combat teams of tanks, assault guns, motorized infantry, engineers, and artillery emerged from the forests on both sides of major highways, enveloping group after group of the roadbound Germans trying to conduct an orderly withdrawal in the face of heavy frontal attacks. Rather than being tied to the good roads like the German rear-axle-drive trucks and horsedrawn wagons, the Soviet motorized infantry could move on marginal dirt roads across country, bypassing the German roadblocks. Once the Soviet trucks had passed the roadblocks on the better roads, they resumed travel at a speedy 30 kilometers per hour rather than 30 kilometers per day. Facing this threat, when a defense zone was broken, the Germans were forced to flee immediately. The German units that did not withdraw expeditiously were surrounded and captured.

The American-made trucks could probably have overcome the difficulty of the Pripyat Marshes that formed the southern side of the White Russian salient. During the early planning of the White Russian operation, Rokossovskiy, commander of the 1st White Russian Front, planned to launch a tank army from the left flank of his front directly north toward Baranovichi. Crossing the Pripyat Marshes with a tank army would have been a difficult task since the only improved route was the rail line leading through Luninets to Baranovichi. However, the attacking Russians would have faced little opposition. By inserting Rotmistrov's 5th Guard Tank Army in the south rather than in the center, a huge amount of rail traffic would have been diverted to the line passing through Gomel instead of the overburdened line passing through Smolensk. Given the change in the deployment of Rotmistrov's army, the timetable might have been achieved and the offensive launched in mid-June before the rains came. The Pripyat Marshes might have been less daunting than the swollen Drut and Berezina Rivers after the rain.

In fact, the 5th Guard Tank Army was not even needed at Orsha. It could have been replaced by a more agile horse-mechanized group. The 1st White Russian Front had two tank corps and two cavalry corps in reserve, double the number required to form an additional horse-mechanized group. The success of the other two cavalry groups was a result of greater mobility. A 30-ton pontoon bridge was sufficient for a cavalry group, which had no group organic support or service components and had little if any need for 60-ton pontoon bridges, probably the most troublesome part of the tank army support element.

Regardless of the possibility offered by a Soviet strike in the south, within a few days after 22 June, the German defenses were broken and Soviet armored columns ranged wide and deep. Late in the first phase, Rotmistrov's 5th Guard Tank Army, delayed in the early part of the operation, advanced 125 kilometers in 3 days, from 26 June to 28 June, and the 2nd Mechanized Brigade of the 3rd Guard Mechanized Corps advanced 70 kilometers in 1 day.[12] If the Germans at Kursk in July 1943 had averaged 20 kilometers per day from the north and south (a total of 40 kilometers per day to close a 200-kilometer gap), they would have closed the trap in 5 days and surrounded the Soviet armies in the salient before the latters' reserves could arrive.

After the accelerated first phase of the White Russian operation, the Russians continued to advance from 4 July to 16 July, although at a slower pace. Army Group Center received reinforcements from the OKH reserve, Army Group North Ukraine, and Army Group South Ukraine. Shortages of fuel hampered the road movement of the panzer divisions, while the railroads were under constant attack from the Red Air Force and Partisans. However, by 17 July, the Germans had reestablished a front and slowed Soviet progress to as little as a kilometer per day.[13]

Slow progress increased casualties. Unfortunately, the Soviet statistics do not separate the losses sustained in the first 2 weeks of the offensive, when the Red Army advanced rapidly, from the later stages, when combat returned to the grinding battles of attrition. The four fronts involved had a total of 2,331,000 Russians, plus 80,000 Poles in the 1st Polish Army. Permanent battle-related losses (killed, missing, and permanently disabled) were 180,000, including 1,500 Poles. Sick and wounded totaled 590,000, including 3,500 Poles. Most of the Soviet casualties came in the final 7 weeks, in contrast to the initial 2 weeks when the Germans experienced their greatest losses while facing the Soviet blitzkrieg.

To place these numbers in perspective, the United States lost 405,399 killed in all theaters in World War II, and of those only 291,557 were combat related. In the entire war, 670,846 Americans were wounded, only 100,000 more than the Russian sick and wounded in the single Battle for White Russia. The Union forces in the U.S. Civil War totaled 2,213,000, about equal to the number of Russians engaged in the Battle for White Russia. Of the Union forces, 364,511 died in the 4 years of the war. Of these, 140,414 were battle related, fewer than the permanent losses of the Russians in this single offensive. Many Americans remember the Civil War as a terrible bloody conflict of lasting impact on U.S. history and politics. The Soviet forces lost as many in 2 months as the Union lost in 4 years.[14]

On 1 July 1944 the German army had 892,000 men in the west and 2,160,000 on the Eastern Front.[15] From June to September 1944 the German casualties were 54,754 dead and 338,933 missing in the west, while 214,511 were killed and 626,641 missing on the Eastern Front and Italy.[16] Of about 700,000 Germans in Army Group Center, 130,000 were killed and 66,000 made prisoners at Vitebsk, Orsha, Mogilev, and Bobruysk in 1 week.[17]

Not only did the Germans suffer heavy losses in manpower, but the nature of the battle with multiple pockets, created and destroyed by the Russians, resulted in heavy losses in equipment and the destruction of entire divisions. In June alone, twenty-five divisions (twenty-one infantry, one panzer, one panzergrenadier, and two air force divisions) were destroyed. Another twenty-eight German divisions were destroyed in July.[18] The loss of these German divisions came at a crucial period when a similar annihilation of German forces was occurring in France. Therefore, there were no reserves available except a few divisions in Norway and the Balkans.

The combined advantages possessed by the Red Army—concentration of forces, deception, surprise, leadership, timing, use of terrain, training, and technology—gave the Soviet forces an edge to inflict a staggering defeat on the German army in White Russia. The psychological culmination of the Soviet victory was the parade of 57,000 German prisoners through the streets of Moscow, the only time such an event occurred during the war.

In the final analysis, the Soviet victory in White Russia was the result of good planning. Stalin had learned at great cost not to meddle too much in the details. Because the Soviet planners had provided a generous margin of resources, almost to the point of overkill, the delayed move of Rotmistrov's 5th Guard Tank Army and its subsequent weather problems had little if any impact on the outcome. To paraphrase the carpenter's adage of measure twice and cut once, the Russians planned twice and fought once, a good formula for success.

The greatest battle of World War II, the Battle for White Russia, not only helped bring the war to a close, but opened the way for the Soviet Union's domination of Eastern Europe. The Western Allies' request to Stalin to start a diversion in the East in June 1944 to dilute German attention and strength in the West during the invasion of France not only was effective, but gave the Russians an incentive to march into Poland, the gateway to the West, and occupy more of Europe than anyone had dreamed. The mighty bear had been unleashed, and only many decades later would it be bridled again.

The Western Allies had needed Soviet help to stop the dreaded Wehrmacht before Hitler could develop weapons of mass destruction, and to save thousands of British and American lives. The die was cast long before Yalta. Roosevelt and Churchill did not hand over Eastern Europe on a silver platter; the Red Army grabbed the platter with hard-fought battles. The victories were won with Soviet lives and weapons and with a significant amount of Lead Lease assistance. At the end of hostilities, the Russian bear did not return to its cage like a docile circus performer, but retained control of the countries that it had liberated from German oppression. The lines drawn at Yalta only reflected the anticipated situation at the end of the war and applied an age-old principle that had ended so many wars in the past: you keep what you possess when the war ends. The Soviet stranglehold on Eastern Europe would remain until the end of the Cold War 40 years later, when the Russian people would no longer submit to a philosophy of guns instead of butter.

Notes

1. David M. Glantz and Jonathan M. House, *When Titans Clashed, How the Red Army Stopped Hitler* (Lawrence: The University Press of Kansas, 1995), p. 207; Trevor N. Dupuy and Paul Martell, *Great Battles on the Eastern Front: The Soviet German War 1941–1945* (Indianapolis: Bobbs-Merrill Company, 1982), p. 153.

2. G. Niepold, *The Battle for White Russia: The Destruction of Army Group Centre, June 1944* (London: Brassey's, 1987), pp. 216–221; Albert Seaton, *The Russo-German War, 1941–45* (New York: Praeger, 1970), p. 442.

3. A. M. Samsanov, ed., *Osvobozhdenie Belorussii, 1944* (Moscow: Nauka, 1974), p. 134.

4. Glantz and House, p. 208; Earl F. Ziemke, *Stalingrad to Berlin: The German Campaign in Russia, 1942–1945* (New York: Dorset Press, 1968), p. 326.

5. Samsanov, p. 438.

6. Ibid., p. 439.

7. Seaton, pp. 440–441; Ziemke, p. 326.

8. V. I. Chuikov, *The End of the Third Reich* (Moscow: Progress Publishers, 1978), p. 10.

9. Glantz and House, p. 360; Dupuy and Martell, p. 163.

10. Chuikov, p. 9.

11. Niepold, p. 45.

12. Dupuy and Martell, p. 164.

13. Seaton, p. 441; Dupuy and Martell, pp. 163–164.

14. G. F. Krivosheev, *Grif Sekretnosti Snyat', Poteri Vooruzhenikh Sil SSSR v Voinakh, Boevikh Deistviyakh i Voennikh Konfliktakh* (Moscow: Voenizdat, 1993), p. 145; U.S. Department of Commerce, *Historical Statistics of the United States: Colonial Times to 1957* (Washington, D.C.: U.S. Government Printing Office, 1960), p. 735.

15. Krivosheev, III, p. 174.

16. Ibid., III, pp. 171, 266.

17. John Erickson, *The Road to Berlin* (Boulder, Colo.: Westview Press, 1983), p. 224; Ziemke, p. 325.

18. Dupuy and Martell, p. 165.

Appendix: Red Army Reserves

Moscow Military District (1 June 1944)

(Units marked with an asterisk were sent to one of the five fronts in the Battle for White Russia in June)

37th Guard Rifle Corps (98th, 99th, and 100th Guard Rifle Divisions)
77th, 91st, and 157th Fortified Regions
11th, 12th, 13th, and 16th Guard Parachute Divisions
47th Mechanized Brigade
272nd*, 273rd*, 274th*, 275th, 283rd, 284th, 285th, and 286th Mechanized Battalions
6th and 32nd Guard Tank Brigades
29th, 149th, and 232nd Tank Brigades
3rd, 7th, 15th*, 28th, 30th*, 32nd, 34th, 35th*, 36th, 48th, 49th, 56th, 57th, 64th*, and 70th Guard Tank Regiments
18th*, 65th*, 148th*, 166th*, 253rd*, 261st, 513th, and 517th* Tank Regiments
333rd*, 334th*, 336th*, 337th*, 338th, 339th, 340th*, 341st*, 342nd*, 343rd*, 344th*, 345th*, 346th*, 347th*, 348th*, 354th*, 377th*, 378th, and 395th* Guard Assault Gun Regiments
1239th, 1434th*, 1456th, 1457th, 1460th, and 1540th Assault Gun Regiments
27th*, 36th, 45th*, and 47th Tank Destroyer Brigades
1160th and 1161st Tank Destroyer Regiments
1st Guard, 2nd*, 3rd*, 4th*, and 5th Corps Artillery Brigades
6th Gun, 16th Light Artillery, 22nd Light Artillery, 112th Howitzer, 122nd Long-Range Howitzer*, 152nd Gun, 153rd Gun, and 156th Heavy Howitzer Brigades
1047th Gun Regiment

4th, 322nd, 328th, 330th, 331st, 402nd*, and 406th* Artillery
  Battalions
6th Guard Mortar Division
4th Guard Mortar Brigade*
348th Guard Mortar Battalion
26th*, 34th*, 42nd*, 89th*, 100th*, and 326th* Guard Mortar
  Regiments
6th and 8th Heavy Mortar Brigades
47th*, 66th*, 67th, 72nd, 73rd, and 74th Antiaircraft Divisions
1885th Antiaircraft Regiment
67th, 94th, 95th, 104th, and 449th Antiaircraft Battalions

Stavka Reserve (1 June 1944)

(Units marked with an asterisk were sent to one of the five fronts
involved in the Battle for White Russia in June)

2nd Guard Army (8 July 1944, to the 1st Baltic Front in June)

54th Rifle Corps (126th, 263rd, and 346th Divisions)
11th Guard Rifle Corps (2nd, 32nd, and 33rd Guard Divisions)
13th Guard Rifle Corps (3rd, 24th, and 87th Guard Divisions)
113th Guard Tank Destroyer Regiment
150th Gun Brigade
483rd Mortar Regiment
1530th Antiaircraft Regiment

*51st Army (1 July 1944, to the 1st Baltic Front in June;
Additions after 1 June 1944)

10th Rifle Corps (91st, 216th, and 257th Divisions)
1st Guard Rifle Corps (87th, 279th, and 347th Divisions)
63rd Rifle Corps (77th, 267th, and 417th Divisions)
764th Tank Destroyer Regiment
151st Gun Brigade
125th Mortar Regiment
77th Guard Antiaircraft Regiment
3rd*, 15th*, and 64th* Guard Tank Regiments
336th* and 346th Guard* and 1022nd*, 1102nd*, 1489th*, and
  1492nd* Assault Gun Regiments
5th Guard Tank Army* (to the 3rd White Russian Front in June)
Coastal Army (occupation force for Crimea)

8th Air Army (included the 1559th, 1560th, 1600th, 1601st, 1602nd, 1603rd, and 1609th Antiaircraft Regiments)
1st Guard Tank Corps* (to 1st White Russian Reserve in June)
2nd Guard Tank Corps* (to 3rd White Russian Front, 11th Guard Army in June)
1st Tank Corps* (to 1st Baltic Reserve in June)
10th Tank Corps
19th Tank Corps* (to 1st Baltic Horse-Mechanized Group in July)
20th Tank Corps
1st Guard Mechanized Corps
2nd Guard Mechanized Corps
5th Guard Mechanized Corps
7th Guard Mechanized Corps
3rd Guard Mechanized Corps* (to 3rd White Russian Front Horse-Mechanized Group in June)
1st Mechanized Corps* (to 1st White Russian Front Horse-Mechanized Group in June)
8th Mechanized Corps
103rd Rifle Corps (29th and 270th Rifle Divisions)* (to 1st Baltic Front 6th Guard Army in June)
4th Guard Cavalry Corps* (to 1st White Russian Front Horse-Mechanized Group in June)
20th Artillery Division* (to 3rd White Russian Front in June)
26th Artillery Division* (to 1st White Russian Front in June)
4th Guard Mortar Division
4th, 5th*, and 52nd Motorcycle Regiments
8th*, 13th*, 22nd, 41st*, and 53rd Guard Breakthrough Tank Regiments
40th*, 119th*, 510th*, and 516th* Tank Regiments
298th Guard*, 335th Guard*, and 1892nd* Assault Gun Regiments
5th Guard, 5th*, 15th, 16th, and 35th Tank Destroyer Brigades
1174th Tank Destroyer Regiment
4th Howitzer*, 62nd Gun*, 105th Long-Range Howitzer, 117th Long-Range Howitzer, 155th Gun*, 157th Gun, 159th Gun*, 15th Guard Gun*, 30th Guard Light Artillery*, and 32nd Long-Range Howitzer* Brigades
1231st Howitzer Regiment*
315th* and 317th* Artillery Battalions
1st Guard Mortar Brigade
2nd, 4th, 19th, 20th, 44th, 49th, and 67th* Guard Mortar Regiments
29th Mortar Brigade
195th and 197th Mortar Regiments
2nd*, 15th, 18th*, and 19th Antiaircraft Divisions

272nd Guard, 257th, 459th, 622nd, 740th, and 1485th Antiaircraft Regiments

Additions to the Stavka Reserve in June 1944

1402nd, 1490th, 1491st, 1492nd, and 1102nd Assault Gun Regiments
39th Tank Destroyer Brigade

Bibliography

Adair, Paul. *Hitler's Greatest Defeat: The Collapse of Army Group Centre, June* ✓
1944. London: Arms and Armour Press, 1994.

Akalovich, N. *Osvobozhenie Belorussii.* Minsk: Nauka i Texinka, 1989.

Akulov, P., and G. Tolokol'nikov, eds. *V Boiakh za Belorussiu.* Minsk: Belarus,
1970.

Babich, P., and A. G. Baier. *Razvitie Vooruzheniia i Organizatsii Sovetski
Suxoputnik Voisk v Godi Velikoi Otechestvennoi Voini.* Moscow: Izdanie
Akademii, 1990.

Batov, P. I. *V Pokhodakh i Boiakh.* Moscow: Voenizdat, 1966.

Beaumont, Joan. *Comrades in Arms: British Aid to Russia, 1941–1945.* London:
Davis-Poynter, 1980.

Belousov, A. "4-ia Guardeiskaia Tankovaia Brigada v Boiakh za Minsk." *Vizh*
7 (July 1974), pp. 45–49.

Biriukov, P. "Osobennosti Primeneniia Inzhenrnykh Voisk Belorusskoi
Operatsii." *Vizh* 6 (June 1984), pp. 34–40.

Chernyayev, V. "Operativnaya Maskirovka Voisk v Belorusskoi Operatsii."
Vizh 8 (August 1974), pp. 11–21.

Chistiakov, Ivan M. *Sluzhim Otchizne.* Moscow: Voenizdat, 1985.

Chuikov, V. I. *The End of the Third Reich.* Moscow: Progress Publishers, 1978.

Dunn, Walter S., Jr. *Hitler's Nemesis: The Red Army, 1930–1945.* Westport, Ct.:
Praeger, 1994.

———. *Second Front Now 1943.* University: University of Alabama Press,
1981.

———. *The Soviet Economy and the Red Army, 1930–1945.* Westport, Ct.:
Praeger, 1995.

Dupuy, Trevor N., and Paul Martell. *Great Battles on the Eastern Front: The
Soviet German War 1941–1945.* Indianapolis, Ind.: Bobbs-Merrill
Company, 1982.

Erickson, John. *The Road to Berlin.* Boulder, Colo.: Westview Press, 1983. ✓

Fremde Heer Ost. Captured German Records. Washington, D.C.: National
Archives, 1982.

Geschichte des Grossen Vaterlandischen Krieges der Sowjetunion. 8 vols.
Berlin:Deutscher Militarverlag, 1964.

Glantz, David M. *Soviet Military Deception in the Second World War.* London:
Frank Cass, 1989.

———, ed. *1985 Art of War Symposium, From the Dnieper to the Vistula: Soviet*

Offensive Operations, November 1943–August 1944. Carlisle Barracks, Penn.: U.S. Army War College, 1985.

Glantz, David M., and Jonathan M. House. *When Titans Clashed, How the Red* ✓ *Army Stopped Hitler.* Lawrence: The University Press of Kansas, 1995.

Glantz, David M., and Harold S. Orenstein, eds. *Belorussia 1944: The Soviet General Staff Study.* Carlisle, Penn.: David M. Glantz, 1998.

Harrison, Mark. *Soviet Planning in Peace and War, 1938–1945.* Cambridge: Cambridge University Press, 1985.

Haupt, Werner von. *Die 260. Infanterie-Division, 1939–1944.* Bad Nauheim and Dorheim: Verlag Hans-Henning Podzun, 1970.

———. *Geschichte der 134. Infanterie Division.* Weinsberg: Herausgegeben vom Kamardenkreis der Ehemaligen, 134. Inf. Division, 1971.

———. *Heeresgruppe Mitte 1941–1945.* Dorheim: H. H. Podzun, 1968.

Heidkemper, O. *Witebsk.* Heidelberg: Vowinckel, 1954.

Hinze, Rolf. *East Front Drama—1944: The Withdrawal Battle of Army Group Center.* Winnipeg, Manitoba: J. J. Fedorowicz Publishing Inc., 1996. ✓

The Illustrated Encyclopedia of 20th Century Weapons and Warfare. 24 vols. New York: Columbia House, 1969.

Keilig, Wolf. *Das Deutsche Heer, 1939–1945.* 3 vols. Bad Nauheim: Podzun, 1956–1972.

Kiriukhin, S. P. *43-ya Armiia v Vitebskoi Operatsii.* Moscow: Voenizdat, 1961.

Kir'ian, M. M. *Fronty Nastupaly.* Moscow: Nauka, 1987.

———. *Vnezapnost v Nastupatelnykh Operatsiyakh Velikoi Otechestvennoi Voiny.* Moscow: Nauka, 1986.

Krivosheev, G. F. *Grif Sekretnosti Snyat. Poteri Vooruzhenikh sil SSSR v Voinakh Voevikh Deistviiakh i Voennikh Konflitakh.* Moscow: Voenizdat, 1993.

Liudnikov, I. I. *Pod Vitebskom.* Moscow: Voenizdat, 1962.

Losik, O. A. "Primenie Bronetankovykh i Mekhaniziro Vannykh Voisk v Belorusskoi Operatsii." *Vizh* 6 (June 1984), pp. 20–24.

———. *Stroitelistvo i Boyevoye Primeneniye Sovetskikh Tankovykh Voysk v Gody Velikoy Otechestvennoy Voyne.* Moscow: Voyenizdat, 1979.

Luchinsky, A. "28-ia Armiia v Bobruiskoi Operatsii." *Vizh* 2 (February 1969), pp. 66–75.

Mikhailkin, V. "Boevoe Primenenie Artillerii v Belorusskoi Operatsii." *Vizh* 6 (June 1984), pp. 25–33.

Militarakademie M. W. Frunse. *Der Durchbruch der Schutzenverbande Durch eine Vorbereitete Verteidigung.* Berlin: Ministerium fur Nationale Verteidigung, 1959.

Milward, Alan S. *War Economy and Society 1939–1945.* London: Lane, 1977.

Niepold, G. *The Battle for White Russia: The Destruction of Army Group Centre, June 1944.* London: Brassey's, 1987.

———. *Mittlere Ostfront Juni' 42.* Herford und Bonn: E. S. Mittler & Sohn, 1985.

Mitchell, B. R. *European Historical Statistics, 1750–1970.* London: Macmillan, 1978.

Mueller-Hillebrand, Burkhart. *Das Heer, 1933–1945.* 3 vols. Frankfurt am Main: E. S. Mittler & Sohn, 1959–1969.

Parrish, Michael. *The USSR and World War II: An Annotated Bibliography of Books Published in the Soviet Union, 1945–1975.* New York: Garland, 1981.

Patika, F. "Tilovoe Obespechenie Frontov v Operatsii "Bagration." *Vizh* 8 (August 1974), pp. 22–29.

Platanov, S. P., ed. *Vtoraia Mirovala Voina.* Moscow: Voenizdat, 1958.

Plotnikov, F. V. *Osvobzhenie Belorussii*. Moscow: Voennoe Izdatelistov, 1984.
———. *V Srazheniia za Belorussi*. Minsk: Belarus, 1982.
Radzievskii, A. I. *Army Operations: USSR Reports Military Affairs.* Washington, D.C.: Foreign Broadcast Information Service, 1985.
———. *Tankovyi Udar*. Moscow: Voennoe Izdatelistvo, 1977.
Rokossovsky, K. "Dva Glavnykh Udara." *Vizh* 6 (June 1965), pp. 13–17.
Samsanov, A. M. ed. *Osvobozhdenie Belorussii, 1944*. Moscow: Nauka, 1974.
Schofield, Brian B. *The Russian Convoys*. London: B. T. Batsford, 1964.
Seaton, Albert. *The Russo-German War, 1941–45*. New York: Praeger, 1970.✔
Shimansky, A. "O Dostizhenii Strategicheskoi Vnezapnosti Pri Podgotovke Letne-Osennei Kampanii 1944 Guda." *Vizh* 6 (June 1968), pp. 17–28.
Shtemenko, S. M. *The Soviet General Staff at War, 1941–1945*. Moscow: Progress Publishers, 1970.
Telegrin, K. "V Boiakh za Osvobozhdenie Belorussii." *Vizh* 6 (June 1969), pp. 82–91.
Tessin, Georg. *Verbande und Truppen der Deutschen Wehrmacht und Waffen SS in Zweiten Weltkrieg, 1939–1945*. 14 vols. Osnabruck: Biblio, 1965–1980.
Tornau, Franz Kurowski. *Sturmartillerie: Fels in der Brandung*. Herford and Bonn: Maximilian, 1965.
Urlanis, B. *Wars and Population*. Moscow: Progress Publishers, 1971.
U.S. Department of Commerce. *Historical Statistics of the United States: Colonial Times to 1957*. Washington, D.C.: GPO, 1960.
Van Tuyll, Hubert P. *Feeding the Bear: American Aid to the Soviet Union, 1941–1945*. Westport, Ct.: Greenwood Press, 1989.
Vasilevsky, A. M. *Delo Vsei Zhizni*. Moscow: Belarus, 1984.
Vysotskiy, F. I., M. E. Makukhin, F. M. Sarychev, and M. K. Shaposhnikov. *Gvardeiskay Tankovaya*. Moscow: Voenizdat, 1963.
Yakovlev, N. "Operativnye Peregruppirovki Voisk Pri Podgotovka Belorusskoi Operatsii." *Vizh* 9 (September 1975), pp. 91–97.
Zaloga, Steven J. *Bagration 1944*. Oxford: Osprey Publishing, 1996. ✔
Zaloga, Steven J., and James Grandsen. *Soviet Tanks and Combat Vehicles of World War Two*. London: Arms and Armour Press, 1984.
Zhukov, G. K. *Reminiscences and Reflections*. Moscow: Progress Publishers, 1989.
Ziemke, Earl F. *Stalingrad to Berlin: The German Campaign in Russia,*✔ *1942–1945*. New York: Dorset Press, 1968.

Index

241

About the Book

Walter Dunn reports—for the first time in English—the details of a battle on the Eastern Front that was perhaps the largest of all time and certainly one of the most significant of World War II. Nearly three million soldiers (two million Soviets and almost a million Germans) participated in a campaign in which five Soviet break-throughs advanced 275 kilometers in two weeks over bad roads and marshy terrain, destroying 50 German divisions and capturing 50,000 German troops—an event celebrated by marching the prisoners of war ignominiously through the streets of Moscow. Hitler would never again have the wherewithal to launch a major offensive in the east.

Soviet Blitzkrieg demonstrates convincingly that by the summer of 1944 the Red Army had mastered the German style of warfare and was capable of turning the tables on the Germans. Using recently declassified Soviet Orders of Battle and his own monumental files of German and Soviet unit histories, Dunn traces each of the blitzkrieg offensives from the initial breakthrough to stalemate.

Walter S. Dunn, Jr., is author of several books, including *Hitler's Nemesis: The Red Army 1930–1945* and *Kursk*.

Stackpole Military History Series

Real battles. Real soldiers. Real stories.

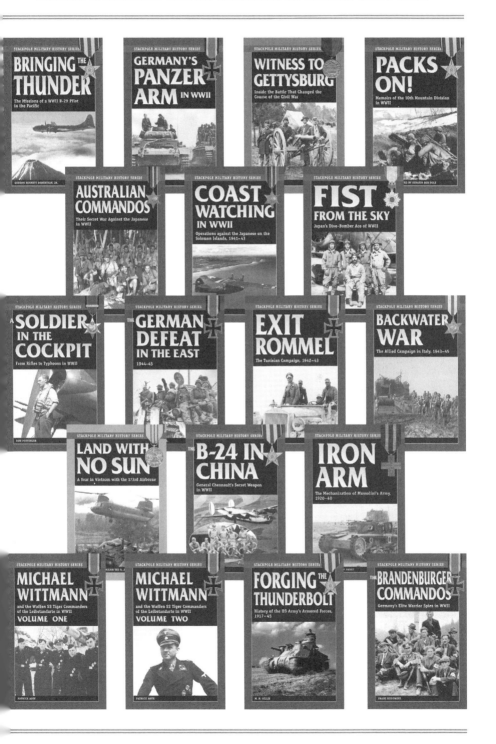

Stackpole Military History Series

Real battles. Real soldiers. Real stories.

Stackpole Military History Series

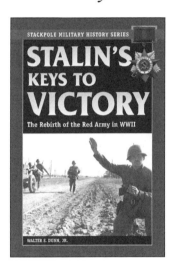

STALIN'S KEYS TO VICTORY
THE REBIRTH OF THE RED ARMY IN WWII
Walter S. Dunn, Jr.

When Hitler invaded the Soviet Union in June 1941, the German Army annihilated a substantial part of the Red Army. Yet the Soviets rebounded to successfully defend Moscow in late 1941, defeat the Germans at Stalingrad in 1942 and Kursk in 1943, and deliver the deathblow in Belarus in 1944. Eastern Front expert Walter Dunn examines these four pivotal battles and explains how the Red Army lost a third of its prewar strength, regrouped, and beat one of the most highly trained and experienced armies in the world.

$16.95 • Paperback • 6 x 9 • 208 pages • 12 photos

WWW.STACKPOLEBOOKS.COM
1-800-732-3669

Stackpole Military History Series

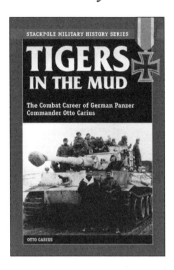

TIGERS IN THE MUD
THE COMBAT CAREER OF GERMAN PANZER
COMMANDER OTTO CARIUS

Otto Carius,
translated by Robert J. Edwards

World War II began with a metallic roar as the
German Blitzkrieg raced across Europe, spearheaded
by the most dreadful weapon of the twentieth century:
the Panzer. Tank commander Otto Carius thrusts the
reader into the thick of battle, replete with the
blood, smoke, mud, and gunpowder so common
to the elite German fighting units.

$19.95 • Paperback • 6 x 9 • 368 pages
51 photos • 48 illustrations • 3 maps

WWW.STACKPOLEBOOKS.COM
1-800-732-3669

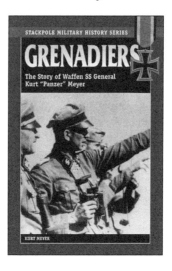

Stackpole Military History Series

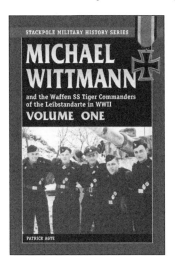

MICHAEL WITTMANN AND THE WAFFEN SS TIGER COMMANDERS OF THE LEIBSTANDARTE IN WORLD WAR II
VOLUME ONE
Patrick Agte

By far the most famous tank commander on any side in
World War II, German Tiger ace Michael Wittmann destroyed 138
enemy tanks and 132 anti-tank guns in a career that embodies the
panzer legend: meticulous in planning, lethal in execution, and
always cool under fire. Most of those kills came in the snow and mud
of the Eastern Front, where Wittmann and the Leibstandarte's
armored company spent more than a year in 1943–44 battling the
Soviets at places like Kharkov, Kursk, and the Cherkassy Pocket.

$19.95 • Paperback • 6 x 9 • 432 pages • 383 photos • 19 maps • 10 charts

WWW.STACKPOLEBOOKS.COM
1-800-732-3669

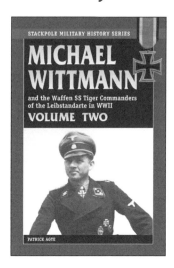

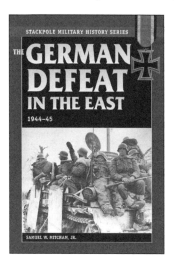

Stackpole Military History Series

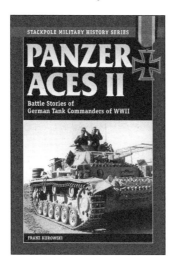

PANZER ACES II
BATTLE STORIES OF
GERMAN TANK COMMANDERS OF WORLD WAR II
Franz Kurowski,
translated by David Johnston

With the same drama and excitement of the first book,
Franz Kurowski relates the combat careers of six more
tank officers. These gripping accounts follow Panzer
crews into some of World War II's bloodiest engage-
ments—with Rommel in North Africa, up and down
the Eastern Front, and in the hedgerows of the West.
Master tacticians and gutsy leaders, these soldiers
changed the face of war forever.

$19.95 • Paperback • 6 x 9 • 496 pages • 71 b/w photos

Stackpole Military History Series

GERMANY'S PANZER ARM IN WWII
R. L. DiNardo

No twentieth-century military organization has been as widely studied as the German war machine in World War II, and few of its components were as important, influential, or revolutionary as its armored force. Nevertheless, there are almost no truly integrated studies of the organizational, economic, personnel, doctrinal, and tactical factors that affected the panzer arm's performance. Drawing on military documents, memoirs, battle reports, and other original sources, DiNardo fills that gap with this detailed look at the rise and fall of German armor.

$16.95 • Paperback • 6 x 9 • 224 pages • 27 photos • 17 diagrams

WWW.STACKPOLEBOOKS.COM
1-800-732-3669

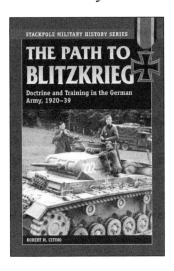

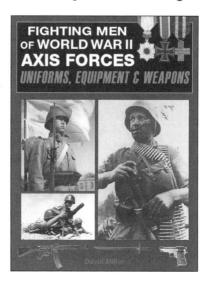